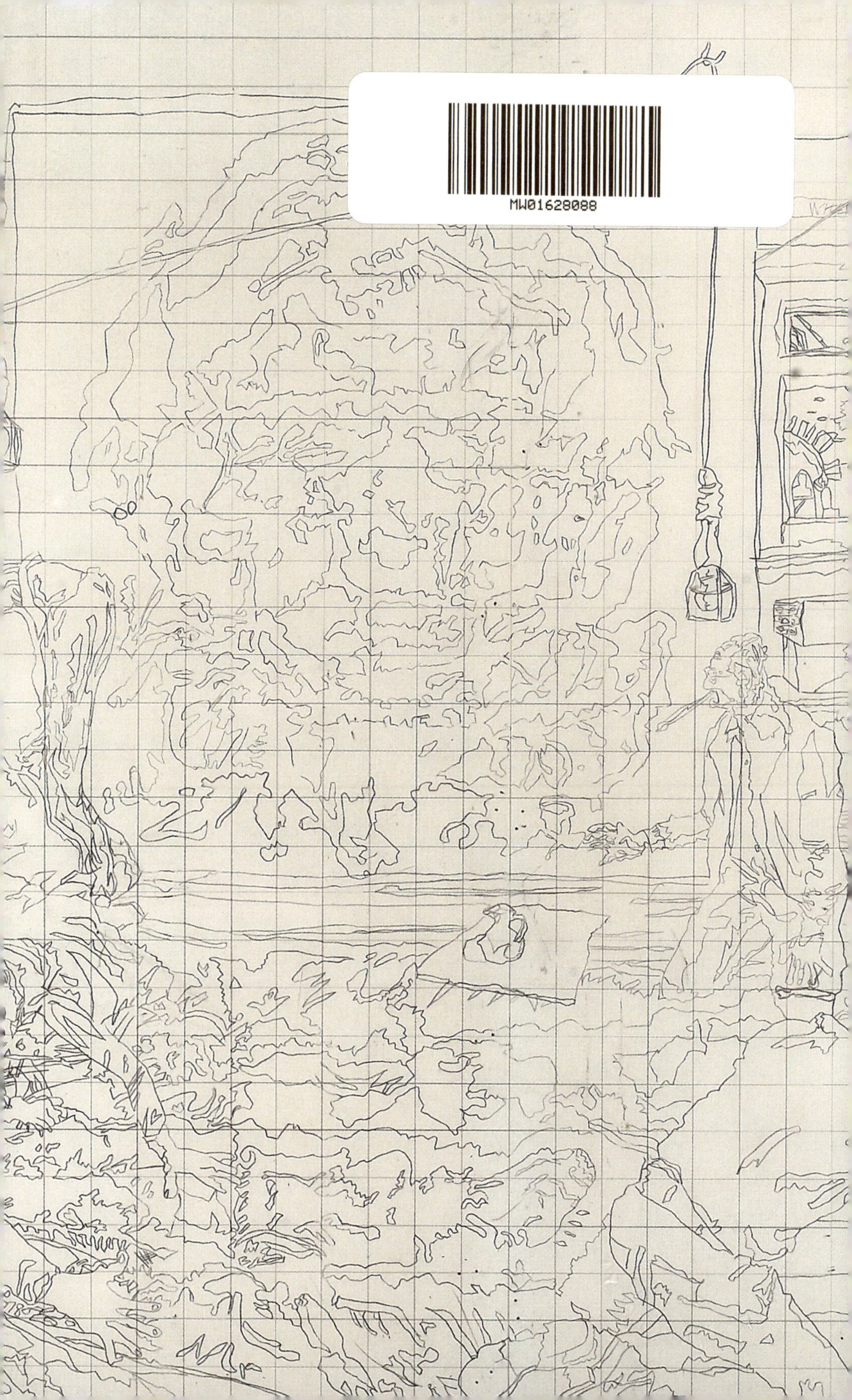
MW01628088

Since 1950

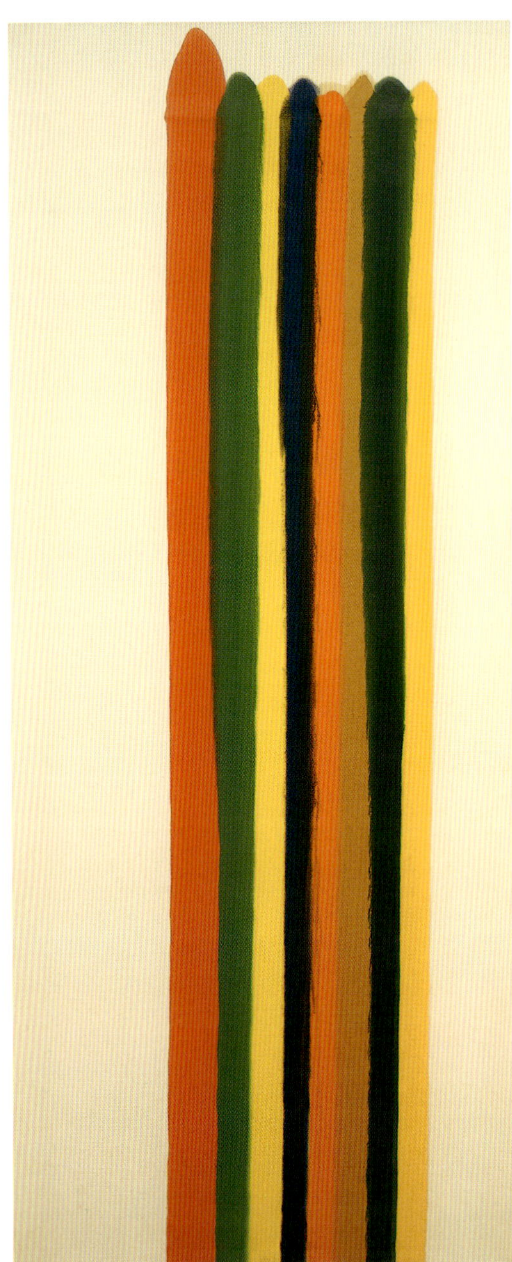

CHARLES HARRISON

# Since 1950

## ART AND ITS CRITICISM

WITH A PREFACE BY

ALEX POTTS

YALE UNIVERSITY PRESS

NEW HAVEN AND LONDON

Designed by Gillian Malpass

Printed in China

**Library of Congress Cataloging-in-Publication Data**

Harrison, Charles, 1942–
Since 1950 : art and its criticism / Charles Harrison.
p. cm.
Includes bibliographical references and index.
ISBN 978-0-300-15186-2 (cl : alk. paper)
1. Art, Modern–19th century–Philosophy.
2. Art, Modern–20th century–Philosophy. I. Title.
N6447.H37 2009
709.04–dc22

2009001836

A catalogue record for this book is available from the British Library

*Endpapers* *Index: The Studio at 3 Wesley Place Painted by Mouth I (ii)* (details of fig. 39), 1982, crayon on paper, 93 × 174 cm, author's collection

*Frontispiece* Morris Louis, *Red Go*, 1962,
acrylic on canvas, 203.2 x 76.2 cm, courtesy Waddington Galleries, London

CONTENTS

# PREFACE

BY ALEX POTTS

In these essays on late twentieth-century art and the critical perspectives it has generated, Charles Harrison offers a particularly compelling and finely argued analysis of the seismic shift that took place when the modernist formalism that had underpinned thinking about art in the first half of the century came to be seen as a spent force. The shift occurred in the wake of the international triumph of American Abstract Expressionist painting in the 1950s – painting that to many at the time seemed to mark the very apogee of modernist abstraction. For Harrison, as for most writers on the period, the crucial turning point came in the late 1960s and early 1970s, when the Conceptual Art movement mounted a systematic critique of the aesthetics of modernism and of its ideological underpinnings. This was the juncture at which a modernist focus on the visual and on pure form gave way to a radically different understanding – one that saw art as needing to be grounded in the intellectual and the textual, and as having to engage with the ideological pressures exerted on its practice by the institutions and apparatuses of the art world. Harrison's analysis of the issues at stake reveals the benefits of his close personal involvement with these developments. He played a significant role in the staging of the milestone exhibition *When Attitudes become Form* when it was shown at its London venue in 1969, and for many years has been actively involved with the British-based practice of Art & Language, which has its origins in the original Conceptual Art movement.

Harrison's writing is fed by a strong sense of commitment that makes it different in kind from standard academic texts. At the same time, the complexity and sophistication of mind-set entailed by this commitment makes his analysis particularly compelling. The book is far from being a celebration of the conceptual in late twentieth-century art or, for that matter, a simple deconstruction of modernism and account of its demise. That a narrow modernist focus on painting and sculpture was displaced by a plethora of alternative, non object-based and often anti-aesthetic practices is not for Harrison a straightforwardly positive development. Quite the contrary. He takes for granted that the modernist outlook had become utterly compromised by the late 1960s, particularly in its latest and most influential variant formulated by Clement Greenberg. But he is also deeply critical of the now hegemonic post-modern, post-conceptual or post-structural critique of the modernist project, and. of what he sees as its intellectual and ethical limits. In his view this critique is for the most part woefully blind to the aesthetic and ethical commitments implicit in the modernist project. In fact, he remains torn between what he sees as the value of an intellectually informed, and committed, formal analysis of art, and his acute awareness of the limits and ultimate bankruptcy of those modernist paradigms of aesthetic value, autonomy and disinterest that were promoted by the mid-twentieth-century art world. This tension in his outlook works productively as he opens up refreshing alternatives to the orthodoxies enshrined in mainstream Anglo-American writing about modern and contemporary art. He is as suspicious of the post-modern paradigms of the present moment as he is of the modernist assumptions that prevailed when he entered the world of art writing and art criticism in the late 1960s and early 1970s.

Harrison's writing is further distinguished from the majority of critically and theoretically aware literature on the subject by the singular clarity of his analysis. Density of critical thought is often conflated with density and turgidity of prose, with the latter covering up for failure to understand the larger issues at stake. These issues Harrison addresses with an uncommon forthrightness that derives from the clearly articulated sense he has of his own intellectual, political and aesthetic commitments. Running through his essays is the conviction that critical thinking about art needs to be grounded in the first instance in a direct engagement with art and its practice – an approach that sets itself against that species of academic correctness in which 'approved' art-theoretical and art-historical paradigms are taken as starting points for interpretation. For Harrison, problems particular to the constitution of the art work must play a leading role. This is a position that might at first seem close to the mid-twentieth century modernism he critiques. He takes one into different territory, however. In the concluding comments to his essay 'Complexity and Disinterest' he speculates on the nature of the art work that might carry some real significance today:

> I would look for an art that teaches us about the problems of representation, and by virtue of doing so teaches us something about the world represented; an art that requires of its spectators – of us, the potential community of learners – that we do not, cannot put it to use for our own established ends.

The art he has in mind is far from being preciously self-referential, and the concept of disinterest at issue certainly not to be identified with the modernist ideal of disinterested contemplation. It is something much more ethically charged and critically self-aware. The spectator is no longer envisaged as a commanding consciousness, but is called upon to examine sceptically his or her engagement with the work of art, and to embark on the rethinking and reimagining of things that art at its most demanding entails.

Harrison exemplifies his approach by focusing on two rather different kinds of art. Firstly, there is the conceptual, and initially largely text-based art with which Art & Language launched itself in the years around 1970. At the same time, he examines instances of late modernist painting and sculpture, produced at the moment of dissolution of the modernist world view, in which the critical impulses that had given earlier modernist art its drive and necessity retained a certain purchase. The scope of his analysis is as broad and comprehensive as any on the subject, but is the more compelling for the relatively unorthodox choice of artists whose work is considered in detail, Ben Nicholson and Roger Hilton among them. These are not artists who usually function as orthodox points of reference in the dominant academic discourse about modern and contemporary art. The same is partly true for Art & Language, though not to anything like the same degree, since their interventions were formative for many of us who had a British as distinct from an American or Continental perspective on the changes taking place in the art world from the 1970s onwards.

The critical purchase of what Harrison has to offer is considerably strengthened by his independence of viewpoint and approach. He is able to make us see things – particularly unexpected artistic values – of which we were previously unaware. Larger questions regarding the ethical and ideological underpinnings of a serious engagement with art emerge more clearly for being located at one remove from the orthodoxies of current historical and critical writing. This said, Harrison has very telling observations to offer on more mainstream phenomena such as American Abstract Expressionist painting and Minimalism, about which he has clearly thought thoroughly and deeply, and very much from the inside. He also identifies with particular acuity what he rightly sees as crucial legacies of the experimental art of the 1960s and early 1970s, namely an 'ironic awareness of the indirectness of all expression', and a vigilance with regard to the all-too-easy lapse into sentimental aggrandizement of the symbolic or expressive value of art, an aggrandizement that reduces the actual art work to the status of signpost or emotional stimulus.

For Harrison, the truly significant work of art will be realist in some sense. Its realism will consist not in the conventional embodiment of some recognizable truth about the world, but in its being itself a credible or realistic phenomenon. To this end, the work of art requires of the artist and of us as spectators an understanding of the changing historical circumstances out of which it emerges and into which it is launched. This does not mean that we should expect the work to 'provide vivid testimony to the character of social life', in the way that a determinist social history of art might do, but rather that we should acknowledge the work's possession of a systemic character, one that 'may in the last resort be only aesthetic, but, for all that, none the less vivid in intellectual or sociological terms.' The history of art that starts from such a basis promises to yield social or cultural understanding by regarding the art work not as a 'signpost, directing attention to significant aspects of the social and cultural world', but rather as something that bears witness in its very structure as art to social realities we only incompletely articulate in words – and that as critics or historians we can never wrap up and deliver for easy consumption.

*University of Michigan*
*December 2008*

# INTRODUCTION

The texts collected here were written between 1986 and 2007. During that period I have been sustained practically and intellectually by two principal affiliations: with the artistic practice of Art & Language, to which I originally committed myself in 1971 as editor of the journal *Art-Language*; and with the Open University, by which I was first employed in 1977. Among the published outcomes of those affiliations are two volumes of *Essays on Art & Language* and a succession of teaching texts and programmes issued by the Open University, the BBC and Yale University Press. The writings in the present volume fall into a slightly distinct category. They were occasioned by invitations to contribute essays, lectures and papers in my own name to exhibition catalogues, workshops and conferences. They thus represent my various attempts to negotiate between the roles of historian, critic, theorist and almost-practitioner of art – none of which on its own has ever seemed quite comfortable or sufficient as a professional identification, for reasons that are partly made explicit in the fifth and seventh of the following texts ('"Englishness" and "Modernism" Revisited' and 'Feeling the Earth Move').

In collecting these writings for publication, however, I do not mean to claim that they are any more independent in voice or content than those explicitly addressed either to the work of Art & Language or to the demands of teaching. As to the first case, each of the texts included in this volume has benefited from the conversation, critical reading and contribution of Michael Baldwin and Mel Ramsden. They are the artists in whose name the work of Art & Language is issued and the authors with whom I collaborate on literary and theoretical projects and publications. While *Since 1950* may not be a publication of Art & Language, it does not stand apart from that collaboration.

As to the relation of this book to my work in education, while none of the texts was conceived with a student audience specifically in mind, it has been in my employment with the Open University that I have learned to distrust any theoretical arguments on cultural matters which cannot be clearly expounded to non-specialists. Collaborative work within the university's course teams and with my colleagues and co-editors Paul Wood and Jason Gaiger has also served to maintain and to develop that concern for the understanding of Modernism and its crises that I brought to my employment in the first place.

Both that concern and an engagement with Art & Language and its morale are motifs that are common to several of these essays. This has led to some occasional areas of overlap. I hope the reader will accept these as a price paid to keep the arguments of the various texts intact, so that each can be read on its own without the need to observe the sequence in which they are printed. This simply follows the chronological order of their completion.

All but three of the texts (1, 2 and 4) were originally written to be read aloud. It has generally been my practice to accompany lectures and conference papers with as many colour slides as were required fully to illustrate their arguments and support their references, preferably using my own photographs taken directly from the works in question. This has usually meant using a considerable number of slides. Reproduction of works of art has now become a very expensive business, however, and it has been necessary to restrict the illustrations in this book to the minimum necessary to provide appropriate reference for the reader. I am grateful to the Arts Faculty of the Open University for the funding that has enabled their inclusion.

My further thanks are due to those various individuals and organisations whose commissions provided practical motivation to write, to Alex Potts for his very supportive preface, to Gillian Malpass of Yale University Press for offering an outlet for this collection and for overseeing its design and production, and to my wife, Trish Evans, for her companionship over the period in which these texts were thought about and composed.

*Charles Harrison*

# 1 SCULPTURE'S RECENT PAST

This essay was written for the catalogue of the exhibition *A Quiet Revolution: British Sculpture Since 1965*, held at the Museum of Contemporary Art, Chicago, in 1987. The brief was to outline developments in English sculpture from the 1950s to the 1970s.

## 'CERTAIN YOUNGER ENGLISHMEN'

'... the whole world has been astonished to see the emergence of a British School of sculpture whose impact has been world-wide.' The author of those words was Sir Herbert Read, the date 1963, and the occasion an open-air exhibition of contemporary British and American sculpture, held in Battersea Park, London (fig. 1).[1] The sculptors Read was referring to – Robert Adams, Kenneth Armitage, Reg Butler, Lynn Chadwick, Bernard Meadows – belonged to a 'Middle Generation' of artists, one or two decades younger than the senior figures Henry Moore and Barbara Hepworth whose careers had been established in relation to European art before the war, one or two decades older than the 'New Generation' which emerged in the 1960s after the centre of the avant-garde had moved to New York.[2] In Read's view the 'single genius' of Henry Moore had provided the initial impulse to which these artists had made a 'vital response'. Of course, in 1963 Read was no longer the avant-garde spokesman he had been thirty years earlier at the time when it was Moore's work that needed defending. A younger critic would at least have hesitated before comparing the 'impact' of the English Middle Generation sculptors with 'the equally surprising emergence of an indigenous school of painting in the United States' (that is, the Abstract Expressionists), or before reproving the American exhibitors (Calder, Chamberlain, Ferber, Smith and Stankiewicz, among them) for the relative absence in their work of 'a specifically *plastic* sensibility'. In

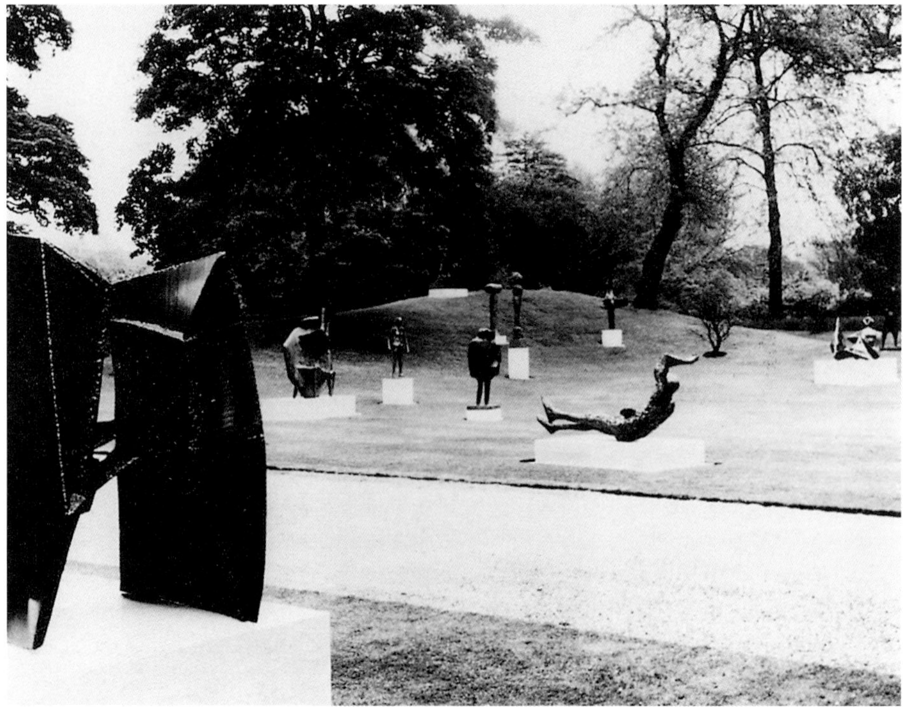

1 *Sculpture: Open-air Exhibition of Contemporary British and American Works*, Battersea Park, London, 1963, general view

the conclusion to his essay, Read struck a particularly conservative note: ‘the best sculptors who are exhibiting here, however free in their fantasy, however experimental in their techniques, respect the limitations of a monumental art that should by definition be imposing, enduring and therefore compact’. When this is taken alongside Read’s denigratory reference to ‘a technique that is neither sculpture nor painting – it has been agreed to call it *assemblage*’, it becomes clear enough that the critical barrier being erected was one designed to exclude from the pantheon the likes of David Smith (represented at Battersea by *Cubi IX* of 1961 (Walker Art Center, Minneapolis)) and Anthony Caro (represented by *Midday* of 1960 (Museum of Modern Art, New York)).

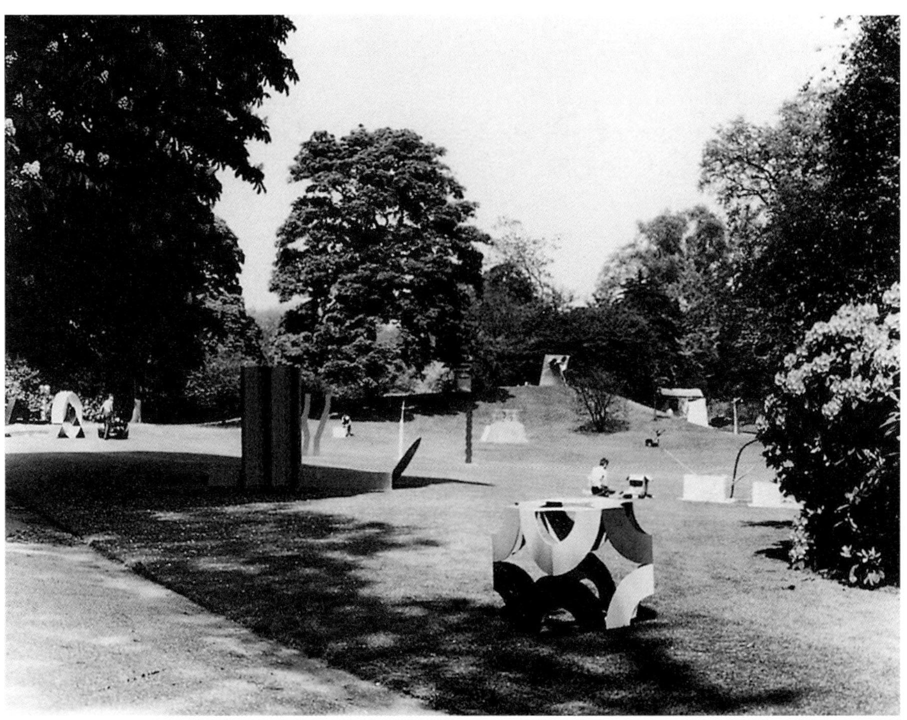

2 *Sculpture in the Open Air*, Battersea Park, London, 1966, general view

Three years later another exhibition of sculpture in the open air was held on the Battersea site (fig. 2). Though Moore was well represented, together with Barbara Hepworth and various members of the Middle Generation, the focus of attention on this occasion fell on the works of Caro and of some younger sculptors who had clearly been subject to his influence. If there was one factor that united this latter group of artists, it was their determined opposition to just that form of contained and imposing monumentality which Read had asserted as a necessary condition of quality in sculpture, and which was associated, above all, with the work of Moore. The 1966 show was 'all-British' with the exception of a single work by Smith, included 'as a homage to a great American sculptor whose death since the last exhibition still seems so untimely'.[3] The catalogue introduction on this occasion was written by Alan Bowness, shortly after the director of the Tate Gallery but then a critic and university teacher of modern art history with a particular interest in British art. Bowness suggested that the exhibition offered a 'confrontation' between generations of modern sculptors and concluded with an even stronger claim than the one Read had made: 'It seems to me more than likely that we are witnessing in this country, here and now, one of the great epochs in the history of the art.'[4]

Various points can be made in relation to this scenario. One is that the notion of a developing 'British School of Sculpture' has been a persistent obsession of English critics and modern-period art historians since at least the early 1930s. Another is that the development of 'British Sculpture' has tended to be seen in terms of separate generations of work, each categorically distinct from the last. A third point is that a kind of autonomy is nevertheless accorded to this development as a whole – as if 'British Sculpture' were a kind of tradition-unto-itself, appropriately valued in its own terms and by reference to its own history and internal critiques. Yet another is that the combination of the first three factors appears to encourage the making of grandiose critical and art-historical claims, in Britain at least, for the achievements of successive generations of British sculptors.

The telling of art history in a linear and hermetic manner has lately become unfashionable, but it is the harder to avoid where a particular discipline – here 'sculpture' – is under review, and especially where that discipline is surveyed in terms of a single national tradition. I hope at least to avoid the worst dangers of provincial rationalisation by setting an account of the conditions of British sculpture in the 1960s and early 1970s, where relevant, in the context of problems and issues within modern art and Modernism as a whole. Given that undertaking, one point to be made about the 'confrontation of generations' in the mid-1960s is that the possibility of a new kind of cosmopolitanism in sculpture was certainly a major issue for the younger of the generations concerned. A demonstrable continuity of style and of practical concepts connects Moore's sculpture with typical works of the Middle Generation. The categorical change associated with Caro's work of the 1960s, however, is not to be explained in terms of the traditional resources and references of modern British sculpture, except insofar as these defined the negatives of ambition at the time.

I do not mean to identify Caro as the sole initiator of a new tradition. It might be more apposite to explain the change in his work around 1960 as representative of a shift in the determinations on the practice of art, and to explain the success of that work in terms of an irresistible shift in the interests of criticism. One way to explain this shift – or at least to hint at its nature – is to note that it was around this time that 'European' became a term signifying critical and curatorial disfavour, a term suddenly heavy with the threat of cultural downgrading. A clear measure of the division between generations which occurred during the late 1950s is the transfer of interest from European to American art.

There are many ways to explain why this should have happened, and should have happened when it did. The most powerful forms of explanation will be those that are built on the findings of political economy. In 1948 Clement Greenberg, a critic not now noted for his forays into the social history of art, observed that 'the conclusion forces itself, much to our own surprise, that the main premises of Western art have at last migrated to the United States, along with the centre of gravity of industrial production and political power'.[5] In the late 1950s and 1960s, Modernism was re-exported from New York to Europe 'like a slow-release Marshall Plan',[6] transformed, metropolitanised, and – at least as regards the functions of criticism – substantially professionalised. It has to be said, however, that though the mechanisms of the 'American (Cultural) Invasion'[7] are traceable into the political and economic spheres, the American painting seen in London in the late 1950s was distinguishable by the undeniable authority of aesthetic quality and newness.[8] English painters of the Middle Generation,[9] still accustomed to looking to Paris as the metropolitan centre of the modern, were for the most part wrong-footed in mid-career. For younger painters there was no such problem. The country they had already identified as the most attractive source of post-war mass-cultural entertainment and consumer novelties could now also be looked to for models of authentically modern high culture. The immediate consequences were discernible in the *Situation* exhibition of 1960, the criteria of inclusion to which were that paintings should be abstract and at least thirty square feet in area.[10] In a second *Situation* exhibition the following year, the compatibility of Caro's work was recognised by the inclusion of one of his recent abstract sculptures.[11]

In order to understand the shift that occurred in British sculpture in the 1960s, it is important to stress the priority of American *painting* in demonstrating Modernism's transatlantic migration. On the one hand the substantial implications of what had been done in New York during the late 1940s and early 1950s were not to be confined within the practical sphere of painting. On the other hand no comparable body of work in American sculpture was available to view. David Smith's work was virtually unknown in England until at least 1959[12] – the date of the second major exhibition of American painting at the Tate Gallery and of an important Pollock retrospective at the Whitechapel – and there was no substantial showing of his work in London until 1966. Anthony Caro initially saw Smith's work at first hand on a visit to America in 1959. His immediate response to that work was certainly a factor in his own decisive change of style and working methods, but some time before then it had already been made clear by the counter-example of Abstract Expressionist painting that the art of sculpture would have to be modernised according to some new set of models.

In 1956, when the exhibition *Modern Art in the United States* came to the Tate Gallery, the painter and critic Patrick Heron had written of his elation at 'the size, energy, originality, economy and inventive daring of many of the paintings'.[13] He continued, 'Their creative emptiness represented a radical discovery, I felt, as did their flatness, or rather their spatial shallowness. . . . Also, there was an absence of relish in the matière as an end in itself.' What Heron was recognising in this response, typical of alert and sympathetic observers among British artists, was that the abstractness of American painting was of a new order from the forms of abstraction typical of previous European art. As well as the obvious bearing on native styles and concepts of painting, there were clear critical implications for the future of sculpture. For example, it seemed in this new phase of Modernism that plausible cosmopolitan art was no longer to be made by veiling naturalistic references under tastefully agitated surfaces. Some quality in the work of Pollock and others of the Americans – maybe the palpable irrelevance to their work of certain conventional ways of reading-in meaning – generated a climate of impatience with that range of metaphorical references and naturalistic similes which had largely sustained British sculpture since the 1920s, and which had significantly underpinned its forms of abstraction.[14]

Though I suggested that Caro was not to be seen as the sole initiator of a new tradition, I referred earlier to a categorical change associated with his work. From 1953 to 1963 Caro taught part-time at St Martin's School of Art in London.[15] During a period of significant change in his own work, his development acted as the focus for a group of younger sculptors, all born between 1934 and 1937, who were associated with the school first as students (variously between 1955 and 1962) and then as teachers: David Annesley, Michael Bolus, Phillip King, Tim Scott, William Tucker and Isaac Witkin. While Caro's contemporaries Eduardo Paolozzi and William Turnbull had for some time been producing sculpture that looked to recent Parisian art rather than to the native tradition dominated by Moore, and while Paolozzi was also teaching at St Martin's from 1955 to 1958, it was in Caro's career that various of the different factors impelling practical and conceptual change seemed to meet around 1960. This was the year in which he made his first non-figurative sculpture in welded steel (fig. 3), the year following a two-month visit to America, during which he had formed friendships with Kenneth Noland and Clement Greenberg. Caro later spoke of the effects of this visit in terms conveying the all-important recognition that Modernism's transatlantic migration had involved a change of aesthetic: 'There's a fine-art quality about European art, even when it's made from junk. America made me see that there are no barriers and no regulations. . . . There's a tremendous freedom in knowing that your only limitations in a sculpture or painting are whether it carries its intentions or not, not whether it's "Art".'[16]

Phillip King, who by 1960 was teaching alongside Caro at St Martin's, has testified to the effect on other sculptors of the latter's apparently sudden abandonment of 'bronze and all that. . . . His example was very

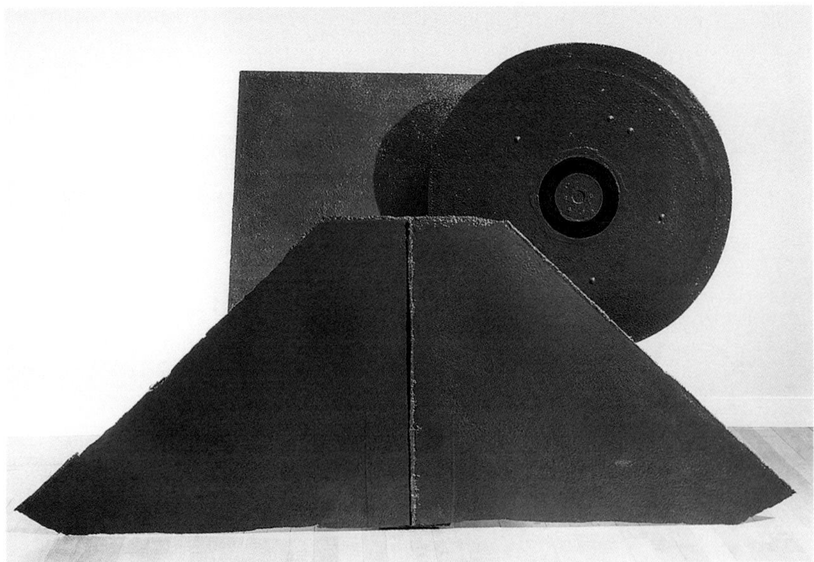

3 Anthony Caro, *Twenty-Four Hours*, 1960, steel painted, 138.4 × 223.5 × 838 cm, Tate

stimulating. He was . . . at an early stage of his breakthrough and was very uncertain as to where he was going, communicating a kind of excitement that sculpture could go anywhere and be very open.'[17] The notion of a 'breakthrough' associated with Caro's work at this time was not simply the invention of British interests. In 1965 Clement Greenberg published an article on Caro's work in *Arts Yearbook*.[18] He began, '"Breakthrough" is a much-abused word in contemporary art writing, but I don't hesitate to apply it to the sculpture in steel that Anthony Caro has been doing since 1960', and continued, 'He is the only new sculptor whose sustained quality can bear comparison with Smith's. With him it has become possible at long last to talk of a generation in sculpture that really comes after Smith's.' In his account of the 'sustained quality' of Caro's work, Greenberg drew attention to the use of ready-made materials, to the 'invasion of space' and to 'an emphasis on abstractness, on radical unlikeness to nature'. He also referred to the debt owed by Caro's work to pictorial art and asserted 'its radical rejection of monolithic structure'. As I suggested earlier, these qualities were the virtual opposites of those associated with the work of Moore and of the British sculptors who followed him most closely. Their explicit assertion as positive values presupposed an entirely different basis for judgement of sculpture from the one which had led Read to stress the priority of monumentality and compactness. Caro (who, it should be remembered, had worked as an assistant to Moore from 1951 to 1953) was now identified as the artist who had effectively terminated a European tradition – 'compelled', in Greenberg's words, 'by a vision that is unable to make itself known except by changing art' – and in the process qualified himself as the rightful successor to America's most distinguished modern sculptor. In 1967 his work was even included by the Los Angeles County Museum in an exhibition titled *American Sculpture in the Sixties*.[19]

Certainly there was some strong compatibility in the 1960s between Caro's work and Smith's on the one hand and Noland's on the other – a compatibility recognised and strengthened by personal friendship. As certainly Greenberg was well placed to identify the particular virtues of Caro's work, the influence of his published deliberations and his personal encouragement and advice giving him some measure of responsibility for its development. But the real importance of the change in Caro's work was not so much that it signified identification with American art as that it asserted commitment to the cosmopolitan values of Modernism in its latest phase – a phase which it is tempting to refer to as 'post-Pollock', since Pollock's work of 1946–50 seemed to set the standard for whatever was to follow. I do not mean to suggest that the impact of American painting cut British sculpture entirely clear of the European sculptural tradition. Nor was the European tradition in sculpture seen by all British sculptors and British critics as appropriately summed up in the work of Henry Moore, not even in the 1950s. Welding was practised at St Martin's before 1960, and considerable interest was then being shown in the constructed work of Picasso and González and in the early work of Giacometti. As regards the technical characteristics of its fabrication, the new British sculpture of the 1960s had some strong precedents in much earlier European art. But it does seem to have been the case that the meaning and identity of sculpture were reconsidered in England in the 1960s and that the reconsidering was done largely by reference to concepts of Modernism first encountered with regard to American painting, and articulated in American criticism, specifically by Greenberg. When Caro first met Greenberg in 1959, the latter had just published an important essay, 'Collage'.[20] One passage in particular might well have served to draw attention to possible practical and conceptual links between the 'alternative' tradition of constructed sculpture and important developments in modern painting.

> The originally affixed elements of a collage had, in effect, been extruded from the picture plane – the sheet of drawing paper or the canvas – to make a bas-relief. But it was a 'constructed', not a sculpted, bas-relief, and it founded a new genre of sculpture. Construction sculpture was freed long ago from its bas-relief frontality and every other suggestion of the picture plane, but has continued to this day to be marked by its pictorial origins. Not for nothing did the sculptor-constructor González call it the new art of 'drawing in space'. But with equal and more descriptive justice it could be called, harking back more specifically to its birth in the collage: the new art of joining two-dimensional forms in three-dimensional space.[21]

This last definition seems tellingly apt in relation to Caro's typical work of the early 1960s (fig. 4).

For some while in the 1960s, the effect of sculpture's strong conceptual dependence on painting was to depress interest in the expressiveness of its material qualities, and to encourage relocation of the ontology of sculpture in a psychological world of experiences, feelings and states of mind. According to William Tucker, 'Sculptors learned from the Cubist painters that no material and no subject was sacred. Sculpture could be made from anything, about anything. Permanence consisted in the strength of the idea, not in the material.'[22] 'I'm fed up with objects on pedestals', Caro declared in 1961. 'I'd like to break down the graspability of sculpture. Sculpture is terrifically tangible, but a painting, however concrete, is partly in the realm of illusion.'[23] In 1967 Tim Scott published a commentary on some notes by Tucker. Tucker had asserted

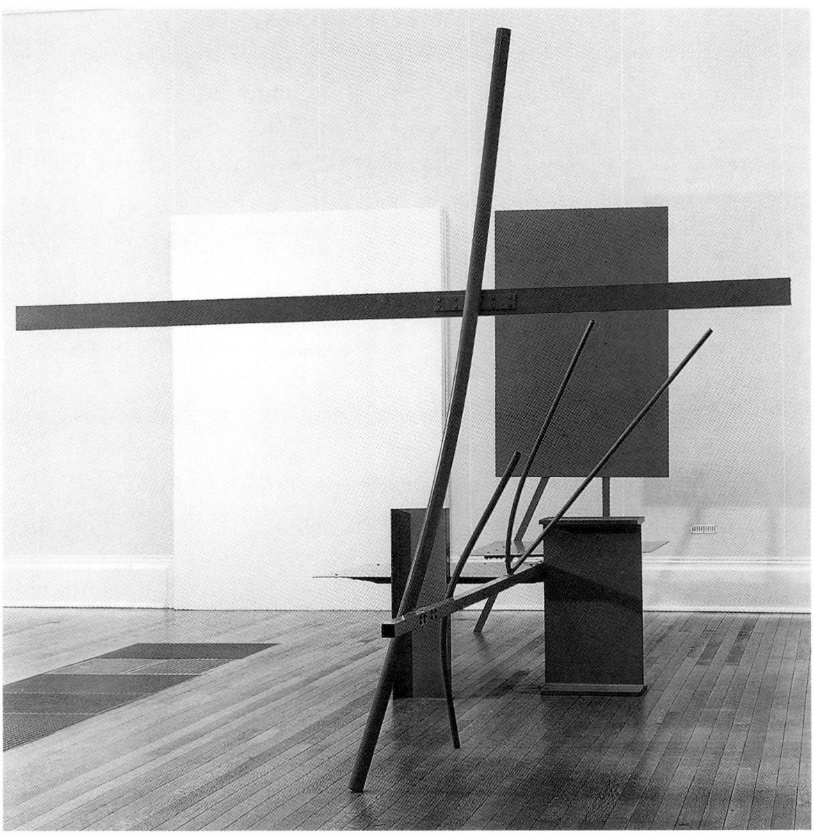

4 Anthony Caro, *Early One Morning*, 1962, steel and aluminium painted red, 290 × 620 × 330 cm, Tate

that 'Sculpture is a proposition about the physical world, about a finite order (completeness), and by implication about our existence in the world.' Scott responded, 'Sculpture acts by displacement; it is the *state* of being, the *state* of feeling, the *state* of experience, the *state* of physical awareness and sensation, the *state* of confrontation by physical phenomena; not these things themselves or an interpretation of them.'[24] (For the sculptors of Scott's and Tucker's generation, this relocation of sculpture in favour of the psychological provided a novel means to think about the significance of physical properties, but without implying that these properties were of secondary interest. In anticipation of the later substance of this essay, it may be noted now that the implications of this conceptual shift were to be taken further by sculptors of a slightly younger generation. Among these, some, like Richard Long, were students at St Martin's in the mid- to late 1960s when Scott and Tucker were among those teaching there. For a few of these younger artists, a more complete identification of 'sculpture' with 'psychological state' was considerably to diminish the status of specific physical properties in the conceptual hierarchy of sculpture.)

By the early 1960s certain characteristics were central to advanced Modernist work in painting and sculpture alike: avoidance of the contained plastic image; pursuit of abstraction to an extent that entailed the purging even of metaphorical reference to things in the world; as regards the 'morality' of practical procedures, a tendency to value the effects of improvisation over the achievement of planned ends;[25] and as regards conditions of spectatorship, the placing of priority on intuitive apprehension over kinaesthetic response. In the most professional criticism of the time, these characteristics were identified as necessary conditions of quality in art. Once he had effected the appropriate change in his working procedures and in his concepts of what kind of thing a sculpture could be, Caro very quickly carried with him both the sympathies of Modernist critics on either side of the Atlantic and the interests of those younger sculptors in England whose response to American painting had already been decisive.

A break had been created in the 'line of succession' of British sculpture and a new agenda of concerns set for prospective practitioners of the art. In 1960, at the end of his apprenticeship as a sculptor, Phillip King had visited the *Documenta* exhibition at Kassel. He later described the European sculpture he saw there as 'dominated by a post-war feeling which seemed very distorted and contorted. . . . It was somehow terribly like scratching your own wounds – an international style with everyone showing the same neuroses.'[26] In contrast the American painting shown at the same exhibition seemed to offer a 'message of hope and optimism, large-scale, less inbred'. A year later, King's contemporary William Tucker responded to a question about the tradition on which current work was based: 'Not a sculpture tradition. The precedents are probably in painting and poetry.'[27] This sudden sense of freedom from sculptural precedents – specific to the two or three years either side of 1960 – was shared among the members of the relatively small community based around St Martin's. No adequate explanation of the development of British sculpture over the past twenty-five years can be given without some acknowledgement of the importance of that moment.

The change in the direction of British sculpture was made public with far less than the usual delay, thanks in part to the interest of Bryan Robertson, then director of the Whitechapel Art Gallery. A substantial exhibition of Caro's recent work was staged there in 1963 and it was immediately clear how sympathetic a venue this was to the nature of the new work. In a text written for the catalogue, the American critic Michael Fried drew attention to the significance of 'syntax' (that is, the nature of the relations between discrete parts) in the visual quality of Caro's work and also to the 'achieved weight-lessness' of the sculptures – a quality that, as Greenberg noted, 'belongs, distinctively, to the new tradition of non-monolithic sculpture which has sprung from the Cubist collage'.[28] Two years later the Whitechapel staged an exhibition of work by the 'New Generation' of sculptors associated with Caro and St Martin's: Annesley, Bolus, King, Scott, Tucker and Witkin (fig. 5). Both exhibitions attracted considerable critical interest. By 1966 each of the New Generation sculptors was represented by a major London gallery and each had been given at least one solo show.[29] The Whitechapel staged retrospectives of Scott and King in 1967 and 1968, respectively. A still more telling measure of success was the readiness of New York galleries to exhibit the new British sculpture. Richard Feigen showed Tucker in 1965 and King in 1966. In the latter year Witkin showed at Elkon, Bolus at Kornblee and Annesley at Poindexter. Scott, the youngest of the group, showed with Lawrence Rubin in 1970. Interviewed for the British journal *Studio International* late in 1967, Greenberg appeared to confirm that the claim Alan Bowness had made the previous year was not to be dismissed as mere insular partisanship: 'I think certain younger Englishmen

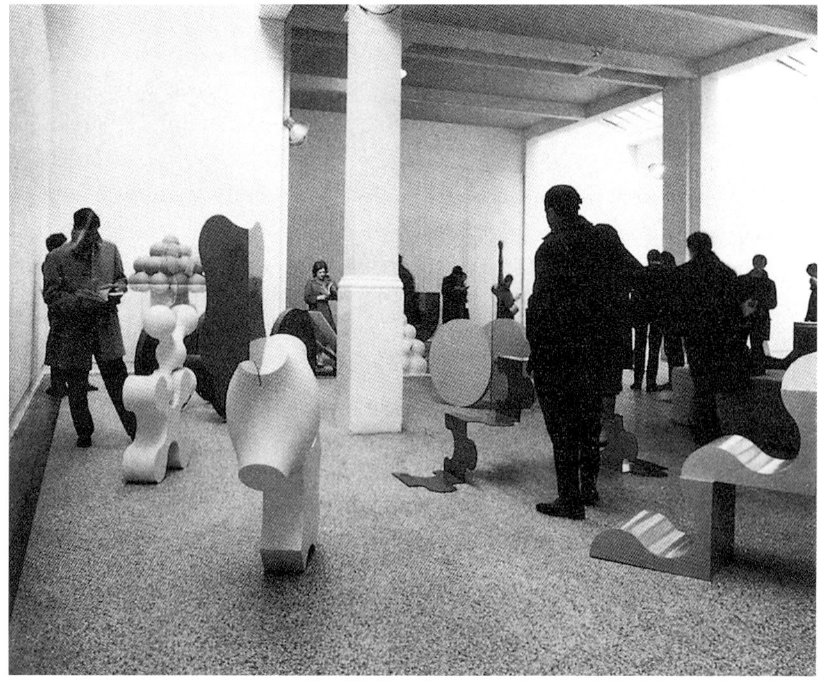

5 *New Generation Sculpture*, Whitechapel Art Gallery, London, 1965, general view

are doing the best sculpture in the world today – sculpture of originality and character. I'd also mention range; variety of effect. That's what makes for "big" art.'[30] American painting and British sculpture had come together, it seemed, with the blessing of the highest critical authority, to constitute the advanced modernist art of the time.

## 'NO PUBLIC REALM'

Though it was inevitable that the names of the New Generation sculptors would remain associated one with another, there was no great homogeneity in their work overall, nor was a debt to Caro as easily discernible in King's work or Tucker's as it was, say, in the welded metal sculpture of Bolus or Annesley. During the 1960s King seemed the most interesting of the group, and until 1969 the most distinctive of his sculptures were based on relatively simple volumetric forms: cones, thick slabs and box shapes. Much of his early work was made in plastic or fibreglass. Tucker also used fibreglass for much of his work of the mid-1960s. Scott made considerable use of glass, perspex and acrylic sheet. For uncommitted observers and for younger students, however, the advanced sculpture course at St Martin's did purvey some strong sense of agreement not simply about the importance of sculpture, but also about the kinds of practical concepts and critical terms that were appropriate to the business of teaching, discussion and evaluation. As regards the climate of debate in general and the occasional semi-formal 'Sculpture Forum' in particular, opinions tended to differ widely among witnesses divided by a mere four or five years in age. Bruce McLean is one of various alumni who have recorded their disenchantment: 'The St Martin's sculpture forum would avoid every broader issue, discussing for hours the position of one piece of metal in relation to another. . . . Twelve adult men with pipes would walk for hours around sculpture and mumble!'[31]

The pace of change from enthusiasm to scepticism was surprisingly rapid. Even as the sculpture of Caro and the New Generation was being acclaimed on both sides of the Atlantic, those who dissented or felt excluded from the conceptual ambience of St Martin's were already beginning to view it as the enclave of a doctrinaire and self-protective practice. This needs to be explained, especially in view of the importance attached to the 'breakthrough' of around 1958–62.

The apparent element of exclusiveness or defensiveness is certainly not to be accounted for simply in terms of the dispositions of the individuals concerned, nor as a closing of ranks in the face of some withdrawal of critical support. It was rather, I think, a symptom of the broader historical conditions of modern art at the time. A practice so powerfully determined by transatlantic Modernism was bound to take on board many of the current problems of Modernism itself, and thus sooner rather than later to become subject to that hardening and dogmatising of taste and expressiveness which had begun to beset American abstract painting and its attendant criticism – begun, I would now say, in the immediate aftermath of Pollock's unmatchable achievement. It is certainly true that Caro and his friends established a climate of critical interest in the best of American modernist painting (which in the early 1960s was still arguably the best American painting of the time) and in the best of American criticism (which was arguably still being written by Greenberg and by such younger disciples as Fried). It is also true that Caro himself was able to benefit from that element of coherence within the modernist tradition which apparently allowed a well-tried set of aesthetic protocols to be satisfied in the face of *ad hoc* compositional procedures. But the space left in Modernism for sculpture to exploit turned out not to have been as large as promised. In its very faultlessness, Caro's work represents a kind of terminus. By the late 1960s it was becoming clear that all art produced within the now-prescriptive decorum of Modernism was bound to become subject to that mechanism in its production which reduced the area of significant practical problems to problems of design, and the problems of attendant criticism to matters of aesthetic tuning.

This is a judgement made with hindsight. It is most unlikely that any of those involved would have assented to such a view at the time (and improbable that they would assent to it now). But determining conditions are determining conditions and they tend to rule over the possibilities of expression in art. If an air of defensiveness did indeed come to permeate the practical and critical environment of the former New Generation during the late 1960s, it may have been because it transpired that transatlantic Modernism had reached the shores of Britain as a virtually exhausted resource and that 'big' art was not after all within their collective grasp. I do not mean to reduce the work and careers of half a dozen different artists to a single pattern. There was to be considerable variety within King's and Scott's work during the 1970s and 1980s, for instance, and Tucker's work has developed along lines different from both. If there has been a limitation common to the work of all, it has been more than merely stylistic. One way to suggest the nature of this limit might be to observe that neither the modernist criticism nor the modernist art of the late 1960s and early 1970s appeared able to admit the possible conceptual conditions of its own failure.

This implies a loss of realism and of critical imagination. Neither the autonomy of a practice nor the expressive quality of its products can be taken for granted, nor are they to be established by appeals to authority. The grounds of autonomy have to be struggled for, found and established in relation to continuing conditions and circumstances, while the expressive quality of art is always a matter for open inquiry. A distinction between generations in the mid-1960s can be made in relation to the issue of sculpture's autonomy and of the terms on which it was established. The artists of the New Generation, though they deliberated at length over the means of construction of sculpture, tended to take for granted its value as a practice and as a form of experience. The emerging sculptors of the late 1960s, on the other hand, were both more casual and more open-minded about how sculpture was to be made and about what it was to be made from, but treated its means of exhibition – the social, geographical and psychological conditions associated with the art – as matters critical to the nature of the enterprise. In the litany of modernist criticism of sculpture, 'environmental' had been a term resonant with disapproval. It could be said – and was by many in the late 1960s – that the generation of a climate of distaste around such issues was merely a means to protect a conceptually fragile form of art against the full force of their implications.

I have deliberately couched the preceding paragraphs in a dissenting voice, aware that other accounts are feasible. The area of possible dispute needs to be properly defined (and will be filled out in practical terms in the next section). It should first be stressed, however, that much carping at the cosmopolitan modernisation of British sculpture – an achievement rightly associated with St Martin's – came from those left marginalised in their provincialism elsewhere: the self-appointed guardians of British art's naturalistic fussiness, the devotees of an arch semi-abstraction or those beset by the fallacy that non-trivial modernisation of art could be achieved by means of an 'interface' with technology. It is no part of the aim of this essay to justify the protests of insular, conservative or superficial opinion. The case for the virtues of full-blooded Modernism needs to be given its due. Just as the work of Noland in the early and mid-1960s made most other abstract painting look small-town and concocted, so Caro's contemporary abstract sculpture and, perhaps more emphatically, the brightly artificial confections of King and Scott exposed as hopeless anachronisms a whole range of overworked sculptural analogues for man, machine or beast, for the forces of nature, for the underlying structure of the universe and so on.

With that acknowledgement made, an important matter of historical interpretation and of critical judgement remains to be decided – a matter as important to the valuation of British sculpture in the recent past as it is to assessment of the post-painterly abstraction of the 1960s or the new expressionism of the 1980s. The view here offered of the conditions of British sculpture in the late 1960s is based on the assumption that the high period of modernist art, which had opened in France in the 1860s, closed in America in the early 1950s; that the possibility of a first-order expressive art was significantly exhausted by the Abstract Expressionists, and by Pollock in particular; and that subsequent art in the modernist tradition staggers under claims for a critical expressive content which become increasingly hard to sustain. There was, as it were, a progressive loss of moral strenuousness in modernist art after Pollock.[32] If this assumption is valid, it is likely to follow that criticism committed to the continued vitality of modernist art in the 1960s and 1970s will have tended to overestimate its expressive qualities, and to misrepresent the academic attenuation of style as critical change and newness. (In this connection consider the North American abstract painting of the late 1960s and early 1970s – Edward Avedisian, Darby Bannard, Jack Bush and Gene Davis, for example – and its interpretation in modernist criticism.) It is also likely to follow that some significant development in art post-Pollock will be found to have been characterised by acknowledgement of *limits* on the possibility of expressiveness, though one would not expect such a development to be acknowledged as significant by observers of a modernist persuasion. (In this connection consider so-called Minimal art and its reception in modernist criticism.)

According to the view advanced here, the art of the period since the 1950s has offered two alternative modes of practice, or modes of conceiving practice. The first – identified with the modernist mainstream – has been predicated on the values of expression, sensation, spontaneity, newness and integrity of effect, has been supported by the dominant critical order, but has involved the reduction of aesthetic problems to the discrimination of formal effects by highly attuned ('sensitive') observers. The second mode rests on the presupposition that such values as expressiveness, sensation, spontaneity and newness have become irredeemably conventionalised, and that maintenance of art's critical function requires that this conventionalisation be acknowledged – as it was, for instance, in Jasper Johns's work of the late 1950s and early 1960s. In the first instance practical priority is placed on the relative novelty and individuality of formal and visual effects within a range determined by the continuity of the modernist tradition. In the second instance priority is placed rather on the critical function of the work, both in revising the available terms of description of works of art and in questioning those patterns of response to the art object that are supposed to define the observer's psychological experience. Fulfilment of this latter function by some works of Minimal art led the modernist critic Fried, in a notorious article in *Artforum*, to accuse the likes of Donald Judd and Robert Morris of a concern with the theatrical at the expense of the aesthetic.[33]

Fried was an ardent champion of Caro's work[34] and a welcome and informed visitor to St Martin's during the 1960s. At the time his was also the most prominent representation of the elaborated modernist view of art and of its recent history[35] and he did much to establish the theoretical terms of reference according to which the new British sculpture was assimilated to the modernist canon. According to this view – which is in clear contradistinction to the one offered above – the mainstream of art after Pollock involved a further elimination of the residues of figurative techniques, a more radical abstraction in assertion of art's unlikeness to other things and in defence of the autonomy of its quality. Art's essential function was the more decisively exposed as the expression of feeling in terms of a medium progressively reduced to its essentials. This was the supposed purport of authentic modernist art, in which the possibility of meaning and quality in experience was continually struggled for and renewed. As regards sculpture, the example of painting helped to purge certain compromising associations with architecture (the tendency to environmental or monumental effect)[36] and with the theatre (the tendency to rhetorical or dramatic expression, notably through the use of the figure) and thereby brought about a purification of the sculptor's resources of expression. Thus Fried could write of two sculptures by Caro, *Deep Body Blue* and *Prairie*, 'In the radicalness of their abstraction both have more in common with certain poetry and music, and certain recent painting, than with the work of any previous sculptor. And yet this very radicalness enables them to achieve a body and a world of meaning and expression that belong essentially to sculpture.'[37]

It may be noted that while poetry and music are acceptable cognates for sculpture as conceived in modernist theory, architecture and theatre are not. This may be because experience of the former is seen as private and contemplative whereas the occasions of the latter are typically public. Certainly the form of sculpture that Caro initiated in Britain is predicated on a belief in the privacy of the encounter between spectator and work of art:

> Of course there are some wrong settings for sculpture. Just as it would be meaningless to play a quartet in the marketplace so there are some quite unsuitable sites for certain sculptures. I prefer my sculpture to be seen in a tranquil and enclosed space. Almost all sculpture, I guess, needs to be indoors – or enclosed in some way. . . . Up to now, all my sculpture (however large) is un-public.[38]

Through the association with music, the requirement of tranquillity and the assertion of an 'un-public' function, Caro here signalled the identification of his work with a distinct critical and aesthetic tradition, the modernist tradition, according to which the significance of art lies in its preservation of spiritual as against utilitarian values. Opposition to this view of art's significance has normally been expressed on the grounds that it entails the provision of special conditions – physical, social and economic – for a special audience. Democratic aspirations and modernist styles have rarely been easy to reconcile in the face of the actual conditions under which art is encountered and consumed.[39]

The view of sculpture articulated by Fried and by Caro does seem to presuppose the availability of relatively specialised circumstances, physical, social and psychological, for the realisation of an expressive potential. In fact, Caro seems to have suffered from few doubts about the means of presentation of his abstract sculpture in the 1960s, perhaps because he was in a relatively strong position to control viewing conditions. For some of the younger sculptors, however, the ill-adjustment of private content to public context may have had something to do with the apparent disappointment of early hopes. William Tucker drew the connection in 'An Essay on Sculpture', published in January 1969.[40] He referred to 'the rich possibilities of a new subject-matter, new materials and the consequent re-appraisal of the kind of articulation sculpture might have', possibilities which had remained 'largely untapped after the heroic period of Cubism, until recent years'. He continued:

> If the bright morning of those hopes has somewhat dimmed, it may well be because neither the artists themselves, nor those who made themselves responsible for publicising and distributing the work, recognised the nature of the revolution that had occurred. The scale and availability of the new work was public, but its content was private. Society had not asked for it, except in the non-world of galleries, museums and circulating exhibitions. The sculptors themselves were hostile to the problems of public communication, rightly suspicious of the motives of those public organisers whose mission it is to cram new feet into old boots. Sculpture in public places, sculpture and architecture, sculpture for schools and hospitals, playground sculpture, festival sculpture, sculpture in gardens, sculpture as environment: anything to make the new work tame and acceptable, to drain off its real power to subvert a comfortable world-view. And sure enough new armies of bronze generals and marble nymphs disguised in steel geometry and vermiform plastic have emerged to reap the harvest of a dead tradition, a temporary and invented public art. For there is no public realm in our time to which a public sculpture might give visual purpose.

For the aspiring British sculptors of the next generation, the notion of a 'public realm' to be addressed in sculpture was still more remote or

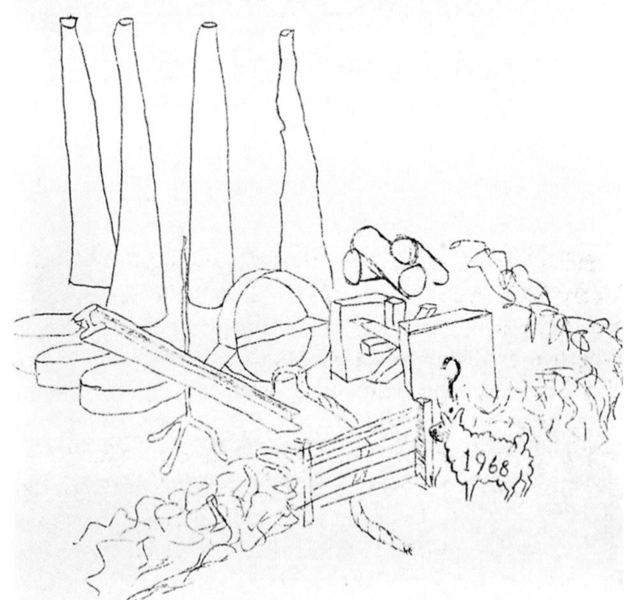


6 Glyn Foulkes, 'St Martin's in the Fields', 1968, cartoon from *Potlatch* (St Martin's student magazine). 'Sculpture then seemed a vast empty field, and we had just climbed over the gate' (David Annesley)

vexed with difficulty. Nor were they likely to identify either with the kinds of concerns Tucker was expressing or with his implication that New Generation sculpture was invested with 'real power to subvert a comfortable world-view'. What they were confronted with in the late 1960s was the apparent success of New Generation sculpture, the prevalence of its exhibition and its theoretical compactness with the dominant aesthetic order (fig. 6). Of those associated with St Martin's as students and new teachers in the mid- to late 1960s – a category that includes Barry Flanagan, Richard Long, Bill Woodrow and Richard Deacon[41] – more than one publicly expressed either some strong dissent from that aesthetic order or some scepticism about the need for specialised viewing conditions, or both. Some attempt to reconcile working conditions with conditions of exhibition was made by one diverse group of sculptors who occupied the premises of a former brewery at Stockwell Depot, London, opening their studios there to the public for the first time in May 1968.[42]

In an article called 'The Concerns of Emerging Sculptors', one of their number, Roland Brener, criticised the New Generation sculptors for having 'lapsed into a form of sculptural rhetoric'.[43] He continued:

> Art can evolve only to a predictable point within an established idiom and the gallery type situation is in itself restrictive enough to limit sculptural possibilities. The New Generation sculptors accepted this limitation and have not up till now questioned or analysed their mode of exposition. The (theoretical) concern with 'realness' and 'openness', the attempt to free sculpture from a descriptive function and associative connotations fail if the work relies for its success on the specialised environment made for it. The contrived social and environmental situation in which it works best is its own contradiction.

Brener's article was printed in the journal *Studio International* in January 1969. This was a special issue devoted to 'Some aspects of contemporary British sculpture' scheduled to coincide with a large retrospective exhibition of Caro's work at the Hayward Gallery in London. The issue included coverage of the sculpture course at St Martin's; Tucker's 'Essay on Sculpture'; a symposium on Caro's work by David Annesley, Roelof Louw, Tim Scott and William Tucker; features on 'Colour in Sculpture' and on the sculptors at Stockwell Depot; and an article by the present author called 'Some recent sculpture in Britain' which featured the work of Brener, Flanagan, Long, Louw and McLean. With the sole exception of William Turnbull, whose steel sculptures of 1963–6 bear a superficial resemblance to Caro's more austere works of the mid-1960s,[44] all those sculptors accorded any significant coverage were or had been associated with the sculpture department at St Martin's as students or teachers or both. Publication of this material drew down on the heads of the editors the accusation that British sculpture had been identified to a quite unwarranted extent with this single school.

If the accusation was justified, however, it was not because the issue lacked variety, a fact that served as testament to the diversity by then associated with the name of St Martin's. Nor was it because dissenting views had been deliberately excluded in the celebration of a distinct line of succession. During the symposium, Annesley eulogised about Caro's

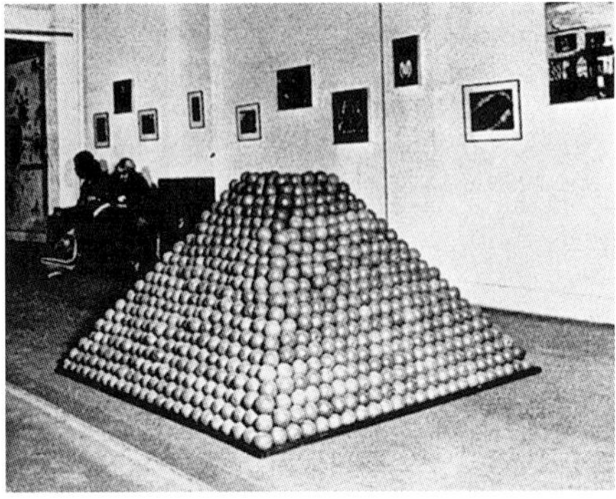

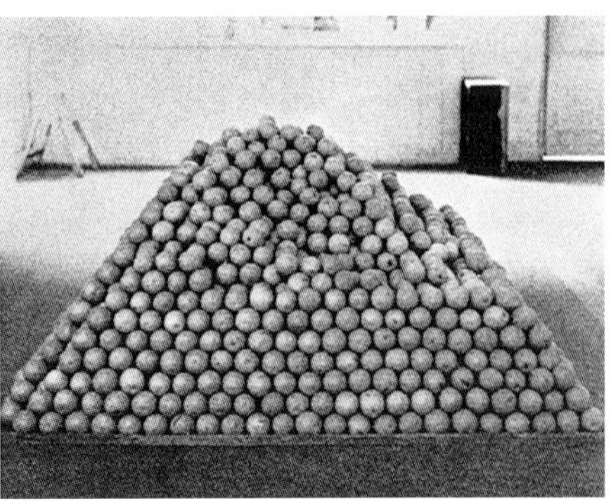

7 *(above and facing page)* Roelof Louw, *Soul City. Pyramid of Oranges*, 1967, around 5,000 oranges stacked, h. 150 cm, base 165 × 165 cm. Installation at Arts Laboratory, London, 1967. Each person who entered was invited to take an orange

work in relation to the painting of Ron Davis, Kenneth Noland, Jules Olitski and Frank Stella. Louw responded with exasperation:

> The way you go on, I feel completely oppressed by Caro's sculptural criteria. . . . It's like being swamped with it. I think it's a question of finding something that is distinctly different from his criteria. There is this 'New Generation' image associated with Caro that persists in English sculpture, and in terms of the sculpture being done *here* now is perhaps not such a good thing.[45]

Though Louw is the exact contemporary of Bolus, King and Witkin, he did not attend St Martin's as a student until the years 1961–5. He was not included in the *New Generation* exhibition of 1965, nor was his work evidently compatible. As one of those working at Stockwell Depot in the late 1960s, he shared in a critical reaction against the hermeticism of recent British sculpture and in that concern for the interaction of sculpture and context that developed in part as a consequence (fig. 7).

There were other factors within the broader conditions of art, however, which served to fuel this and related concerns. During the course of the 1960s, it became increasingly evident that a strong American alternative had developed to the modernist mainstream as

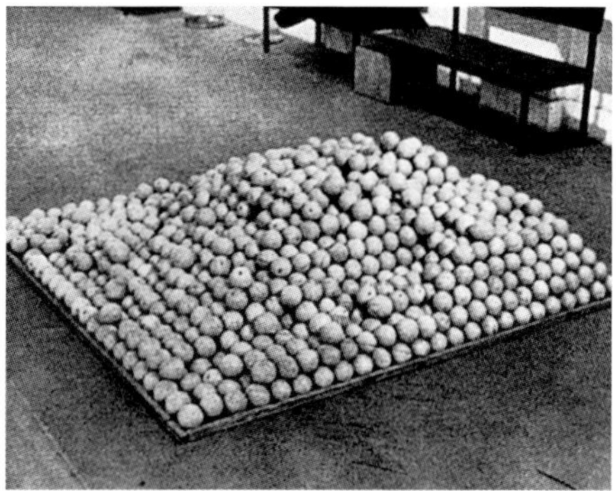

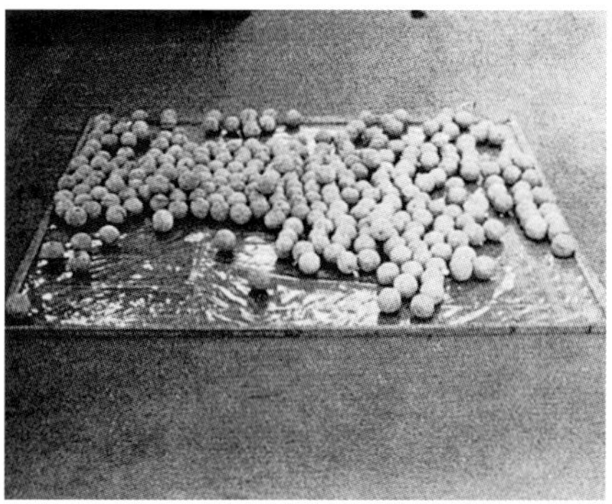

defined by Greenberg and Fried – or rather, perhaps, that Modernism itself had bifurcated along lines such as I suggested earlier, and that its dominant professional forms were no longer to be identified with post-painterly abstraction and constructed sculpture. Exposure in London was relatively piecemeal and haphazard, reflecting changes in the export policies of American dealers and agencies and in the interest of individual curators, rather than the chronological sequence of events in New York. In the early 1960s the Robert Fraser Gallery exhibited the work of Pop artists such as Oldenburg and Warhol. In 1964 the Whitechapel staged large retrospective exhibitions of Johns (whose work Greenberg had referred to pejoratively as singing 'the swan song of homeless representation')[46] and Robert Rauschenberg (whose work Fried was to denigrate as 'theater').[47] Some attentive readers had been alerted to the existence of an individual and often dissenting voice by Judd's criticism published in *Arts* between 1959 and 1965. In his essay 'Specific Objects' in the latter year, he characterised 'present three-dimensional work' in terms that implied that sculpture 'made part by part, by addition, composed', had been practically and conceptually superseded.[48] In the same year *Artforum* became sporadically available in London and was immediately adopted as required reading by those British artists and critics with any serious interest in modern art.

The first of Robert Morris's 'Notes on Sculpture' appeared in *Artforum* in 1966, as did the earliest of Robert Smithson's mannered self-justifications.[49] Morris was concerned to prise the concept of sculpture loose from its association with the qualities of painting since Pollock: 'It should be stated that the concerns of sculpture have been for some time not only distinct but hostile to those of painting. The clearer the nature of the values of sculpture becomes the stronger the opposition appears'.[50] Like Judd, Morris was concerned to re-establish the priority of 'shape' over 'syntax' and in the third set of his 'Notes on Sculpture' struck the same tone of overt antagonism towards the notion of an improvised art for private contemplation. With regard to 'the forms used in present-day three-dimensional work', he wrote:

> Such work which has the feel and look of openness, extendibility, accessibility, publicness, repeatability, equanimity, directness, immediacy, and has been formed by clear decision rather than groping craft would seem to have a few social implications, none of which are negative. Such work would undoubtedly be boring to those who long for access to an exclusive specialness, the experience of which reassures their superior perception.[51]

'Notes on Sculpture, Part 3' was published in *Artforum* in the summer of 1967 in an influential special issue on 'American Sculpture'. Besides contributions from Robert Smithson and Sol LeWitt and articles on David Smith, Oldenburg and Mark Di Suvero, the issue included Fried's sustained attack on Minimal Art, 'Art and Objecthood', which asserted the value of Caro's sculpture as 'a fountainhead of anti-literalist and anti-theatrical sensibility' in contradistinction to the works of Judd, Morris and other Americans. Lines of demarcation had thus become clearly drawn in the artistic culture of the late 1960s, and drawn with specific regard to the nature and valuation of sculpture from both sides of the Atlantic. Symptomatic of the gradual internationalisation of this debate was the publication by *Studio International* in April 1969 of a special issue on 'Aspects of art called "minimal" ', with contributions from Judd, Smithson, LeWitt, Dan Flavin and Carl Andre.[52] In the same month British audiences were finally able to view relevant American works at first hand when the Museum of Modern Art's mixed survey *Art of the Real* opened at the Tate Gallery, with works by Andre, Judd, LeWitt, Morris, Smithson and Tony Smith, among others.[53]

I do not mean to suggest that the appearance of sculpture by younger British artists changed in the late 1960s or early 1970s in response to the impact of American Minimal Art. In fact, comparatively little sculpture was produced in Britain that emulated the styles of Judd, Morris, LeWitt or Andre, and for obvious reasons what there was of it hardly deserves to be recalled. The point is rather that younger British sculptors had already strong grounds for interest in such issues as were at stake in the *Artforum* special issue. Many of those explicit critical divisions and theoretical arguments which were occasioned by the Minimal artists' competition for the avant-garde centre stage in the mid-1960s were easily enough interpreted in terms of controversies endemic to the development of British sculpture over the same period. If my earlier suggestions are valid, these controversies on both sides of the Atlantic were generated by common problems – by a kind of 'crisis of Modernism'[54] – experienced at a deep level.

## 'EVERYTHING ELSE BUT SCULPTURE'

As time passes it becomes increasingly clear that the moment of the late 1960s represents a nodal point of some significance, not simply in the history of artistic styles but in more general aspects of the cultural and political life of the West. The idea of a 'post-modern' or a 'post-modernist' art gained currency in the 1980s and was applied to various forms of painting and sculpture – not to mention those artistic practices that can be included in neither category – with various degrees of theoretical justification, but always with the implication that a certain cultural regime was drawing to a close. It is surely still an open question whether we witnessed a change in the historical character of our culture or merely a redirection of intellectual and artistic fashion. If the former, however, we may have to look back over at least the past forty years for an adequate understanding of the relationship between Modernism and its cultural succession. Central to any analysis of this relationship must be an inquiry into the forms of objects variously designated as artistic and into the kinds of relations supposed to obtain between these objects and interested spectators. What cognitive and other functions are works of art – for our present purposes works of sculpture, specifically – supposed typically or necessarily to fulfil and how have these functions changed (if they have changed)?

In an interview of 1974, Caro looked back to the moment of the early 1960s:

> It was a very exciting time. We could be going to one another's studios, or into the sculpture school; there'd be work to look at, work that would call your own work into question. . . . All of us were questioning the assumptions by which sculpture had said 'I'm Sculpture'. Anything was possible in those years. It wasn't really the material that was important. What was important was the examination of what sculpture could be to you in your life.[55]

Whatever the positive legacy of this questioning and this examination – and it was certainly considerable – four particular practical and theoretical assumptions were left intact in the wake of the New Generation's early success. The first, already mentioned, was the assumption that sculpture rightly claimed for itself viewing conditions that emphasised its hermetic integrity, its radical unlikeness to other things. The paradigm viewing space was the white-painted gallery, empty of all possible distractions. The second assumption was that the spectator's interest in processes, procedures and techniques of fabrication was properly subordinate to the whole effect of the finished work. How a piece was put together was a matter of lower critical priority than what it felt like to be in its presence. The third assumption was that sculpture was properly made out of rigid materials and had one stable and authentic physical form. Although it had been a principle of Caro's teaching that sculpture *might* be made of anything[56] and although Tucker affirmed that 'There is no longer any resistance in the traditional limits of sculpture, Imitation and Material',[57] the technical novelty of New Generation work in the 1960s was generally restricted to those procedures of welding, bolting, moulding and turning of metals, plastics and wood that were already well-established means of manufacture – if not always for objects within the area of fine art. The fourth assumption was that the integrity of a sculpture was a matter of the syntactical coherence of its disparate parts. One sculpture might have two or more physically separated components, so long as these were bound together by some sense of the rightness of the total configuration – though it was far from clear how this 'rightness' was to be defined.

This last assumption was of some importance to the character of New Generation sculpture in relation both to American minimalist work and to the interests of emerging British sculptors. The nature of its implications makes clear how the other assumptions were interconnected in practice. Once sculpture was no longer predicated on the integrity of masses, a basic question which had to be addressed was how different components were or should be or could be related to one another, in what dimensions and across what kind of space (fig. 8). How were separate parts to be brought together, visually and conceptually, to form one work, if not by literal adhesion? For Judd, Morris and Andre, the answer lay in the repetition of identical or similar units. This was a means to preserve 'wholeness' in the perception of a single extensive work. It was also a solution that entailed recognition of the literal nature of the ground plane – or, for reliefs, the wall plane – as the defining physical limit of three-dimensional work. For Caro the solution seemed to reside rather in the achievement of a basically pictorial sense of interconnectedness between discrete parts. Thus works such as his *Prairie* of 1967 are effective insofar as the self-sufficiency of a perceived composition suppresses interest in the actual juncture of literal parts.[58] This, as Greenberg had noted in 1965, involves treating the ground in the same way as the picture plane had been treated in Cubist collage; that is, as if it were a merely notional level in relation to which other surfaces are defined and arranged.[59]

So long as single sculptures could be viewed in ideal conditions, this dependence on pictorial integrity posed no great problem. Once more than one work was shown in the same space, however, or where sculpture had to compete with the unsympathetic details of a busy environment, there was always a risk that the formal integrity of any single work would be lost and its separate components be reduced in perception to the status of accidental objects. Under such circumstances aesthetic collapse could be immediate and complete.[60] Caro has remained master

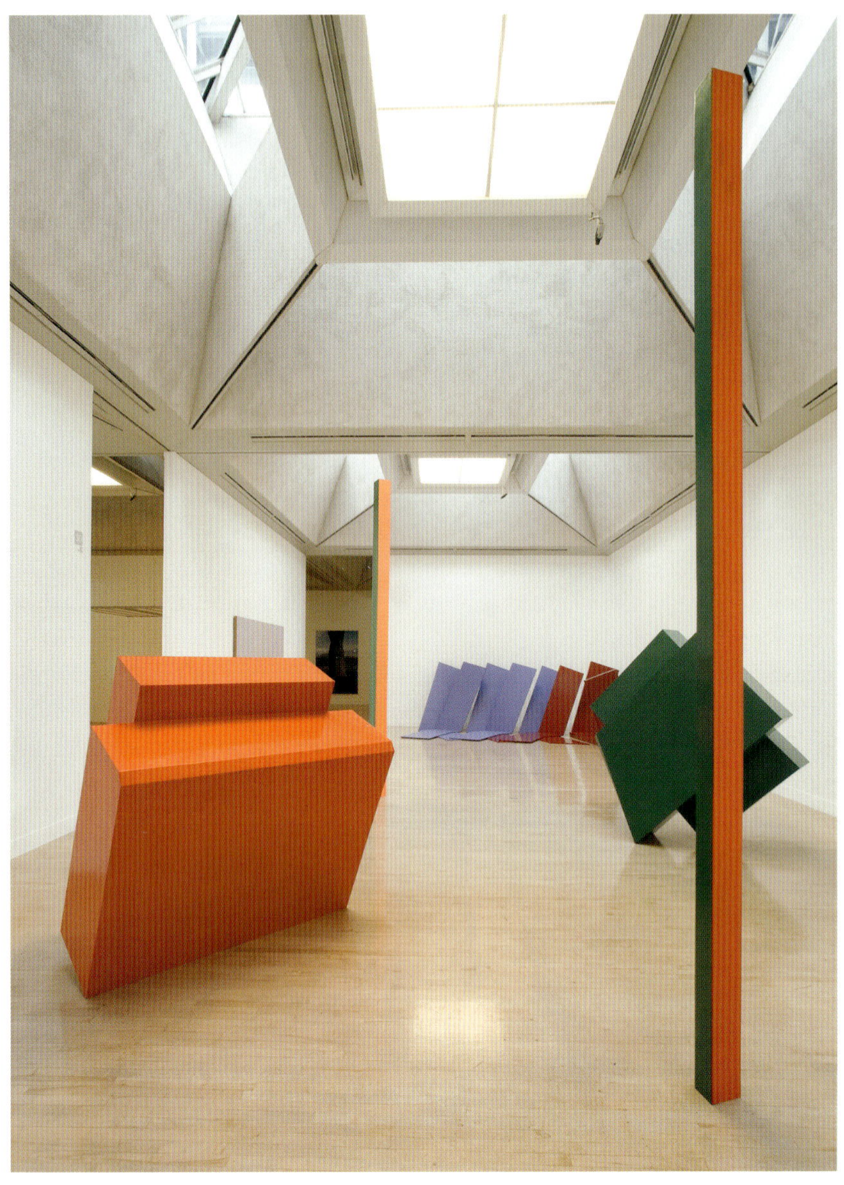

8 Phillip King, *Call*, 1967, fibreglass, 442 × 457 × 487 cm (two pieces each 442 × 15 × 15 cm; two pieces each 152.5 × 183 × 91 cm), background shows *Nile*, 1967, Tate

of the post-Cubist mode he developed in the 1960s but it proved a terminus for those who followed him. The sculptural tradition he initiated in Britain had to become conceptually conservative to continue. There remained the problem of how to extend sculpture physically and notionally without loss of integrity. This issue could be satisfactorily addressed, it seemed, only by those prepared to abandon both the additive and constructive mode and the assumption of coherence which was its justification.

In the most interesting new sculpture of the late 1960s, this and the other three basic assumptions were variously subjected to practical critique. Both Flanagan and Long were producing independent work while still associated with St Martin's as students. By 1965 Flanagan was making idiosyncratic standing objects by filling cloth 'skins' with plaster or sand. The identity of such works was very clearly established in terms of the properties of certain non-rigid materials and of the procedures by means of which these were manipulated into certain configurations. In his first one-person exhibition, in August 1966, Flanagan included a 'sculpture' made simply from poured and scooped dry sand. A year later he installed three separate works for the purposes of photography prior to their exhibition at the Biennale des Jeunes in Paris (fig. 9). The identity of the resulting arrangement led Flanagan to question the relationships between the autonomy of individual sculptures, the autonomy of individual parts of sculptures and the autonomy of a given 'exhibition' in which they were conjoined.

> The ideal state is when each object commands an equal attention to the next, due to its very own identity/separation as an object. When not in this ideal state the observer (accepting the whole convention) uses his faculties to edit out any distractions and confusions to maintain a positive relationship within that convention. As soon as any one object loses its autonomous identity by statement and intention things begin to happen; the whole situation is affected and the nature of 'exhibition' altered.[61]

The three sculptures concerned – *4 casb 2 '67*, *ringl 1 '67* and *rope (gr 2sp) 6'* 67 – have remained together since. Two further points should

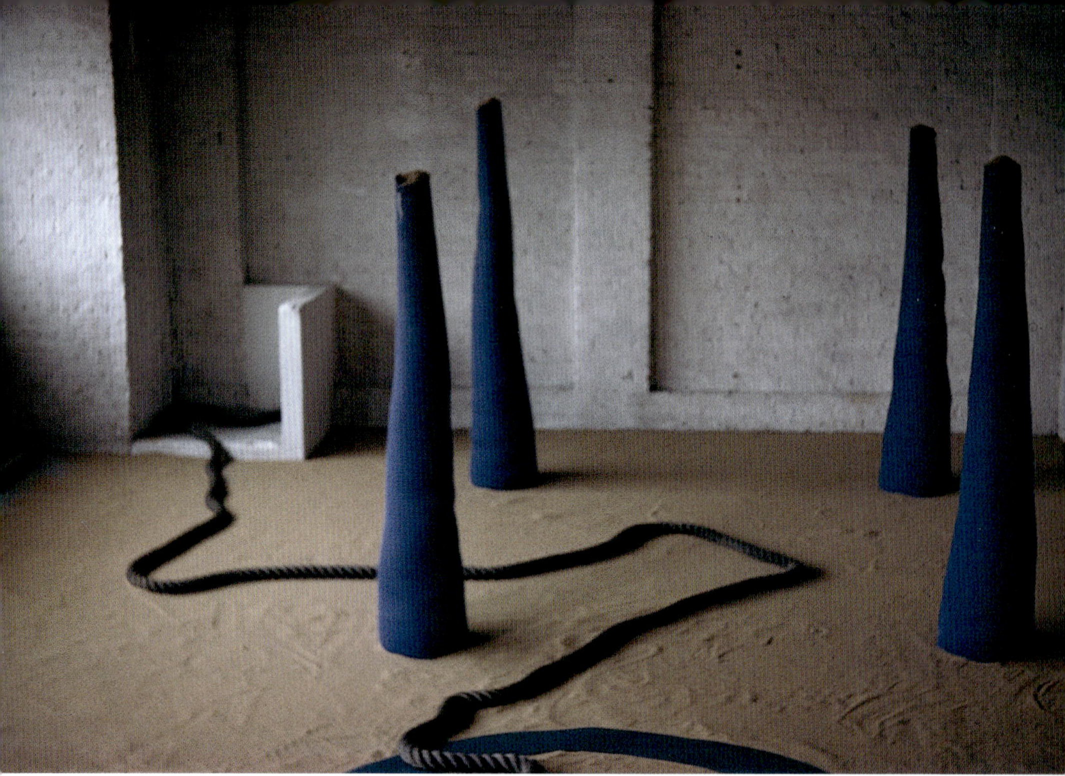

9 Barry Flanagan, *4 casb 2 '67, ringl 1 '67, rope (gr 2sp) 6 '67*, 1967, cloth, rope, linoleum, sand and plastic, uprights each h. 182.2 cm, ring dia. 182.2 cm, Tate

be noted beyond those Flanagan himself was in a position to make at the time: the first is that the spectator's acceptance of 'the whole convention' is by no means to be taken for granted; the second is that other and more inexorable factors than 'statement and intention' may lead to loss of autonomy of sculptural objects.

Richard Long arrived at St Martin's from the west of England in 1966 already interested in the association of landscape with sculpture and in the use of materials specific to certain sites. From the first his work outdoors was characterised by the discreteness of its presence in relation to the chosen location. His avant-garde single-mindedness was noticed within the college and by 1967 his work was attracting considerable interest outside. That December he 'installed' a work to the north-east of London. This consisted, in his own description, of '16 similar parts placed irregularly surrounding an area of 2401 square miles. Near each part was a notice giving the information. Thus a spectator could only see one part (no information being given to locate the others), but have a mental realisation of the whole.'[62] With the notion of a sculpture as something possibly 'realised' in the mind, Long put his work, deliberately and strategically, beyond reach of that minimum requirement for sculpture which had effectively regulated even the most experimental work at St Martin's until then.[63]

Though both Flanagan and Long arrived at their respective concepts of sculpture through idiosyncratic routes, various factors were contributing at the time towards a relaxation of the 'material-character/physical object paradigm' of art.[64] John Latham was among those teaching part-time at St Martin's in the years 1966–7[65] and his own work had for some time been directed at the critique of precedents and the revision of the practice of art in line with a belief that 'The world inferred has no things, as immutable solids . . . it has only event patterns of relative stability.'[66] Latham and Flanagan shared an exhibition in Wales in 1965, at a time when Flanagan was newly interested in the ideas of Alfred Jarry and in Pataphysics, the 'science of imaginary solutions'. In the autumn of the next year, Latham played a considerable part in an international 'Destruction in Art' symposium held at a venue close to St Martin's. Flanagan became involved, together with Yoko Ono, who was then working in London. In England as elsewhere in the 1960s, there was a rapid growth in 'fringe' activities of the kind associated with the idea of a 'counter-culture' and with the development of 'arts laboratories' as meeting places. These activities were pursued in a world in which film, music, performance, poetry and art were seen as the subjects of an overlapping interest and culture, rather than as the strictly defined practical and intentional categories they remained in modernist theory. Flanagan had attended Caro's sculpture class at St Martin's for three months in 1960. In 1963, before his enrolment as a full-time student in the sculpture department, he wrote to Caro,

> the Friday evening evening classes at St Martin's were good meat for my imagination. These classes prompted the writing of poetry, a play, film scripts, songs, the purchase of cine equipment, and work on a means to translate movement and atmosphere into music.

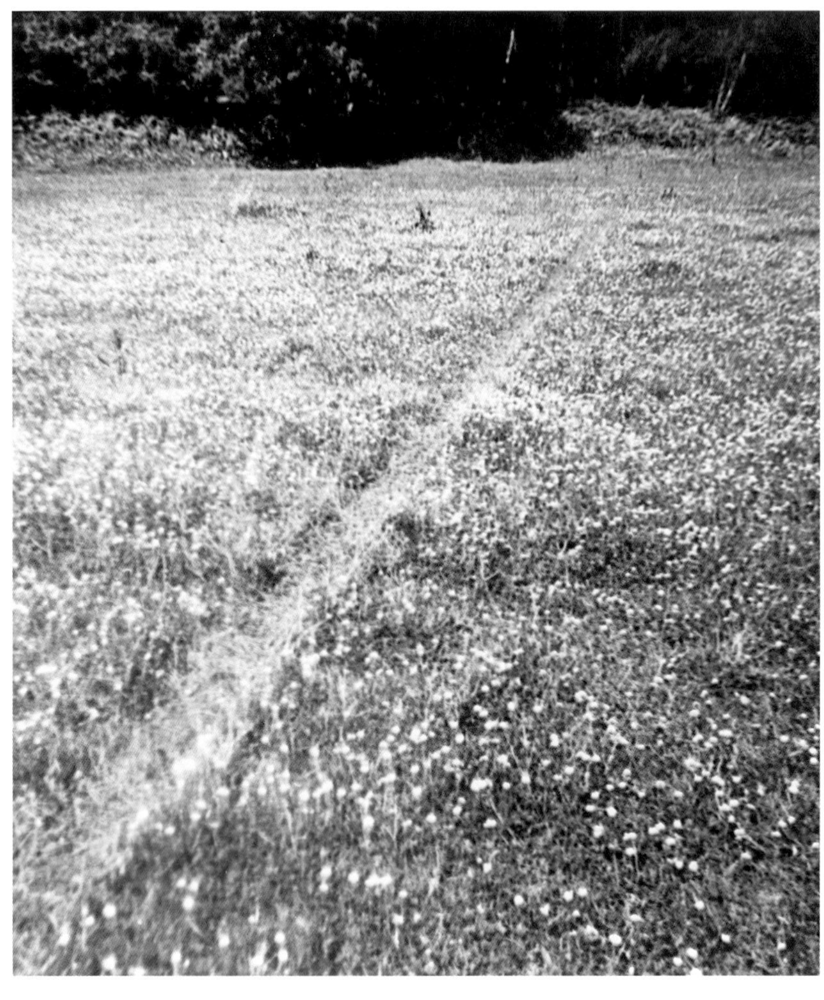

10 Richard Long, *A Line Made by Walking, England*, 1967, public freehold

> I might claim to be a sculptor and do everything else but sculpture. This is my dilemma.[67]

Flanagan printed this letter in a magazine he co-edited at St Martin's in 1964–5.[68] The point he was thus aiming to make public was one to which many of his contemporaries would have been likely to give assent. Even as the 1965 *New Generation* exhibition announced the domination of British sculpture by the aesthetics of transatlantic Modernism, the physical and conceptual autonomy of the art was coming under attack from a variety of directions.

Among the bases of modernist theories of art are a belief in the necessity of specialisation within individual art forms, and a belief in the autonomy of aesthetic experience. That both items of faith were laid open to question in the bohemian fringes of the mid- to late 1960s – in London as in New York or Paris – was not so much a cause as a symptom of diminution in the cultural authority of Modernism. An adequate account of the reasons for this diminution lies well outside the scope of this essay. I have suggested that loss of 'moral strenuousness' in modernist art after Pollock may have been one contributing factor, though this loss itself stands in need of explanation. The deployment and implication of modernist theory in the cultural politics of the Cold War was certainly another factor.[69] One long-term effect of this implication was to generate distrust on the part of 'left-wing' intellectuals during the 1960s towards virtually all claims for 'high art'. During the 1960s the category 'left-wing intellectuals' included the great majority of all intellectuals interested in art, while the most powerful theories of high art were associated with American art and criticism. At the same time the anti-Americanism normally associated with socialism in Britain and Europe was considerably aggravated by reactions to U.S. involvement in Vietnam.

Under the prompting of these and other conditions, younger British artists in the late 1960s were relatively emancipated from that conviction of the authority of American art which had seemed a virtual requirement for serious work in the previous decade. It was a symptom of this emancipation that the tradition associated with St Martin's ceased to be the virtually exclusive source of coherence in the development of British sculpture which it had been during the period of American domination. This said, however, it should be noted how many artists in the British avant-garde of the 1970s and 1980s have been associated with St Martin's at some point in their careers: to the names of Flanagan, Long, Woodrow and Deacon, Gilbert & George and Bruce McLean might be added by virtue of notoriety at least. It may well have been the case that the relative professionalism of the relationship with American Modernism established at St Martin's provided younger artists with a clear ground on which to make their divergent moves and have them seen as such. Well ramified as it was, the term 'sculpture' was available to them not so much to designate a category of three-dimensional artistic objects as to claim a sort of aesthetic privilege for certain types of enterprise and activity as against others. Thus in 1967 McLean designated as 'Floataway Sculpture' some pieces of chipboard and linoleum thrown into a river.[70] Two years later Gilbert & George dubbed themselves 'Living Sculptures', proceeding to perform what they referred to as 'Interview Sculpture', 'Nerve Sculpture' and so forth. Richard Long used the term to refer not only to arrangements of turf or stone or wood in landscape locations, but also to the evidence of subtractive activities – depressions left by walking in long grass (fig. 10), a cross marked out by picking the heads of daisies – and to those configurations marked out only by his own passage across country. This obstinate attachment to the category of sculpture may have served initially to express a spirit of ironic and avant-gardist detachment from the macho ethos of the St Martin's sculpture department. It later came to serve a normal if less defensible strategy: the insistence that how the artist means his work to be regarded should be accepted as defining what that work categorically is.

In September 1967 Flanagan and Long exhibited together with Jan Dibbets (then a student at St Martin's on a British Council scholarship from Holland) and John Johnson (who was doing work similar to Long's at the time) in a little-noticed show at the Galerie Loehr in Frankfurt.[71] (Among the European artists included was Konrad Lueg, alter ego of the dealer Konrad Fischer, who gave Long his first one-person show in Düsseldorf the next year.) This was one of a series of more or less coincident manifestations of what emerged, within the next two years, as a widespread, informal movement – a movement that briefly united disparate factions from both sides of the Atlantic into what seemed at the time a single cosmopolitan avant-garde. In Italy during the same month, Arte Povera was launched with a small exhibition at Galleria la Bertesca in Genoa, to the accompaniment of a short manifesto promising terrible reprisals against the oppressive system. Process Art was in the air in New York by at least September–October 1966, when Lucy Lippard organised a show of *Eccentric Abstraction* at the Fischbach Gallery.[72] Soon after this, Robert Morris was playing impresario to a new 'Anti-Form' movement in American sculpture.[73] Two further components of the new avant-garde mélange were the subject of shows at the Dwan Gallery, *Language* in 1967 and *Earthworks* in 1968. In Germany, Joseph Beuys, a veteran of the Fluxus movement of the 1950s, had for some while been producing strange, obsessive assemblages and picturesque, brownish dog-eared things. He had a cult following at the Staatliche Kunstakademie Düsseldorf, where he had been teaching since 1961, but was not much known outside his country until 1968, when he was included in *Documenta 4* at Kassel and was featured as the doyen of a local movement at *Prospekt*, an avant-garde dealers' showcase in Düsseldorf.[74] By the next year he was accorded widespread recognition as a progenitor, while several of his former pupils were included in major survey exhibitions.

The first of these large surveys came in 1969, the year of public and international recognition of the new tendency – at least of its recognition as avant-garde. The curatorial initiatives came from Europe. *Op Losse Schroeven* ('Square Pegs in Round Holes') opened at the Stedelijk Museum in Amsterdam in March, the same month as *When Attitudes become Form* opened at the Kunsthalle Bern. Flanagan, Long, Louw and McLean were included in both exhibitions.[75] In September of the same year, a revised version of the *Attitudes* show travelled to London (figs 11 and 12). Some idea of the wide catchment area of these surveys is given by the coverall subtitle of the last: 'Works – Concepts – Processes – Situations – Information'. No one seemed sure quite what they were dealing with. This was understandable. One feature that united the best of the widely disparate new work of the late 1960s was its critical

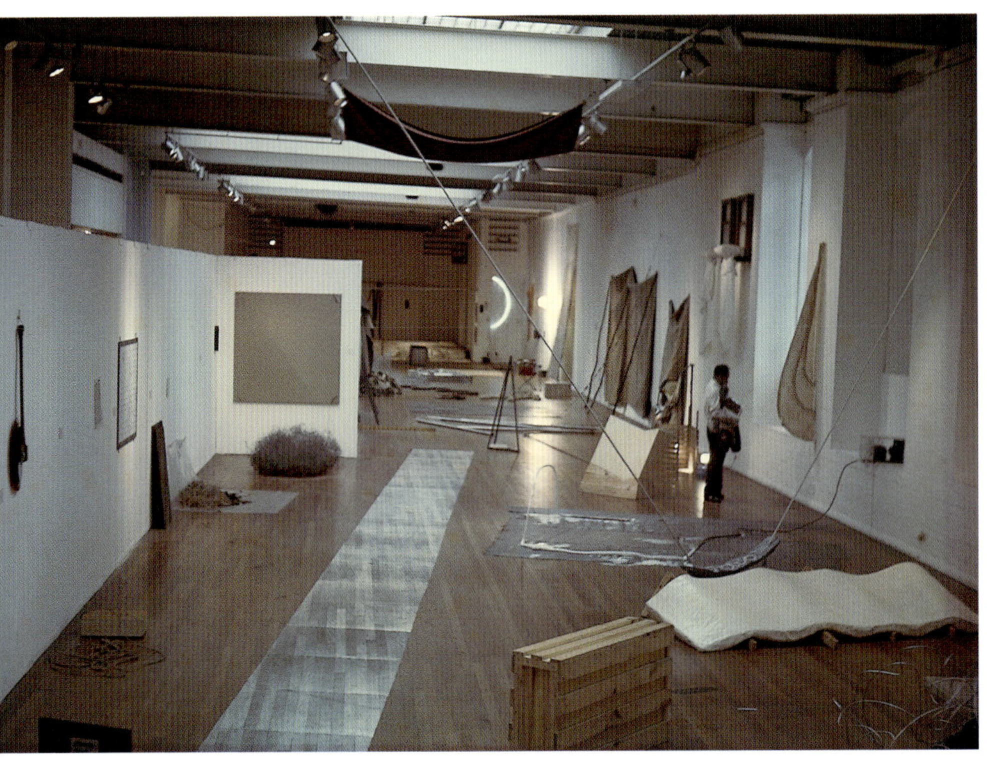

11 (*above*) and 12 (*facing page*) Installation views of *When Attitudes become Form*, Institute of Contemporary Arts, London, 1969, showing *Photo-path* by Victor Burgin (*above*) and hanging rope sculpture by Roelof Louw (*facing page*)

disengagement from formally based concepts of style. Such concepts had served well enough to categorise the mainstream of modernist painting and sculpture up to this point, and normal art criticism and curatorship had tended to presuppose their continued relevance for the purposes of grouping and demarcation. With this security undermined, those slow on their feet were left grasping at straw categories, or listening anxiously for gossip with the ring of authority and authenticity about it. The following are among the many labels variously tried on for the late 1960s avant-garde or for its component parts: Post-Object Art, Multiformal Art, Non-Rigid Art, Concept Art, Conceptual Art, Idea Art, Ideational

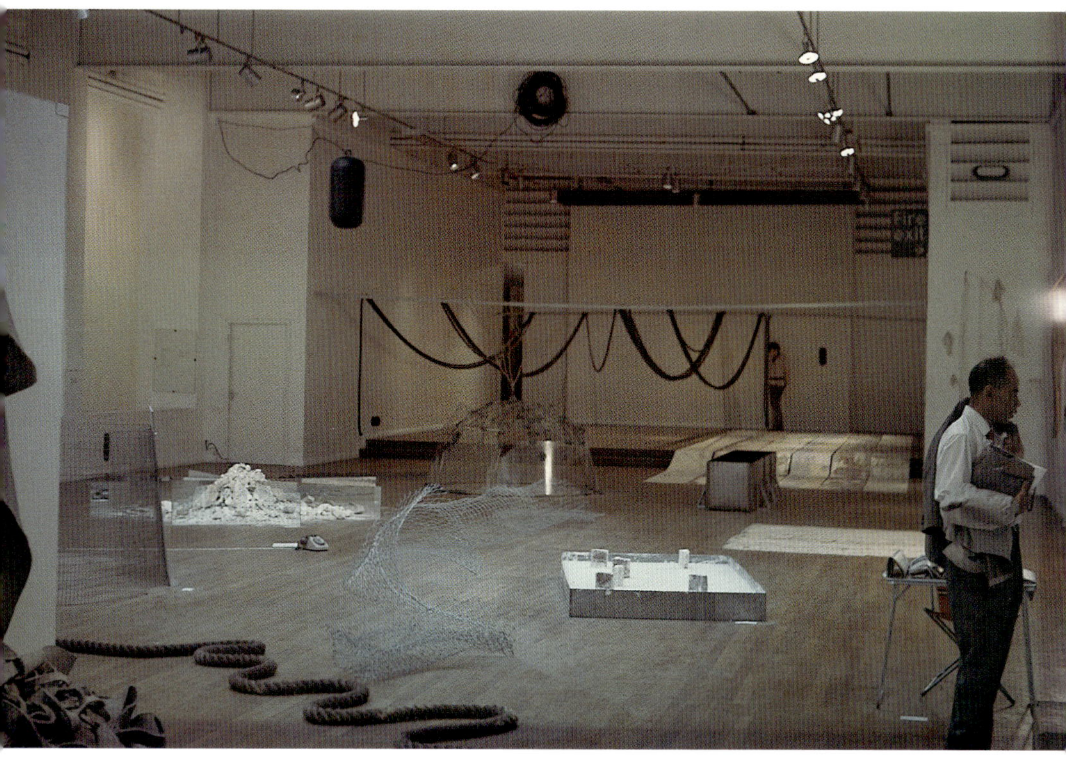


Art, Earthworks, Earth Art, Land Art, Organic-Matter Art, Process Art, Procedural Art, Anti-Form, Systems Art, Micro-Emotive Art, Possible Art, Impossible Art, Arte Povera, Post-Studio Art, Meta Art.

Some large claims were made for the new movement and for the implications of the work. This is Grégoire Muller, introducing the *Attitudes* show:

> For all those polemicists who, from the point of view of the sociology of art, fight against the traditional concepts of the museum, the gallery, the work of art . . . this movement is a godsend. The majority of the artists in this exhibition are, for other reasons, united with their position; their work is made everywhere or anywhere, in newspapers, on the walls of towns, in the sand, in the snow . . . some of these 'works'

> can be redone by no matter whom, others are untransportable, perishable, unsaleable, still others invisible and known solely through documentation. . . .
>
> With this new movement art is liberated from all its fetters.[76]

Such paeans ring hollow enough now, but in 1969 the association of an international artistic avant-garde with the prospect of substantial change still seemed plausible to many – to many of those, at least, who had not noticed the combination of rampant idealism and individualism also associated with the movement, qualities encapsulated in the instruction to 'Live in your head.'[77]

A host of international surveys followed in the next three years. One feature of these shows was that artists were generally invited to install their own works. In some cases the components were so apparently haphazard that curators can have had little confidence in their ability properly to arrange them; in others 'installation' was supposedly conceptually and practically indistinguishable from 'realisation'; in still others the artist's work entailed doing a special 'piece' relating to the specific environment or 'space', to local political or sociological conditions, or whatever. The bringing together of artists from several countries and continents led to a rapid exchange of information and to the establishment of an international network of contacts and friendships. Brief though it was, there may never have been so potentially cosmopolitan a moment in the history of art. Flanagan and Long were included in a significant number of these shows, Louw and McLean in a few. Gilbert & George were taken up in 1970.

Though hindsight has modified the picture, and though some overt incompatibilities were evident even then, it seemed at the time that the art of the heterogeneous new movement could at least be defined on the grounds of its unlikeness to immediately previous work. First there was its distinctive independence from the art of painting. In 1967 Robert Morris had asserted of painting that 'The mode has become antique.'[78] Such exceptional forms of wall-based two-dimensional work as were included in the surveys of the new avant-garde seemed designed to prove this rule. Whatever interests they offered to view, these were not compatible with the priority which modernist theory had placed on the expression of feeling in visual form.[79] It seemed that 'sculpture' – or 'three-dimensional work' – had now prised itself conceptually loose from painting, leaving the latter to fulfil a highly specialised and possibly redundant aesthetic function. Secondly, in so far as an aesthetic object was offered to view in the new 'three-dimensional work', this was not established in terms of some single, necessarily fixed and physically stable configuration. The possibility of change of state was a feature of the ontological character of the art. Thirdly, identification of the 'work' on the part of the spectator was not simply a matter of response to an achieved order; imaginative reconstruction of the artist's procedures and activities was often inseparable from the perception of that order. Fourthly, at least from a theoretical point of view, no privilege was attached to any material or medium as against another. Indeed, the avant-garde tendency in the late 1960s and early 1970s was to avoid just those materials with which the sculpture of the recent past had been identified.

As regards this last characteristic, the continuing tendency of some British sculptors, Richard Long and David Nash among them, has been to locate the physical activity of sculpture within a world separated from the kinds of metropolitan context associated with the development of Modernism. This separation is not so much a matter of distance from the business of the art world (a distance no avant-garde artist can afford to maintain) as of a programmatic abstinence from the use of certain forming techniques and a consistent avoidance of certain materials. To a concept of sculpture as the wilful and expressive exploitation of malleable material, they counterpose a more passive view, predicated on a kind of reconciliation with the natural world. This entails that normal processes of growth, weathering and so on be admitted, and even accorded a necessary role, as forming agencies in the artefacts of human culture. In such work the defeated social idealism of the late 1960s perhaps finds a continued expression. If so, we might view work such as Tony Cragg's and Bill Woodrow's as presenting the other side of the same coin, the critique of modernity achieved in their cases through the aesthetic recuperation of urban detritus. Though the associations of this material and of its history remain accessible in the work, their meaning is critically transformed by incorporation within the range of signification of sculpture.

Certainly the most interesting new British sculptors of the 1970s and early 1980s had in common a sense of disengagement from celebratory concepts of modernity. We should not, however, take this as the essence of radicalism. A complex and critical relationship with concepts of modernity has characterised authentic modernist art since Manet's time, at least insofar as modernity was considered in terms of scientific and technological progress and attendant social change. If we are to identify post-modernism in art, it will have to be on other grounds. So what form has the legacy of the 1960s taken in subsequent art? I would suggest that two particular conditions have had determining effects on avant-garde art since the moment of around 1967–72 and on the concerns of attendant criticism and theory. The first is the realisation that once the authority of any given aesthetic rationale is undermined, claims for the status of artistic objects are revealed in all their fragility and contingency. The second, which follows hard on the heels of the first, is the recognition that the production of works of art and the production of rationales for works of art are mutually implicated moves in a game – a serious game, in which the conditions of play are always changing, so that the values of forms of accomplishment and competence are never stable for long. This is not to say either that competence is irrelevant to quality in art, or that no constant features are picked out by such terms as 'sculpture'. The point is rather that neither can be prescribed.

It was by the Conceptual Art of the late 1960s that the mutual implication of art and language was demonstrated to the art world itself. Conceptual Art represented an extreme position within the general climate of dissent from modernist concepts of the art object, and thus a greater destabilising potential as regards the world of aesthetic business-as-normal. Those of its proponents who were not simply followers of avant-garde fashion formed a kind of militant arm of the wider late-1960s movement. The Art & Language group was formed in Coventry, England, by four artists whose collective experience included an early interest in Minimal Art and in the implications of its theory, and a disenchanted exposure to the advanced sculpture course at St Martin's.[80] Publication of their journal *Art-Language* commenced in the spring of 1969.[81] The development of Art & Language's publications and works for exhibition since that date, through enlargements and contractions of membership, has constituted what is virtually a distinct tradition – a tradition in which limits on the possibility of expressiveness in art are acknowledged as conditions of realism. The awkward presence of Art & Language within the context of British art has perhaps served to highlight locally that general tendency to polarisation within modern art which I would trace back to the 1950s. From the 1970s to the late 1980s, and particularly following the widespread celebration of a renewed figuration, a 'New Expressiveness' in both painting and sculpture, modern work seemed to divide qualitatively over the issue of its own historical continuity. While some forms of art have appeared to offer an uncomplicated restoration of eternal themes and pleasures, others, by the manifest artificiality of their representational modes, have signified that ironic awareness of the indirectness of all expression which was the most telling legacy of the art of the 1960s. The two forms are not easy to distinguish on the mere basis of style and appearance, but morally they are widely distinct. The question of where we should look for the authentic art of our time is not sensibly to be addressed without considering how the art of those decades should be viewed and interpreted. The recent history of sculpture – and of the claims made for sculptural work – is of critical interest in this respect.

# 2 ON WRITING ABOUT . . .

This text was originally published in *Kunst & Museumjournaal*, no. 6, Amsterdam, 1990. On that occasion it was illustrated with three 'black' paintings: Kasimir Malevich's *Black Square* of 1929 (Tretiakov Gallery, Moscow), Ad Reinhardt's *Abstract Painting No. 5*, 1962 (Tate), and Mel Ramsden's *Two Black Squares – The Paradoxes of Absolute Zero*, 1966 (author's collection). It was provoked in part by a visit to the substantial exhibition of Malevich's work held at the Stedelijk Museum in 1989. Its aim is to represent and review various means and ends in the criticism of art.

> 'You can argue only against a proposition, not against a vocabulary. Vocabularies get discarded after looking bad in comparison with other vocabularies, not as a result of an appeal to overarching metavocabularies in which criteria for vocabulary choice can be formulated.'
>
> Richard Rorty, 'Philosophy without Principles', in W. J. T. Mitchell, ed., *Against Theory*, Chicago, 1985

Imagine a gallery. In this gallery there are many works, but we are concerned only with one. For the sake of argument let it be a painting, in oil on canvas, about a metre square, its surface relatively smooth and of an apparently unvaried black. Let it have been produced some time between 1915 and 1969. The task is to write about this painting – to produce a text, let us say, 3000 words in length. How is this requirement to be met? What are the conditions of 'about . . .'?

A conventional way to answer this question – or rather a conventional recommendation as to how the materials for an answer may be acquired – has been that one should stand before the painting, the mind emptied of all contingent considerations, all everyday preoccupations, that one should *look*, and that one should let the imagination like a blank tablet take whatever imprint the painting has to offer it. But, in the words of N. R. Hanson, 'Seeing is not only the having of a visual experience. It is also the way in which that experience is had.' Modes of seeing must be considered as conditions bearing on the meaning of 'about'. Among the factors determining modes of seeing will be beliefs and presumptions both about what is being looked at and about the forms of words in which the objects of this attention are most appropriately or most usefully described, explained or interpreted. By what kind of disposition, what knowledge, what beliefs, what interests is one qualified to write *about* . . . Of whose 'seeing', whose 'imagination' are we speaking?

A: 'When I look at the painting, I see a black cat in a coal cellar at midnight.'

B: 'When I look at the painting, I see a dungeon full of black snakes.'

C: 'All that is significant here is that there are no grounds on which to decide between the respective interpretations of A and B. Both readings are arbitrary and incompetent. Both speakers are the prisoners of expectations which the painting itself treats as irrelevant. Only the vulgar and the naive look for figuration where figuration is absent. The painting is not a picture. The very absence of figuration directs the viewer to a different sort of meaning. In fact, the meaning of the painting lies in the very absence of reference to the things of the world. To concentrate on the rigorously unmodulated surface of the painting is to be imaginatively absorbed into a dimensionless space – to be transported into a state of not being. This is what the painting is about. It is a profound meditation on death and the infinite. The originality of the creator is revealed in the extremism of his statement. What the painting requires of the spectator is a matching resoluteness: the courage to confront the void. The business of criticism is to provide relevant exhortation: to guide the viewer towards a proper appreciation of the meaning and value of the artist's work.'

D: 'C is guilty of a vulgarity more gross than A's or B's. To view the surface of the painting as a doorway into the infinite is to indulge in a form of wanton superstition; it is to make the painting the arbitrary object of a personal and neurotic search for meaning. Nothing is discovered in the process. A highly questionable if not absurd belief is mindlessly affirmed, that's all. It is the culturally induced expectation of metaphysical grandeur, and not the painting, that produces C's "experience". The search for metaphysical meaning is merely a sophisticated version of the search for figurative content. If I say that the painting in question offers an optimistic celebration of corporeal existence, is the argument I have with C open to any less arbitrary and unsatisfactory resolution than the argument between A and B? Interpretation must be constrained by criteria of relevance: and what I mean by relevance is relevance to the effects of art. Furthermore only those effects will count for the purposes of criticism which can be explained as the consequences of technical characteristics. A well-grounded criticism will be one which takes adequate account of the formal and technical aspects of the work in question, and which makes no claims for the meaning of that work which cannot be connected to descriptions of those aspects.

'To talk about technical characteristics is to address painting as a specialised activity. The modern artist derives his chief inspiration from the medium in which he works. Originality in painting consists in the production of new painterly effects. This newness is relative to the state of development of painting itself, and it involves a critical and self-critical attitude towards received models and exemplars. What is required for the appreciation of this newness is acquaintance with painting itself, with its intrinsic concerns, its conventions, its problems and its limitations.

'Every painted surface sustains some illusion of depth, however shallow. In the black painting the boundaries of the pictorial space are closely identified with the physical limits of the painted surface, so that the illusion of space is maximally compressed. The essential originality of the painting inheres in the relative closeness of this identification and in the force of this compression of illusionistic space. Previous abstract painting had eschewed the form of pictorial space within which physical objects might be represented or physical events transpire. The author of the black painting has continued the critical thrust of abstract painting to a further stage. Not only does this work eliminate the furniture and the stagings of the pictorial; it purges painting of those suggestive atmospheric effects which were the means by which all previous abstract work had secured some continuing – if fugitive – reference to the world of the picturesque. It is in pursuit of this critique of the atmospheric, and not in the name of death and despair, that the artist has reduced his palette to one extreme and opaque tone. The business of criticism is not to interpret the effects of art but to characterise them, to explain how (and perhaps why) these effects are produced, and to bear witness to the quality of experience which they in turn produce in the attuned spectator.'

E: 'The autonomy which D accords to painting amounts to a powerful closure on inquiry. His emphasis on formal characteristics and intrinsic concerns serves to distract attention from the social and historical functions of art. The painting as he describes it is simply an illustration of the technical presumptions of his theory. It takes its place in a prescribed development as an object otherwise insulated from history. In fact, the black painting means nothing unless its production can be represented as an intentional act in the context of some history. To uncover the meaning of the painting we will need to know about the network of practices and discourses within which it was possible to conceive and to make such a thing. In assessing its critical character, that's to say, we will need to know just how to read it as a symbol. And this entails that we consider how it was proposed and situated in relation to the various alternative forms of practice and of signification obtaining at the moment of its production. We will need to be able to locate it within a context of contemporary debates about the function of art and the role of the avant-garde. And in turn we will need to know to what extent the materials of these debates were furnished and inflected by wider historical events and tendencies.

'For example if we know that the painting was produced in Russia in 1915 it may be appropriate to interpret it as expressing dissent from the prevailing canons of taste at a time of impending social and political change. In particular it may be seen on the one hand as critical of that taste for sensuous gratification which was associated with the mimetic imagery of bourgeois culture, and on the other as affirming the possibility of a radically transformed visual morphology appropriate to the needs and interests of an envisaged post-revolutionary society. Viewed in the context of history the painting may be revealed as the vivid repository of contingent interests and aspirations. The real measure of assiduousness in criticism is that those historical meanings should be uncovered which have been overlaid by subsequent ratification and appropriation.'

F: 'On first reading it seems that D and E hold diametrically opposed views (though they no doubt share a dismissive attitude towards the views of C). In addressing the task of writing "about" the black painting, for example, they will embark on quite different preliminaries, and it will be surprising if their respective accounts are not very different one from another. And yet they are bound together in the same dialectical world; the world which defines itself between the supposedly opposite poles of Modernism and Marxism. It is a feature of this world that in any context in which the one voice strives to be heard, the discourse of the other must be available to thought as a resource of negative example or as a counter. For instance, the work of art features in the discourse of the modernist as an object of transcendental value. As such it is generally implausible. But under conditions in which all values are supposed to reduce to market value this very implausibility becomes a matter of critical interest. And for analysis of this reductive tendency, it is to the Marxist account of the mechanisms of Capital that we normally look. And for his part, the Marxist or Historical Materialist confronts the most interesting anomaly to his basic thesis – the thesis that the requirement that we work to live is what defines humans as a historical species – if and when he attempts to explain how that which modernist theory distinguishes as art was possibly produced.

'Modernism and Marxism are bound into a rhetorical structure of reciprocating necessities – in the same way and for many of the same reasons as the political West and East were bound together during the long period of the Cold War. Each, that is to say, needs that account of the other which serves its own ends, and each needs the other's account of itself to provide the negative ground against which its own self-image may then be positively established.

'This is to point to the historically specific and contingent nature both of those positions from which the discourses of D and E are uttered and of that dialectical world in which they have for so long been joined. What these discourses have in common is a misplaced faith in the power of theory to discover truth. Their argument is an argument about which theory is most likely to offer a true account of objects such as the black painting. In the one case the true account envisaged is an account of aesthetic quality and effect, in the other it is an account of embedded historical meaning. But if theories constitute their objects rather than discovering them, the argument is not one which will be testable against the true face of the black painting – or of anything else. There is no such true face, no "painting" to be discovered which is independent of the interests of theory and thus capable of acting as the final arbiter of its claims. There is only ever another interpretation in the endless competition of interpretations. Beneath the grand claims to an enlightening function made by the one form of theory and the grand claims to explanatory potential made by the other, each alike emerges as a kind of conditioned response to the utterance of the other.

'We are heartily weary now of this unreal battle for the unattainable truth. In whatever accents they are uttered the rallying cries now fall on deaf ears. Why should we not frankly acknowledge the partial and instrumental nature of our interpretative acts? The black painting I am interested in is the black painting which serves my ends, which is the point of departure for my own imaginative activities. To write about this painting is not to fathom its true meaning nor to characterise its effects nor to explain its production. It is to set beside it another artefact, another text. In the critical practice I have in mind, the meaning of "about" is radically changed. The intention it declares is not that a predication should be made but that a process should be commenced. "About . . ." does not promise directness of address to the object of thought. It announces circumambulation in its neighbourhood.

'We have suffered long enough under the oppressive regime of relevance. Concepts of relevance impose rules for the formation of categories, decide conditions of entry to areas of thought, set principles of decorum to regulate comparison. Relevance requires consistency and inhibits discovery. Criticism liberated from the spurious requirement of relevance is criticism empowered and unafraid to forge new relationships, to be creative, to be poetic. The measure of competence to write about must in the last instance be a measure of competence in *writing*. The most demanding assessment to which criticism can be subjected is the assessment of its literary quality.'

G: 'Let us consider some types of text and the various forms of relationship they might bear to the black painting. A given text might be connected to the painting through some relation of similarity, albeit analogical, metaphorical, allegorical or in some other way formal. This is to say that in some manner, however indirect, the order of this text will be determined by the structure of the painting. It will thus in some sense propose or avail an interpretation of that structure. In such a case the text will be subject to an assessment of its relevance. Another type of text might reveal a causal connection in some other way, for instance by departing from a recorded encounter with the painting in pursuit of a trail of associations. However apparently divergent, these associations will nevertheless be open to assessment in relation to some perception of the painting and of the load of inference which it can feasibly be made to bear. This is to say that such a text will still be subject to some evaluation of its relevance. There is a third form of text we might envisage, however. In this case the relationship between painting and text involves neither evident similarity nor evident causal contact. The conjunction of text and painting appears arbitrary except in so far as it is simply stipulated.

'If F is proposing any substantive change in the requirements on criticism, he must be arguing for some text of this third type. That's to say, what he must be proposing is that a relation of significant contiguity can be established between text and painting in the absence either of a relation of significant similarity or of a relation of significant causal contact. Given that the production of the text must be an intentional act of some kind, we are entitled to ask, "Why this painting?" In the absence of any other form of relation securing text to painting, the reason for F's stipulating a relation of contiguity with a specific painting may be assumed to be that it serves his own interests as author; that's to say that it serves to establish the significance of the text. The answer to the question, "Why this painting?" must thus come in the form, "Because it is good, notorious, interesting, important or etc." What we are in effect witnessing, then, is a reversal of the conventional relation of critical enterprise to object of criticism. Rather than the critical text serving to publish and to defend an intuition of the value of the painting, the already assumed value of the painting is mobilised to enhance the value of the text. The painting is reduced to the status of conversation-piece. Nor is the assumption of the value of the painting either examined or defended in the new "poetic" text. How can it be when the very status of the text depends on that value being unquestionably accepted? Criticism which insulates itself against examination of the bases of its own claims to significance is criticism in a state of decadence. The point is not that such criticism is possessed of an inadequate theoretical apparatus. The point is that its character is manipulative. In so far as a text of this order can be *about* a specific work of art, it must treat it not as an end but as a means – a means, that's to say, to exploit an available vocabulary.

'This is criticism in bad faith. It is a condition of some object's being an object of thought that it is allowed to impose some necessity on the thinker. It is a condition of the possibility of criticism that the work of art – that which is written *about* – be allowed to impose some necessity on the vocabulary of the critic. I suppose it might still be asked why an intuition of quality in some artistic work should precede the generation of a critical text. But thought is thought about – *something*. Criticism is criticism about – *something*. Something is the case. Something is the origin of our intuitions and experiences. Something alerts us to the inadequacy of an accustomed and available vocabulary. The world in which this something exists and is the case is a kind of transcendental world. D has a point with his requirement of relevance. F's discourse is discourse or criticism as caprice. His freedom from relevance is freedom as caprice. As he means to live it, the critic's life is an incessant succession of paradigm shifts in which even aesthetic enhancement seems vapid. Criticism thus "liberated" is criticism in thrall to the voluntaristic fantasies of choosing. F will in the end be unable to say whether the conditions of his choosing are established by the dialectical exigencies of discourse or by fear, hunger and the secret police.'

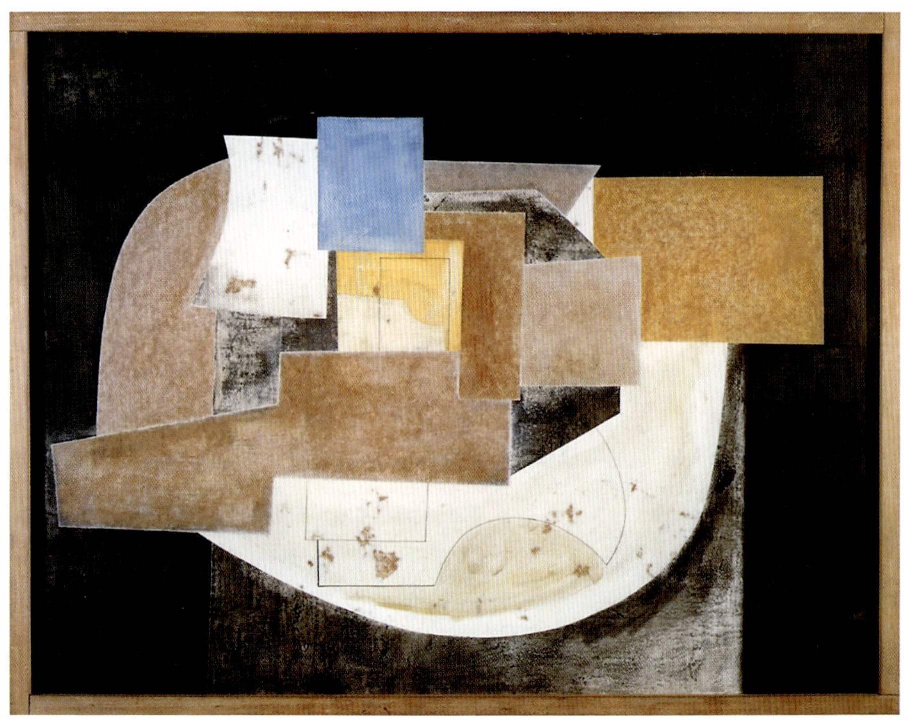

13 Ben Nicholson, *November 1955 (still life – nightshade)*, oil and pencil on board, 96.3 × 127 cm, collection Elizabeth and Hans C. Bechtler, Zurich

# 3 BEN NICHOLSON AND THE DECLINE OF CUBISM

This paper is concerned with the passing of critical initiative from English to U.S. abstract art in the 1940s and 1950s. In its original form it was written for a conference on Cold War culture, held at University College, London, in 1993. It was substantially revised for a conference on Ben Nicholson at the Courtauld Institute, London, in 2007. It has not previously been published.

This essay has its origins in the near-coincidence of an exhibition and a colloquium more than a dozen years ago. The exhibition was the last major retrospective of Nicholson's work, held at the Tate Gallery (now Tate Britain) in 1993. During its planning stages I received a 'phone call from a member of the curatorial staff. After some awkward preliminaries, it emerged that the business of the call was to discover what I might write supposing I were invited to contribute to the catalogue. The caller appeared to have two ends in view. The first was to place me in the position of someone soliciting for work. The second was to secure the catalogue against contributions made in the wrong tone of voice. The curator was successful in this second aim at least. As is the custom on such occasions, the exhibition represented Nicholson as an unqualified success.

What follows may be seen as an attempt to open Nicholson's work to criticism and thus to help rescue it from that kind of success. It has some of its roots in that moment when I felt a need to explain – to myself at least – why I was not properly equipped to join the celebratory rites for someone I had been happy to think of as a kind of mentor and even a friend. How should I account for the unmarketable disappointment in the artist's later career that I had come to feel, and that I expected the Tate exhibition to confirm – as indeed it did? To be more specific, how might one connect the two principal observations that that work had seemed to invite? On the one hand, some of Nicholson's still-life compositions of the mid-1950s are as demanding of consideration in aesthetic terms as anything he produced during the course of a career that spanned seven decades. I take the *Still Life – Nightshade* of 1955 (fig. 13), for example, to be one of the strongest of all his works. On the other hand, these paintings of the 1950s are without significant issue in Nicholson's own work or in anyone else's. They seem to mark a practical and critical zenith, although he remained productive for another twenty-five years after the first of them were painted. During the 1960s he produced a series of abstract reliefs (fig. 14) that aspire to a form of modernist monumentality. For all that Nicholson himself regarded these as equivalent in importance to the white reliefs of the 1930s, I came to see them as for the most part hollow and mannered in their effects, while the majority of the works on paper that accompanied and followed them appeared whimsical and slight.

I do not pretend that the reasons for such disappointments are easily attributed. The difficulties have been much rehearsed in criticism and art history. How can we justifiably speak of artistic objects as though they were somehow inherently good or less good or bad, when it is only in the blinding light of our own personal interests and prejudices that we perceive them at all? To put the matter in broader terms, how, from within the sphere of influence of a cultural apparatus, are we to distinguish the aesthetic or other effects of the art that that apparatus enfolds or extrudes?

In the field of modern art criticism, to talk of spheres of influence – at least where the art of the 1950s and 1960s is concerned – is inescapably to raise the issue of American Modernism and its hegemonic effects. This takes me to the second event by which my present speculations were originally provoked. In the year following the Tate retrospective of Nicholson's work, a conference was held in London on 'Cold War Culture'. It was the consequent opportunity to reconsider Nicholson's work in the light of wider concerns in post-war art and criticism that I propose now to revisit.

The reference flagged in my title is to Clement Greenberg's essay 'The Decline of Cubism', originally published in *Partisan Review* in 1948. If we accept the author's processes of reasoning as he then repre-

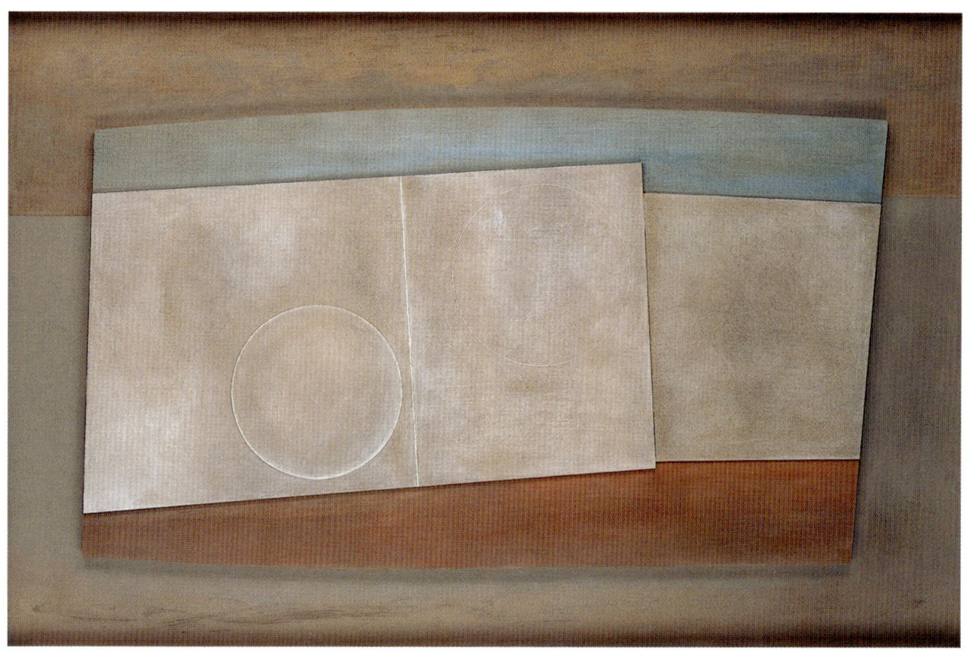

14 Ben Nicholson, *1966 (Erymanthos)*, oil on carved board, 121.2 × 183.4 cm, private collection

sented them, he was following John Ruskin, Clive Bell and other notable predecessors in diagnosing social and economic conditions on the evidence of relative aesthetic achievements. 'If artists as great as Picasso, Braque and Léger have declined so grievously', he wrote, 'it can only be because the general social premises that used to guarantee their functioning have disappeared in Europe.' By contrast, he took the emergence of Arshile Gorky, Jackson Pollock and David Smith as surprising evidence that 'the main premises of Western art have at last migrated to the United States, along with the center of gravity of industrial production and political power.'[1] Greenberg's implication was clear. European art had become decadent because Europe was decadent, while the vitality of American art was sustained by American political and economic ascendance.

Let us say that someone with an eye attuned to Jackson Pollock or to Mark Rothko detected in Nicholson's work of the late 1950s and 1960s the kind of persistent mannerism that signifies attachment to a critically exhausted style. One might ask that person which came first: the pejorative judgement on Nicholson's work or a theorised conviction of the decline of Cubism. To put this another way, there needs to be some testing of the grounds of relative judgement in this and similar cases which is neither just a restatement of the now largely discredited Greenbergian model of self-critical stylistic progress, nor just a pseudo-post-modernist restatement of conservative and insular loyalties. At issue, as so often, is the vexed relationship between concepts of stylistic development, concepts of conservatism and modernism, and aesthetic judgements. I do not pretend to know how the logic of these relations is to be pinned down. I merely mean to offer a small-scale case study of the problem.

Modernist criticism does indeed present a simple and well-rehearsed formula by means of which my inquiry into Nicholson's apparent decline might seem to be satisfied. It goes like this. On the one hand Nicholson's works of the mid-50s are of some interest and vividness as recapitulations of the formal and decorative repertoire of Cubism on the part of an artist who had been more deeply engaged with that repertoire over a longer period than any other English artist. On the other hand it had become clear by the time Nicholson's later still lifes were painted that the development of a critical Modernism in painting no longer rested on the particular modes of compositional discipline that Cubism had imposed. It might be observed, for example, that *Still Life – Nightshade* was painted during the year in which New York's Museum of Modern Art launched 'Modern Art in the United States' on its triumphal European tour. In the conventional wisdom of art history, it was the concluding section of this exhibition that served to inform observant Europeans that the post-Cubist art of the American Abstract Expressionists was now the dominant source for paradigms of Modernism in painting. When he wrote 'The Decline of Cubism', Greenberg had been looking to America for a 'new efflorescence' of the 'cubist tradition'. Seven years later, however, in the year of *Still Life – Nightshade* and of

'Modern Art in the United States', he was ready to specify what was required of a painterly practice seeking *emancipation* from Cubism. The essay in question was published under the telling title 'American-Type Painting'. In order 'to say what they had to say', Greenberg informs us, the American painters had to

> loosen up the rather strictly demarcated illusion of shallow depth [Picasso] had been working within, in his more ambitious pictures, since he closed his 'synthetic' Cubist period. With this went that canon of drawing in faired, more or less simple lines and curves that Cubism imposed and which had dominated almost all abstract art since 1920. They had to free themselves from this too.[2]

It is hard to imagine a more economical account of the stylistic canon within which Nicholson's work was to remain confined. Once American-type painting gained the ascendant, work such as his was left on the wrong side of a critical and art-historical divide. As England's senior provincial modernist, the account might conclude, Nicholson achieved his most lucid and compelling summation of the legacy of Cubism at the very point when that legacy was shown to be effectively exhausted.

This account of the development of painting is not so much wrong as limited and limiting in its scope, as it has been widely suggested that modernist criticism as a whole became some time during the Cold War years between 'The Decline of Cubism' and 'American-Type Painting'. In 1948 Greenberg gives us plausible material reasons for a revival of the Cubist tradition in America. In 1955 he tells us how American-type painting *freed* itself from Cubism. The possible renaissance of one style becomes the triumph of another in a Wölfflinian process of alternation. But what Greenberg does not explain – not, at least, without our reading between the lines of other essays – is just why liberation from Cubism had become a necessary condition of going-on. If we could find an answer to that question we might better understand why Nicholson's persistence with an art based on Cubist principles appeared to entail a failure of the critical spirit. Just at the point when the question is raised, however, it becomes the discernible tendency of modernist criticism to disconnect its global narrative of self-critical developments in art from those basic mechanisms – be they political, economic or biological – that we expect to discover at work beneath the surface of cultural change. According to some accounts of the development of modernist criticism from the late 1950s through the 1960s, it is through this very process of autonomising of artistic style that that criticism reveals itself as an intellectual agency of the Cold War.

I shall take this latter suggestion for what it is worth as a cue to return to Nicholson's late work, to the painted reliefs of the 1960s and to the contemporary and subsequent works on paper – I think particularly of the series of spanners from the early 1970s (fig. 15). In the hollowness of the one and the slightness of the other a single kind of failure may, I think, be diagnosed: a failure of realism. As I intend it here, realism is a term capable of properly conflating a philosophical demand with a mode of sociological critique. On the one hand the suspicion of idealism must always fall on those, like Nicholson, who evoke naturalistic structures without seeming to convey an acceptance of their substantiality; on the other it might be said that to derive whimsical patterns from a clutch of engineering tools is to play the aesthete in the most damaging sense of the term; that is to say, in a circumstance that might be thought to connote the division of labour and its consequences, it is to make decorative capital out of aspect blindness.

Now aspect blindness of this order is certainly consistent with that amnesia about Marx's critique of capital that was a condition of normal cultural life in the Cold War West. Protection of Nicholson's work from critical exposure of this blindness and of its causes might also without difficulty be connected to the hegemonic interests of those sponsoring and curatorial institutions that support celebratory exhibitions. ('Whatever you do, don't mention the War' – the class war, that is.) It might seem that I have stumbled into an observation that ties the weakness of Nicholson's later work to a historically specific aspect of the culture.

Yet we need to be careful here. The decorative graphic virtuosity that Nicholson exploits in his late drawings was always the least of his competences – though by no means the least marketable. From the start of his maturity as an artist in the 1920s he had a tendency to spend his

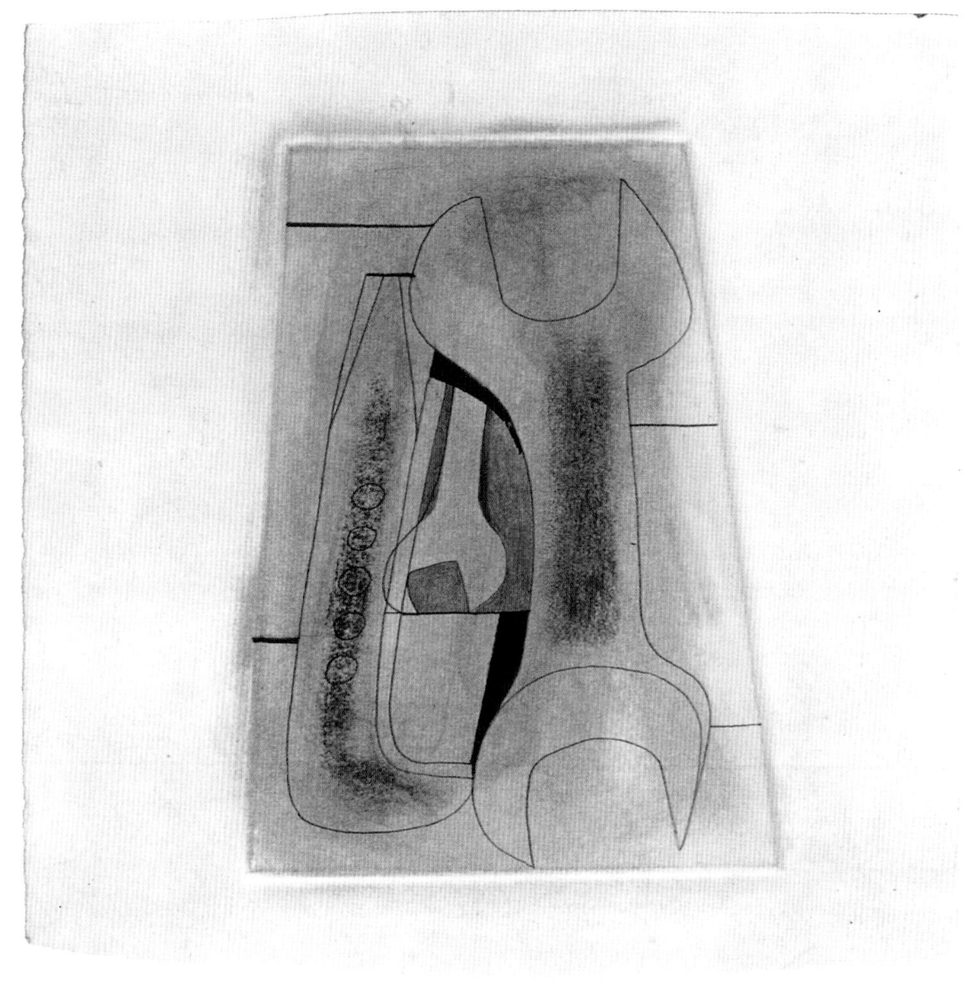

15 Ben Nicholson, *three moonstruck spanners with nearly six holes*, 1974, watercolour, pencil and oil wash on paper, 45.6 × 41.7 cm, private collection

good taste in displays of charm. Though the least nostalgic artist of his generation, he could always be sentimentally distracted by the handle of a pottery jug or the lettering on a French shopfront.

Given this revealing tendency to tweeness in his taste, what we should perhaps be asking is how Nicholson managed to sustain his critical concentration when he did. The answer, I think, is that in his works of the 1930s and 1940s it was his determination to be modern – which is to say his preparedeness to submit to the established discipline of Cubism, and subsequently of abstract art – that held his sentimentality in check. And it was the experience of working in relief – or rather it was that commitment to the facticity of the painted surface that led him to carving in the first place – that gave the same body of work its saving substantiality. In the mid-1930s the same combination of engagements brought his work practically and theoretically into conjunction with the art and aspirations of the European Modern Movement. This conjunction served in turn to reinforce his belief in the idea that Modernism was necessarily a cosmopolitan achievement. And commitment to cosmopolitanism is a powerful check on nostalgia.

The value of this commitment can be sampled by placing Nicholson's wartime paintings (fig. 16) in context with typical works by his contemporaries and near-contemporaries Graham Sutherland (fig. 17), John Piper and Henry Moore (fig. 18) – artists who were more often identified as appropriate representatives of British humanism by the functionaries of the War Artists Advisory Committee, the Council for Encouragement of Music and the Arts, and the British Council. Whatever accusations may be levelled at Nicholson, he cannot be said ever to have been effective in reviving the British romantic tradition, in celebrating the British heritage or in solemnising the universal values of the British family. It is not because Nicholson's work is lacking in overt signs of engagement with modern social and political life that I diagnose a lack of realism. On the contrary; during the 1940s there were strong ethical implications to his disengagement from the national stereotypes of profundity, and to his distaste for the coercive illustrative modes by which these were entrenched.

Isolated in Cornwall during the war and the early 1950s, even when churning out his still-life-and-landscape potboilers, he seems to have held on to the central commitment of that transcendental socialism by which the European Modern Movement had been sustained: I mean the idea that the making of a work of art is a kind of model for the making of a world – a world in which individual partialities and investments are not so much set aside as assumed to be assimilated to the achievement of a greater harmony. This was the last optimistic platform for a modern artistic culture that the Western world would be able to accommodate. No wonder it took so long for it to be finally dismantled.

Let us allow a kind of poignancy to Nicholson's wartime and early post-war work. The conclusion it seems to propose to the retrospective view is that if you were a British artist during the years 1940 to 1956, out of it – in Cornwall or wherever – was the best place to be, even, or especially, during that great reassertion of British self-satisfaction and sentimentality, the Festival of Britain. And if there was a virtuous project to undertake during those years, what better than to maintain a connection between the domestic culture and the legacy of the Modern Movement, in hope of better times. The point I am trying to make is that the technical and stylistic resources available to Nicholson under the long regime of Cubism were such as to minimise the effect of his weaknesses and to maximise his abilities. I also mean to suggest that those abilities were of some continuing critical interest.

Of course we know now, as many no doubt knew at the time, that the realisation of the Modern Movement's dream had been ruled out well before the outbreak of war. I have argued elsewhere that British art's *littérateurs* had been waging a kind of Cold War against modernist cosmopolitanism since at least 1936.[3] *Plus ça change.* Now that liberal capitalism has been proclaimed the global state of nature, it can sometimes seem hard not to surrender to the post-modernist propaganda of today's *littérateurs*, who would have it that the political adventure of the twentieth century was really over before it had even properly begun. It has to be said that the hope of better times must already have worn very thin by the end of the 1940s. I think Nicholson's work had begun to

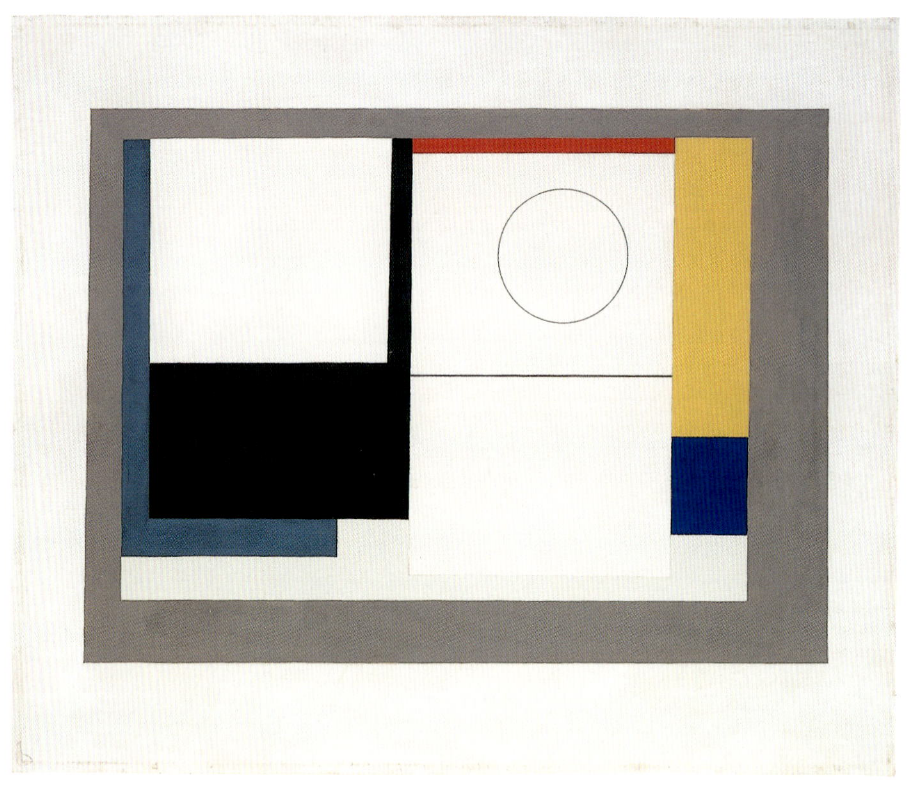

16 Ben Nicholson, *1943 (painting)*, pencil and gouache on board, 34.3 × 41.9 cm, British Council Collection

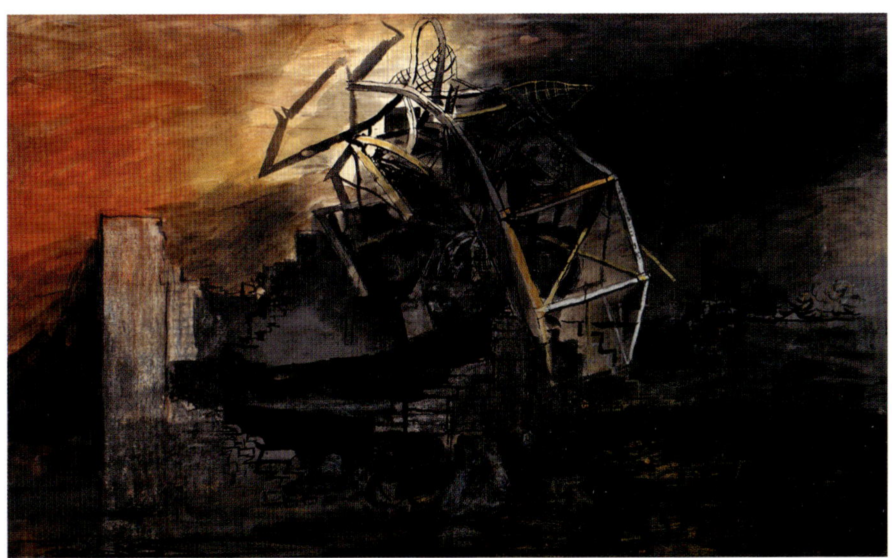

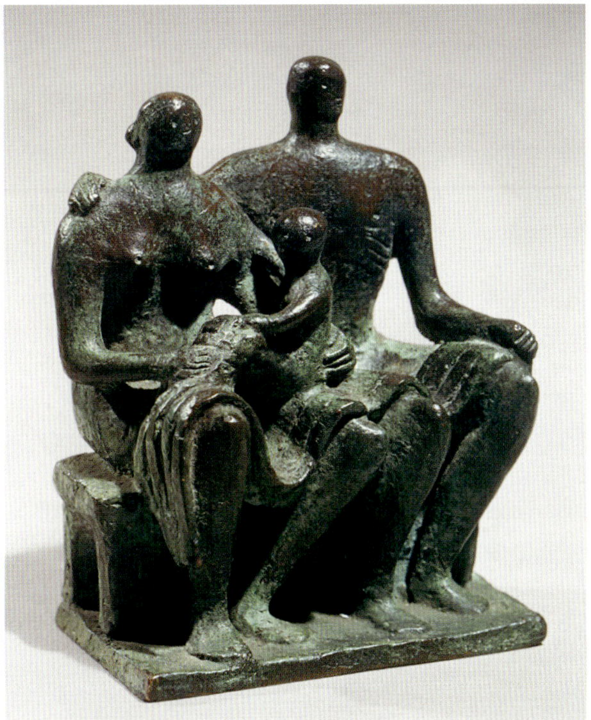

17 (*above*) Graham Sutherland, *Devastation in the City*, 1941, pencil and gouache on board, 37 × 45.8 cm, Imperial War Museum

18 (*left*) Henry Moore, *Maquette for Family Group*, 1944, bronze, 137 × 114 × 67 cm, Tate

wear thin by then too, for reasons that cannot be wholly disconnected. An aesthetic language is not critically sustainable for long without some realistic nourishment. The decorative panels he made in 1949 for the steamship *Rangitane* look like just that: mere decoration – which is to say abstract art without either critical direction or substantial content.

If we play Greenberg's game and diagnose underlying conditions from aesthetic effects, we might conclude that the Modern Movement's project of universal social harmony had altogether lost virtue through lack of contrast or resistance in the sphere of culture. In the new world order of the late 1940s and early 1950s, it was from the formerly oppositional project that new stereotypes of profundity were being drawn. In the modernisation of art education effected in Britain during the 1950s, for instance, the bureaucratisation of self-expression took place largely in the name of the Cubist tradition and its extensions. It is telling that this, the period of some of Nicholson's weakest work, the time of his separation from his modernist partner Hepworth, was also the time of establishment of his international reputation. His first New York show was held in the year of the steamship commission. Three years later he was awarded first prize at the Carnegie International in Pittsburgh and in 1954 he won the Ulisse award at the Venice Biennale.

The glittering prizes notwithstanding, it was perhaps the prospect of a total blockage in the critical direction of abstract art that led Nicholson in the mid-50s to reinforce the Cubist armature of his work. Certainly it is a more plastic kind of Cubism that sustains the large still lifes of 1955–6. It appears as though he was able to preserve the possibility of some robust emotional content in his work only by once again moderating its claims – by allowing that the task of the artist is after all categorically distinct from the work of the architect, the designer and the planner, and that the critical power of the aesthetic is in the end to be contained within the painting's framing edges. It is tempting to attribute the uncharacteristic gravitas of *Still Life – Nightshade* to the pathos involved in this acknowledgement. The Modern Movement project of world harmony surrenders finally to the modernist pragmatism of resolution in one painting. If Cubism could no longer sustain its autonomy as experiment, it could at least be classical.

The question remains, why then? Or, to put the question another way, if, as Greenberg claimed, the American painters had to free themselves from Cubism in order to 'say what they had to say', just what was the necessity that both connected their message to the historical moment of the mid-century, and prevented its articulation within the language of Cubism? Presumably some indication may be found by looking at the message in question; that is, by considering the new properties that distinguished significant modern painting at the time around 1950 when it was evident from art such as Nicholson's that the rich seam of the Cubist tradition was finally running out.

It might seem that we are back again with 'American-type painting' and with Greenberg's lucid description of stylistic characteristics. In fact we find ourselves now in territory to which neither the Greenberg of 'The Decline of Cubism' nor the Greenberg of 'American-type painting' can be taken as an adequate guide. Indeed, the most influential of all the American critic's essays, his 'Modernist Painting' of 1960, serves to trail a kind of red herring across the work of the Abstract Expressionists. He does not actually deny that reiterated emphasis on existential conditions and emotional content that we find in the statements of the painters themselves. The point is rather that his account of a century of development in modern painting is one in which that emphasis is accorded no explanatory role.

So far as painting is concerned, the problems of renewing emotional rather than merely iconographic value depend on the possibility that the relations between the literal and the metaphorical can be rendered newly palpable in the experience of the engaged spectator. The technical demands entailed are specific to painting, but the terms of reference for the literal and the metaphorical are not. They are conditions of cognitive existence as these are experienced under contingent and everyday circumstances. Whether they are registered in self-consciousness or not, they will bear down on artist and spectator alike.

The new compositional discipline to which the Americans submitted involved not only the avoidance of 'Cubist fragmentation' but also a determined pursuit of 'the sense of the whole thing' – to borrow two phrases from Don Judd.[4] This sense of the whole thing depended on a new means of tuning the relationship between the painting's literal properties and those properties that it held metaphorically. This means of tuning is most clearly at work in the paintings of Mark Rothko and Barnett Newman. On the one hand the literal surface, however marked and differentiated, was conceived by them as a single uninterrupted frontal plane; on the other that surface was made to function illusionistically so as to induce the engaged spectator into a kind of imaginary emotional exchange, variously referred to by the painters themselves as 'a consummated relationship' and a 'real transaction'.[5] An abstract art based on Cubism could not have been made to do this work. A painting dependent for its animation on the relating of its internal planes would not seem to confront the spectator on equal terms. Nor could the job be done by means of a realist art rooted in the illustration of the human figure. A painting containing a picture of the human figure could not itself be metaphorically endowed with personality – though of course it could be endowed with iconographical content *ad nauseam*.

The competent viewer presupposed by these new paintings is someone who comes to them 'free from the conventions of understanding', equipped with 'both need and spirit' (the words are Rothko's);[6] someone endowed, in Newman's terms, with 'the feeling of his own totality, of his own separateness';[7] someone able and willing to consummate that unreassuring but equal relationship that the painting holds out in its capacity not as a picture but as a form of equivalent for the value of another person. Such viewers were in short supply in the late 1940s and early 1950s. 'A painting lives by companionship', Rothko wrote in 1947. 'It dies by the same token. It is therefore a risky and unfeeling act to send it out into the world. How often it must be permanently impaired by the eyes of the vulgar and the cruelty of the impotent who would extend their affliction universally.'[8]

It seems that what the painters had to say that was unsayable within the optimistic language of Cubism and of concrete abstract art was that painting could no longer discover its philosophical or psychological justification in the prospect of a better world. As for the modern figurative tradition, if regarded from a position free both from Stalinist dogmatism and from liberal sentimentality, what it was bound to present, in

Rothko's memorable phrase, was 'a *tableau vivant* of human incommunicability'.[9] (In case it seems that I am trying to set Nicholson up in a disadvantageous contest with the American painters, I should make clear that he had the highest regard for Rothko's work in particular and that the two artists exchanged paintings.)

The defeat of revolutionary optimism was regarded both as a necessity and as a prospective triumph by the Western ideologues of the Cold War – as it still is. The critically important paintings of the late 1940s and early 1950s are those that acknowledge the defeat but give the lie to the triumph. Therein lies their realism. The state to which Newman's and Rothko's paintings seem to testify is one of being hunted back to the minimum conditions of social exchange and of decency in human relations.

That which finds expression in art cannot thereafter be unsaid. This may be why art matters at all. To proceed through the 1950s and beyond on the philosophical basis that had sustained the idealism of the pre-war years was to be condemned to conservatism. This, I think, is what happened to Ben Nicholson. The effect in technical terms was that the endemic strains of idealism and sentimentality in his taste ceased to be conditions *in face of which* he had to do his work; they now defined the very circumstances of going on doing it. That persistence of this order is often represented as a *sine qua non* of unqualified success tells us nothing we do not already know about the institutions doing the representing. Which returns us full circle to my 'phone call from the Tate.

My conclusion, such as it is, is vulnerable to two forms of misunderstanding, which I should like to pre-empt. The first potential misunderstanding is that I mean to blame Nicholson for the late weakness of his art. It needs to be borne in mind that in 1955 he was a man of 61, a decade older than Newman and Rothko and nearly two decades older than Pollock. He was the contemporary of Joan Mirò, André Masson, Alexander Calder, Milton Avery and Stuart Davis – company in which even his late work stands up well. On these and other grounds it would be absurd to hold Nicholson to account for failing to become an Abstract Expressionist. But in any case, my purpose has been to suggest that the commitments and competences that go to make a modern artist under one set of historical circumstances can turn out to be disenabling under another, for reasons that may be altogether beyond that artist's control. The more restricted the competences in the first place, the more likely this is to happen, but it is enough to do the best one can. My primary interest is not in finding fault but in examining what happens to artistic styles and techniques. To see how these serve or fail the requirements of modern expression is to learn a kind of history – or at least it is to be availed of modes of vivid retrospect independent of those types of representation to which the title of History is more commonly given.

My second disavowal is implied by the first. The problems of restoring or renewing human emotional values are perennial in the arts. It may be said that the possibility of facing those problems is a condition of the very possibility of art. The decline of Cubism was a practical issue. It was also for some an ideological opportunity. I have suggested that specific problems of renewal of emotional value in painting can be seen to coincide with the establishment of the Cold War. However, co-occurrence is not in itself the sign of a causal relationship. In the rhetoric of the Cold War, a liberal and exploratory Modernism was contrasted with a dogmatic and conservative Realism; or a historically grounded and heuristically charged Realism was contrasted with a mystificatory and elitist Modernism – the form of this contrast depending on the political and intellectual location of the speaker's platform. This is the reciprocating system ironically pictured in Art & Language's *Portraits of V. I. Lenin in the Style of Jackson Pollock* (fig. 30). The rhetorical creatures of the Cold War do indeed seem to coincide at points with the practical and conceptual issues that painters faced during the late 1940s and early 1950s in negotiating between Cubist abstraction and some possible figuration. But it would be invidious simply to accord priority to the rhetoric, and to conceive of the Cold War as the historical and political agency by which the issues in question were put on the agenda of art. We need to remember that Cold War rhetoric was above all opportunistic and parasitic. It seized on tendencies relatively independent of political direction and recast them in the image of its own fantasies of power and opposition, of vitality and effeteness. We need to understand the conditions under which the work of Rothko and others came to have ideological use value. Yet if the art is not *simply* to be Cold War art we also need some means to distinguish the conditions of production of its use value from the problems of production of aesthetic value – ideological as these last may also be. Among the hardest such distinctions to make are those that would insulate judgements of aesthetic worth against the hegemony of American Modernism on the one hand and the promptings of insular affections on the other. I have tried to explain what I judge to be a falling off in the aesthetic value of Nicholson's work, and to do so by situating it in a kind of historical ground. But if any rhetorical plausibility attaches to my argument, it remains the case that a convincing revision of the aesthetic judgement is all that is required to call both the relevance and the motivation of that argument into question.

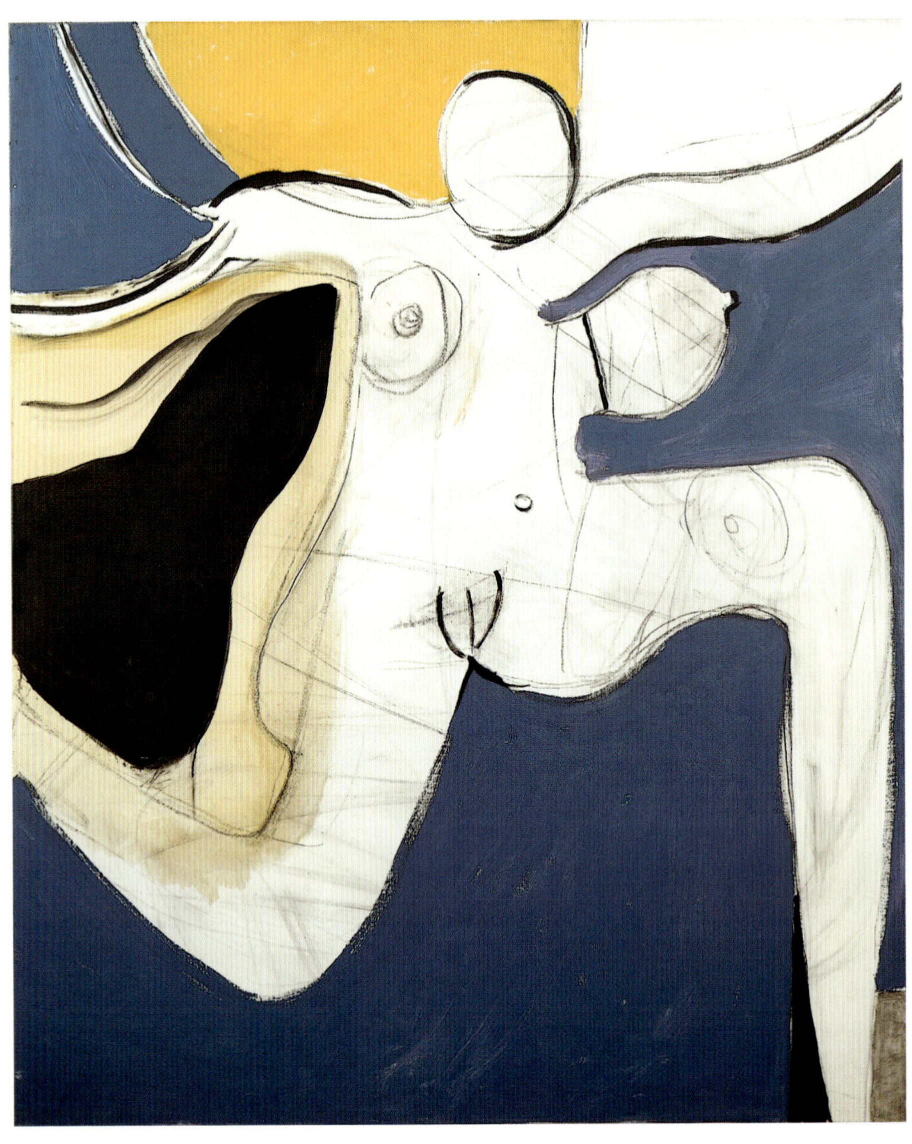

19 Roger Hilton, *Dancing Woman, December* 1963, oil and charcoal on canvas, 152 × 127 cm, Scottish National Gallery of Modern Art, Edinburgh

# 4 ROGER HILTON: THE OBLIGATION TO EXPRESS

This evaluation of Hilton's work was originally written for the catalogue of a retrospective exhibition held at the Hayward Gallery, London, in 1993. In a letter to Lawrence Alloway, Hilton wrote, 'Art precedes the artist. I don't mean works of art, I mean the machinery of art.' The aim of this essay is to consider the machinery of painting as Hilton was engaged with it. It has been slightly revised for the present publication.

## FIGURATION AND ABSTRACTION

Hilton's mature paintings are both attractive and difficult. Their attractions are difficult to explain. Their difficulty is somehow attractive. The means and materials of their facture are flaunted on their surfaces, as if those surfaces had been conceived of as mere literal planes in need of decoration. Yet even at their most abstract Hilton's paintings remain as emotionally and psychologically suggestive as works far more evidently reliant than they on forms of pictorial illusion. This is not to say that these paintings are without significant illusory properties. They could not be so redolent of human states as they are unless some form of mimesis had been established in the process of their composition. But however it is that these states are evoked it is not through the picturing of emotional or psychological dramas. On the contrary, it was in part his determined resistance to narrative and to illustration that led Hilton to invest his art with emotional content by other means.

Even those of Hilton's paintings which do unquestionably contain pictures of animals or birds or human figures seem in fact to depend for their effect on that manifest artificiality which commits the image to its role in the composition of the surface, thus limiting the possibility of its being exploited in furtherance of a sentimental interest. Of all Hilton's mature paintings in oils the composition most apparently conducive to being read as a narrative drama is one which exists in two versions, both painted in December 1963, both featuring a nude female figure, the first known as *Oh Yoi Yoi* and the second as *Dancing Woman* (fig. 19). Hilton himself recounted an anecdote in explanation of the first of these. He referred to a scene on holiday in France following a row with his second wife to be. She was jumping up and down naked on a veranda shouting.[1] Meanwhile a nearby hayrick had caught fire.[2] In this case it is certainly tempting to see the painting as a kind of illustration of the remembered scene, of its tensions, its absurdities and its drama. Yet all that this anecdote really does – as Hilton no doubt knew – is explain the title of the first of the two paintings in question, this being what the pictured woman is supposed to have been shouting.[3] To describe *Oh Yoi Yoi* as a picture of an angry woman jumping up and down on a veranda against a background of flames is actually to do very little to elucidate its composition or its effects. To assess how little, we have only to imagine on the one hand how unlikely it is that anyone would have deduced the anecdote from the painting, and on the other how radically different a picture someone would be likely to conceive who had heard the anecdote but not seen Hilton's painting. The relationship between the event and the painting, that is to say, is such that the memory of the event imposes few conditions on the painting. It is rather a virtue of the art of painting as Hilton conceived it that it imposes critical limits on the relevance of remembered experience. Art must be made of something – of the materials of some actual experience – but the demands of that making are only trivially satisfied by depiction.

The most distinctive improvement Hilton made to the second version of his composition was to change the colour surrounding the nude from red to blue, thus disconnecting the work still further from the remembered moment (if, that is, we assume that the warm colouration of *Oh Yoi Yoi* is appropriately seen as iconic – that is, as signifying fire).[4] Here it is not the figure's imagined part in a story that gives it its individuality and its animation, but rather the life it is made to live on the contained surface of the canvas. It is significant that the figure is so arranged on that surface that the outlines of its limbs break the edges in places. It is also significant that the effect of this incompleteness in the figure is not such as to imply some continuation of its existence outside the world of the painting. On the contrary, it is to identify figure and ground more closely both with each other and with the literal plane of the canvas.

It is telling that when Hilton does base a composition on a single recognisable figure – usually a recognisably female figure – the resulting effect is generally less one of intimacy than of something like irony, an irony which does not so much serve to pick out the figure represented as to embrace the very means of representation. True, as opposed to merely attitudinal, irony entails acknowledgement that forms and means of expression are subject to an evacuation of meaning which is outside the individual's control. One problem which Hilton faced in common with other significant painters of his time was how to sustain the emotional charge of painting under conditions in which, as Mark Rothko put it in 1958, 'None of us could use the human figure without mutilating it'.[5] An inability, or perhaps a principled unwillingness, to put the individual figure to expressive use under these conditions was one factor distinguishing the English painters of Hilton's generation – the so-called Middle Generation – both from the neo-Romantics, whose highly theatrical work was in the ascendant at the end of the 1940s, and from those painters nowadays associated with the School of London, Francis Bacon and Lucian Freud foremost among them. For these latter the depiction of the human individual – whether mutilated or whole – was to remain the definitive vehicle of emotional expression in painting.

The example of the *Dancing Woman* is indicative of Hilton's taste and priorities as they operated from the early 1950s until his death in 1975. In particular, it is clear that the experience of abstract painting which he gained in the early 1950s remained of crucial relevance even to the explicitly figurative paintings which he made after the late 1950s. This experience was itself both a consequence and a confirmation of his commitment to a modernist ethic, a commitment which he never revised.

* * *

## THE VOCATION OF MODERNISM

The effective preliminaries to Roger Hilton's career occupied two periods of about half a dozen years each, divided by the Second World War, for part of which he was interned in a German prison camp. The works which survive from this long apprenticeship are mostly relatively modest. Many can be dated only circumstantially. Works from the early 1930s betray an interest in the dry touch and light tonality of Vuillard's works of the 1890s. Some pictures from the late 1930s show him absorbing the effects of Cubism as those effects were diluted through the Ecole de Paris of the 1920s. Others which explore the modern European styles of the 1930s may not have been painted until the late 1940s, when Hilton, like a number of his contemporaries, was trying to make up for England's lost time. What is clear is that from his early twenties Hilton was capable of drawing with a distinctive concentration and intelligence. The strength of his drawing is felt throughout his work, even at its most abstract.

It was Hilton's expressed conviction that painters are born and not bred.[6] For all the apparent dilettantism of his pre-war career, he came to be driven by a sense of vocation that would have done credit to a French Symbolist in the 1890s. But that in itself says something important about his breeding as a painter. Though he spent far more time in England than in France both before the war and after, his understanding of the modern in art was largely formed in Paris. In his mature work he was to draw strength not simply from his early technical grounding in the French modern tradition, but also from the beliefs and values by which that tradition had been sustained. In a correspondence with Terry Frost preserved in the Tate Gallery archives, the substance of Hilton's regular encouragement to his hard-pressed friend is a reiterated reminder that painting is not only its own reward but a virtual form of self-sustaining life in itself. This idea may not have originated with the Modern Movement, but it was within French modernist theory that it was elevated to the status of a creed.

Though lip-service was paid to this idea within English artistic circles during and after the war, there was little real appetite for its practical implications. Full-blooded Modernism has been a rare phenomenon in English art, and its demands are not easily registered among the familiar challenges of the native culture. There are two particular demands that Hilton's paintings make of the viewer. The first is that their practical, factive aspects should be accorded due weight. The abstract works of 1953–4 come alive in the awareness of the viewer as they reveal the accumulated evidence of cancellation and change. Similarly in the less densely painted and more atmospheric works of the late 1950s and early 1960s the final position is usually defined as the product of a sequence of practical moves. The apparent evidence of the painting's genesis is typically carried through lines drawn both beneath and across painted areas. These range from the light and vestigial to the broad and emphatic. Their effect is usually to suggest a manner of proceeding from tentative exploration, through deliberative revision to decisive spontaneity.

The significance of this effect is not simply to define the character of a painting. In so far as it is associated with a sense of value in the experience of the spectator, it implies value in the type of procedure for which the painting serves as token. The suggestion is that if we could always conduct ourselves in such a manner, the outcome would be a condition such as the painting itself metaphorically exemplifies. We may or may not find that condition desirable in imagination. But it would be a trivial form of liking of the painting which was not also an opening of the heart to its implication.

It should be stressed that this implication is not primarily a function of whatever it is that Hilton's paintings may depict. Rather it is a function of the practical ethic by which they happen to have been shaped. As already suggested, even those works which evidently contain pictured figures tend to reveal their intentional character largely through the details of their formal organisation and their facture, details which may have little to do with the requirements for defining a figure (apart from the 1963 *Dancing Woman*, see for instance the 1957 *Grey Figure*, the 1961 *Figure*, the 1963 *Figure and Bird* and the untitled work of 1968 in the Powell Collection).

The demand for recognition of the work's practical character is thus a demand that its implications be acknowledged, for better or worse, and whatever associations its pictorial settings may conjure. The second demand made by the paintings is that their content be allowed to be unamenable to translation. However suggestive and however stimulating they may be to processes of interpretation, to reduce this content to literary form would be to restore those habitual forms of conceptualisation from which the paintings seek a critical independence.

These two demands are clearly connected. On the one hand the viewer frustrated in the search for narrative is directed to the literal evidence of the painting's composition, that is, to its surface and to those properties of the surface that serve to establish and to individualise its decorative integrity. On the other it is precisely so that that surface may be experienced as the self-sufficient medium of the painting's content that the expectation of narrative is necessarily frustrated.

## MODERNISM AND REALISM

It could be said that the requirement of integrity and self-sufficiency in composition is to all intents and purposes the requirement of aesthetic unity, and that this is a condition to which all art alike is subject. In the last instance this may be true, but last instances appear under some confusing guises when viewed through the incidental demands of contingent culture and the actualities of studio practice. Both for those who approve and for those who disapprove the idea of art for art's sake, it is a truism of the age that aesthetic experience is supposed to be an end in itself. At least in the modern period, however, the aesthetic has never been pursued in practice as an end or value in itself – or never to any critically significant purpose. What we may conceive as the aesthetic achievement of a given body of work is typically a kind of residue. It is the by-product of a series of disassociations, critical moves which artists make with regard to those ends and purposes and values with which, for one reason or another, they are unable to identify. As regards the modern period at least, to talk of a vocation for art is to put a positive cast on this inability comfortably to identify with generally approved purposes and values. The modernist vocation, that is, has tended to entail dissent from the self-imagery of modern societies. Even when this dissent has been expressed in the form of a utopian modelling of alternatives, the dissatisfaction motivating the artist's critical moves has been necessarily specific and relative to historically defined conditions. Therein lies the guarantee of realism in the achievement of the aesthetic. To put the matter another way, the true mark of realism in art is an indifference to dead issues. And such indifference is in turn of critical interest in identifying a given body of painting as the modern painting of its time and place.[7] In Hilton's case it was largely through his consistent and unerring distaste for the appearances and technical instruments of insularity and sentimentality that he came in the early 1950s to develop a style of abstract art fully deserving of international recognition.

Prominent among the dead issues of the mid-century were the various arguments in favour of illustrative forms of expression and figurative forms of 'realism'. Nevertheless, and despite the brief rise of an abstract tendency led by Ben Nicholson and Barbara Hepworth in the 1930s, at the end of the war illustrative techniques were still widely regarded in England as the predominant artistic means of establishing a bearing on the world and of connecting with a wider culture. The prevalent English style of the 1940s and early 1950s was a form of insular neo-romanticism. The predominant critical attitude of the time is expressed in Robin Ironside's *Painting Since 1939*, a survey of *British* painting published in 1947.[8] Ironside disparaged 'the idea of an exclusive and all-sufficing beauty in plastic values' and noted the inappropriateness of such extremism in 'a culture so ill-conditioned to uncompromising theories'. He singled out the work of Nicholson as typifying the form of modernist outlandishness to which the native culture was properly resistant, concluding with satisfaction that 'The best British painting relies, for its final justification, upon an amateur stimulus', and that there was no prospect of a return to abstraction.

To speak of an amateur stimulus is to assume that art's justification must come in the end from its subservience to some larger sense of obligation, whether it be to a literature, to a party or to a nation. As Hilton conceived it, however, his vocation needed no justification, since art as he conceived it was its own justification. A conviction along these lines could never of itself make an artist, but it could do much to save a talented painter from the dangers of provincialism. For those availed as Hilton was of some distance from the prevailing ethos of the culture, a different value was attached to the figurative styles widely practised by British artists and supported by Ironside and other writers. Viewed against the legacy of the larger Modern Movement, they appeared as repositories of sentimental and insular interests, and thus of conservatism, even in the hands of artists whose avowed aims were not apparently conservative.

There were two basic technical assumptions that had tended to distinguish the composition of figurative art. The first was that the way to establish significance was to position relatively concrete and plastic figures within relatively vacant and spatial grounds. The second was that the illusion of weight and density should be decreased and the illusion of spatial distance increased as one moved up the canvas, as it were from foreground to middle distance to background to sky, so that the bottom and lower edges of the canvas would always be more heavily stressed than the upper edges and the top. In fact, these assumptions had been shown to be insecure by the work of Cézanne as early as the late nineteenth century, and had been rendered largely irrelevant by the work of the Cubists. The mature work of Mondrian had demonstrated not so much that figuration was unnecessary to painting as that a highly concrete form of aesthetic order could be sustained when these technical assumptions were abandoned. That they had become the conditions of conservative concepts of representation was a realisation that was long overdue in England.

In the context of English art at the mid-century Hilton's relative Modernism thus entailed a form of reconnection to the Continental Modern Movement. The implication was that Modernism itself had become the inescapable condition of art's capacity to sustain unsentimental content. Sentimentality is a form of evasion of the actual currency of our lives. It entails a failure of realism. Modernism was revealed, in fact, as the very condition of realism in representation. And if Modernism did not entail abstraction, it did at least require the avoidance of those forms of figure–ground relation and of spatial illusion that had become associated with the conservation of dead culture. In other words, these became the very practical conditions that a work would have to evade if it was to be modern in its effects. For Hilton in the early 1950s, as for the Americans Jackson Pollock and Mark Rothko in the late 1940s, the specific technical implication of the demand for integrity in modern painting was now that all areas of the surface had to be invested with an equal potential. This envisaged form of integrity became a significant qualification on the painting's relationship to its spectator, and thus of the spectator's experience as these painters wished to effect and to define it.

Hilton was not the first or the only English artist to have reached this conclusion in practice, but among his generation he was the most unrelenting in pursuing its consequences. The clearest observable tendency in his painting from about 1947 to 1953 is one of dispersal outwards of those plastic effects that had previously concentrated at the centre of the canvas to establish a motif, whether a single figure, a head or some less easily translatable form. In paintings of 1950–52 (*Composition 1* is a typical example; fig. 20) this process of figurative constitution is still observed, but its function is spread across the canvas on relatively informal grid-like structures. These are lightly anchored to the bottom of the canvas, just failing to reach its edges and thus leaving a residue of atmospheric emptiness around them.

After the war Hilton's inclination had been to re-establish a sense of connection to the French modern tradition. These transitional paintings of the early 1950s testify to his acquaintance with the kind of informal, brushy, semi-abstract painting that had been developed in Paris in the late 1940s by Manessier, Estève, Bissière (one of Hilton's teachers from the pre-war period) and others. They are similar to paintings of 1948–50 by Alan Davie and William Gear, who had both had comparable grounds for emancipation from insular interests.

While Hilton's works of the early 1950s assert a positive cosmopolitanism, however, they also serve to indicate the limitations of what could then be learned in Paris. The crucial move in his work came at the point when the interstices of his grid-like structures were filled up with opaque paint and when the remainder of allusive space was forced out as it were

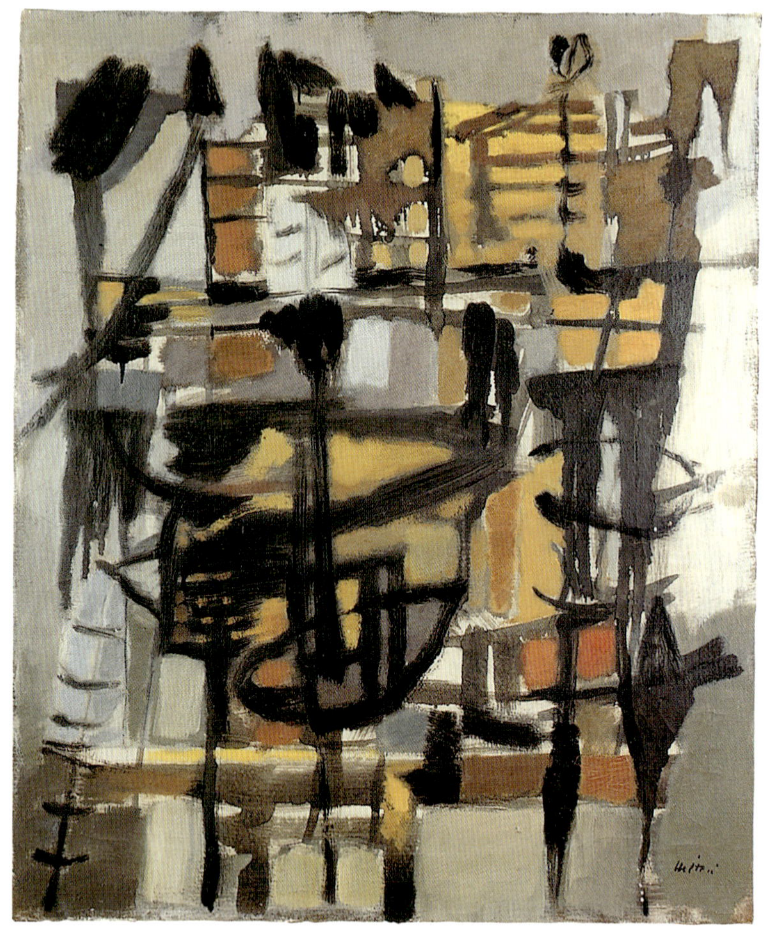

20 Roger Hilton, *Composition*, c.1950–2, oil on canvas, 66 × 55.9 cm, formerly collection John Hilton

beyond the literal edge of the canvas, until the effect of plastic density became a property of the painting as a whole. This was also the point at which Hilton finally achieved independence from the legacy of the Ecole de Paris. The concrete effect that he first achieved in paintings of mid-1953 was alien to the French tradition. Its precedents were to be found rather in forms of abstract painting that had been produced in Russia and in Holland in the second and third decades of the century, at a time when French hegemony over the development of modern art had first been decisively challenged.

A *terminus post quem* is established by the painting *June 1953 (Deep Cadmium)* in the Scottish National Gallery of Modern Art. From this point on, from the abstract configurations of 1953–4 to the *Nude* of 1967 or the Tate's untitled painting of 1971, the forms of Hilton's paintings regularly fill out their surfaces, so that the depicted shapes and images of his compositions become fully integrated and identified with the literal shapes of his canvases.[9] It becomes a consistent feature of his individual style that shapes are attached to the sides of his paintings, and that forms and lines are run out to intersect their edges, as it were to raise the stakes in that contract according to which the divisions between painting and larger world are negotiated. In a statement written at the time, Hilton indicated the nature of this contract as he understood it. 'I am only interested in pictures which turn their faces outwards, whose action is outwards, and which are received outwards by the spectator. Any picture which does not give an immediate effect of space, not inside the picture, not illusionist space, but outside it in the heart of the spectator is, to me, without interest.'[10] It was at this stage in his career that Hilton both achieved an individual style and identified himself as a painter of fully abstract paintings.

A number of factors must have helped bring him to the point at which he could make this identification. He clearly drew strength from the contacts he had formed with a circle of British contemporaries that included William Gear, F. E. McWilliam, Terry Frost, Patrick Heron and William Scott. His friendship with the expatriate Stephen Gilbert led to contact with the Dutch painter Constant, with whom Gilbert was associated in the COBRA group. And early in 1953 a trip to Holland in Constant's company brought Hilton first-hand experience of Mondrian's painting.

It is the precedent of Mondrian's work above all that seems to lie behind Hilton's abstract paintings of late 1953 and 1954. Consciously or not, he absorbed that precedent, and the utopian form of Modernism for which it was the vehicle, and reworked it with a realistic regard for the changed conditions of the post-war years – conditions under which utopian forms of expression appeared to have been emptied of all critical power and pertinence. In an untitled painting of October 1953–March 1954 (fig. 21) Hilton seems deliberately to have felt for that remarkable form of aesthetic tuning by which Mondrian's procedure was animated. Yet in doing so he gave practical effect to the very different considerations by which the procedures of painting were then bound to be inflected. The geometry buckles as if under an inexorable spoiling force: the requirement that painting give expression to images of individuality. Not even at the level of the aesthetic, it seemed, could the model of a harmonious social order be plausibly established.

Hilton's position at this point should not be mistaken. I mean to suggest that the sense of individuality was an inescapable determinant on the painting of the 1940s and 1950s – a determinant acknowledged by Hilton among others. But to say this is not *per se* to offer justification for pictures of dramatically solitary human figures, though subjects of this order were rife in French and English painting at the time.[11] In fact, given both the prevalence of such subjects and the thoroughness of Hilton's own grounding in the figure-drawing tradition, his avoidance of the figure as explicit subject can reasonably be taken as confirmation that his dissociation was intentional and principled. The untitled painting may testify to a kind of rejection of geometric abstraction, but it also manages in the end to resist becoming just another tortured figure.

It was clearly not Hilton's desire or his intention to join in the establishment of an individualistic type of art. At the time his untitled work was painted he was occupied by thoughts of painting's possible role in the shaping of a larger world. For many of those he was talking to it still seemed possible that this role could be discharged either through a form of Constructivism or through some less idealistic form of social engagement. It is significant that Constant was working in 1953 on quasi-architectural projects and that he came to be associated with the anarchic urbanism of the Situationists. The point in Hilton's case was that it seemed necessary that the individual need for expression be acknowledged not as an end in itself but as the limiting condition on any search for higher truths. 'One must express oneself', he wrote at the time. 'There

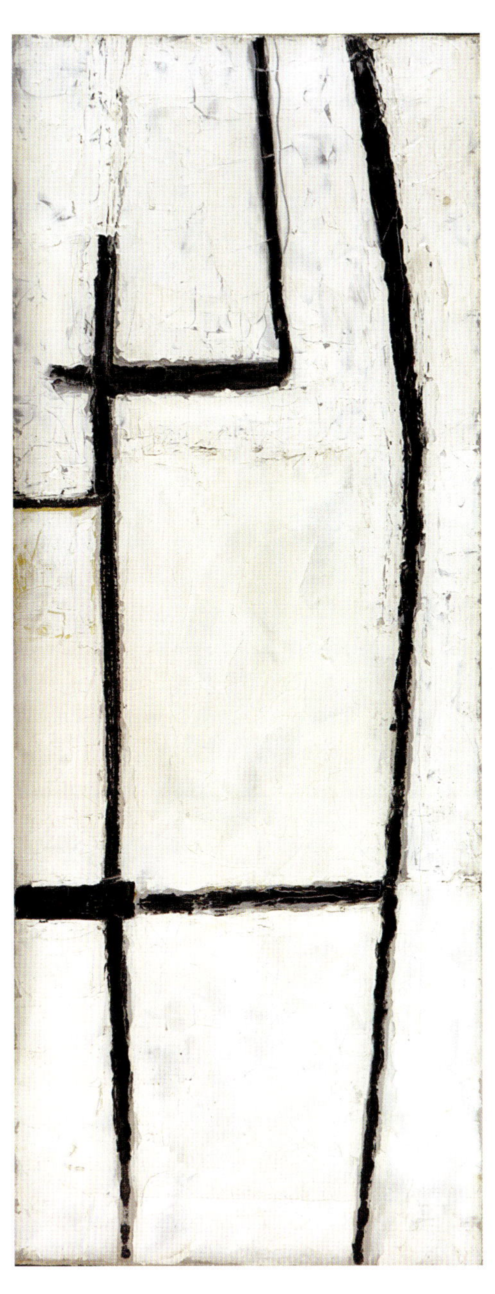

21 Roger Hilton, *October 1953–March 1954/Black on White March 1954*, oil on canvas, 76 × 30.5 cm, Southampton Art Gallery, formerly collection David Brown

are situations, states of mind, moods, etc. which call for some artistic expression; because one knows that only some form of art is capable of going beyond them to give an intuitive contact with a superior set of truths.'[12]

## FIGURATIVE CONTENT AND UNCONSCIOUS CONTENT

The conditions Hilton confronted in the early 1950s may be recapitulated with regard to those faced by the advanced American painters during the previous decade. On both sides of the Atlantic, traditional styles of figuration had become widely and, it seemed, irredeemably associated with sentimental and parochial forms of content. In America, non-academic figuration tended to entail either the idealisation of the American scene or subordination to one or another programme for the prescription of realism. In England, such modernised forms of figuration as the neo-romanticism of the 1940s and early 1950s offered no more than a half-hearted domestication of the critical legacy of modern painting. At the same time, the geometrical bases of pre-war forms of Modernist abstraction seemed to be invested with a form of idealism that rendered them implausible as models for post-war practice. As late as the mid-1930s, it had seemed to Nicholson and Hepworth among others that a significant form of 'content' could be assured by associating the work's design with the proposed lineaments of a larger social world.[13] But such beliefs had been stripped of credibility by the history of the intervening years. The question facing Hilton in the early 1950s was the one the American Barnett Newman had posed in 1948: 'how if we refuse to admit any exaltation in pure relations, if we refuse to live in the abstract, how can we be creating a sublime art?'[14] And Newman's answer could be used to represent Hilton's own conclusion: 'We are making it out of ourselves, out of our own feelings.'

Of course this left open the further question of just how it was that 'our own feelings' were to become the stuff of significant art. The answer could only be given in the development of practice, which meant that it had to be found in the very process of negotiation between the Scylla and Charybdis of conservative figuration and idealistic abstraction. What this meant was not simply that the artist had to find a kind of middle style, though it is indeed the case that forms of semi-abstract art proliferated among modern painters throughout the West during the late 1940s and the 1950s. The demand that mattered concerned the effect of the finished work: the form of exertion it elicited from the engaged spectator, the experience that resulted and the relevance to that experience of the spectator's attempts to read the work respectively as figurative and as abstract. What was required was firstly that the spectator should be so positioned that neither form of reading could be entirely discounted, and secondly that a significant form of remainder was left when either or both forms of reading were tried. It is this effective form of aporia that accounts in large measure for the difficulty encountered in interpreting Hilton's work. The burden of my argument has been that that difficulty was an inescapable condition of originality, given the culture, the history, within which the work had to be done; that is, it was a condition of the possibility of safeguarding the meaning of the work against co-option to conservative ends; a condition, in fact, of Modernism.

It should be stressed that the difficulty in question is not *prima facie* a matter of complexity or of undue specialisation in the techniques of art. It is first and foremost a social and ethical difficulty – the kind of difficulty we confront in holding on to our real desires and intuitions in face of the pervasive simplifications and misrepresentations of our political and economic culture. In that sense it is not only a condition of Modernism but also a condition of realism in expression. If a 'private' form of painting – a painting that had the individual's emotional condition as its working materials – were to take the place of the Modern Movement's aspirations for a socially pertinent modern art, then the borders of that private world would have to be elastic and penetrable. It could not be easy. The collapse of the aspiration to improve the social world was not a licence to be comfortable with the world as it was, nor to cultivate one's favourite motifs like so many more wares on display.

An example may help both to fill out what is meant above by the concept of a remainder, and to take us further into a characterisation of the difficulty of Hilton's work. In pursuit of a figurative reading we might

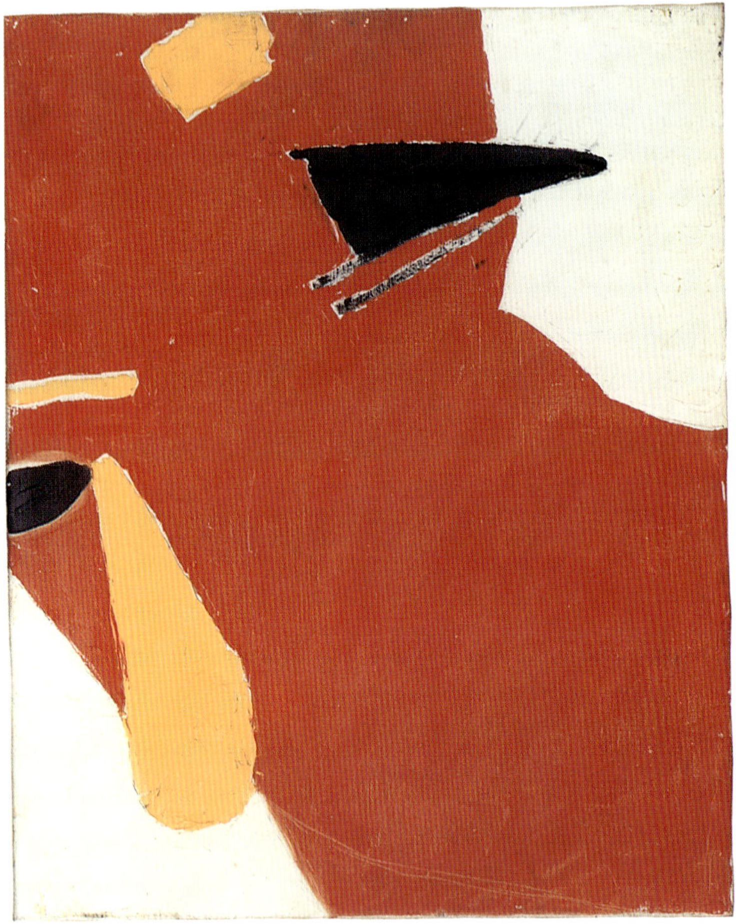

22 Roger Hilton, *August 1953 (Red, Ochre, Black and White)*, oil on canvas, 61 × 51 cm, Southampton Art Gallery, formerly collection David Brown

interpret the red form of *August 1953* (fig. 22) as the central portion of a reclining torso, going on to rationalise the black and yellow shapes as forms of reference to breasts, arms and so forth. In paintings as dependent as Hilton's typically are on the use of complex and irregular shapes and contours, such resemblances can usually be discovered if we seek them. In this case the resemblance we have found may seem to explain the sense that the painting evokes a human presence.

Yet unless this form of identification is consistent with all aspects of the painting, it will be open to correction. In finding a figure in *August 1953* we may in fact be allowing a familiar and convenient type of *gestalt* to distract us from the evidence offered both by the character of the drawing and by the evidence of facture. For the whole tendency of the painting's spatial organisation is actually to deny the kind of simple figure–ground relation that a straightforwardly figurative reading presupposes. For example, the larger black patch both serves to break the contour of the red area and to prevent too marked a spatial separation of red from white, while the concreteness of the painting's effect depends to a large extent on the impression that the diagonally opposed areas of white are both fully substantial parts of the painting's surface and notionally equidistant from the eye. Attention to the handling of the paint will also reveal that the red surface was laid on around the black and yellow patches, so that they appear not as its adjuncts but as isolated and embedded within it. The reading of the painting as a reclining nude may be persuasive in the context of a reproduction, but the hold this reading exerts over the imagination is so weakened by experience of the actual painted surface as to be rendered largely incidental.

None the less, it has to be acknowledged that simply to describe *August 1953* as an abstract painting is to fail to do justice to its effect – to the sense, mentioned earlier, that it somehow evokes a human presence. In fact it is perhaps precisely because its surface does not recline that the painting seems to address the viewer with an identity of its own to offer. Its surface faces us, upright and indivisible, and in that sense – not as a picture, but metaphorically – as if it were the animate form of another person. It is the poignancy of this sense of 'as if' that directs us to the work's irreducible and inescapably human aesthetic remainder.

One explicit function of abstract art in its first phase had been to liberate painting from its subservience to the self-enchanted spectator, whose incurable tendency it was to look into paintings in search of congenial likenesses and reflections. In the second major phase of abstraction during the late 1940s and early 1950s it was clearly necessary that the concrete identity of the painting should be re-established, that it should still resist the regard that would open up its space indiscriminately to occupation in fantasy. 'A picture is a thing', Hilton wrote in 1954, 'no longer looked into but something which energises and activates.'[15]

Once this identity had been established, however, as it was in Hilton's work by 1953, it seems to have been possible to reopen the painting to association, though as it were on the painting's own terms. It could be done without risk of compromise, that is, so long as the associations in question were subordinate to what Hilton, taking his cue from Constant but ultimately from Mondrian, conceived of as the 'plastic' effect of the painting; so long, in fact, as these associations did not act as vehicles for redundant conventions.[16] Such associations might contribute to the effect of the painting, but they would do so as it were *post hoc*, accidentally and not as necessary aspects of its composition. It is in this light that we should perhaps understand Hilton's apparently disingenuous delay in recognising that his *February 1954* (fig. 23) could be read as a 'big red woman'.[17] In his manner of conceiving the painting, it appears, the woman as subject played no conscious part.

Of course, not all forms of content are consciously introduced. Hilton was presumably acknowledging as much in allowing that the woman visible in *February 1954* had now become inseparable from the painting. There is no making sense of the suggestiveness of his work – its untranslatable remainder – without making due allowance both for the involuntary manner in which much of its content must have entered the working procedure, and for the automatistic mechanisms by which that content is insinuated into the imagination of the spectator. A decided loosening and complication of the surface is certainly evident in works painted by Hilton in the autumn of 1955 (see, for instance, the paintings titled *October 1955* and *November 1955*), and as surely the effect of this development is to reopen the work to naturalistic atmosphere and reference.

We need to be careful, however. It does not follow that we should accept the recognition of mere pictorial resemblance as satisfying the demand for interpretation. Strong expression entails metaphor. Though there is no metaphor as such in painting, that complex faculty that we

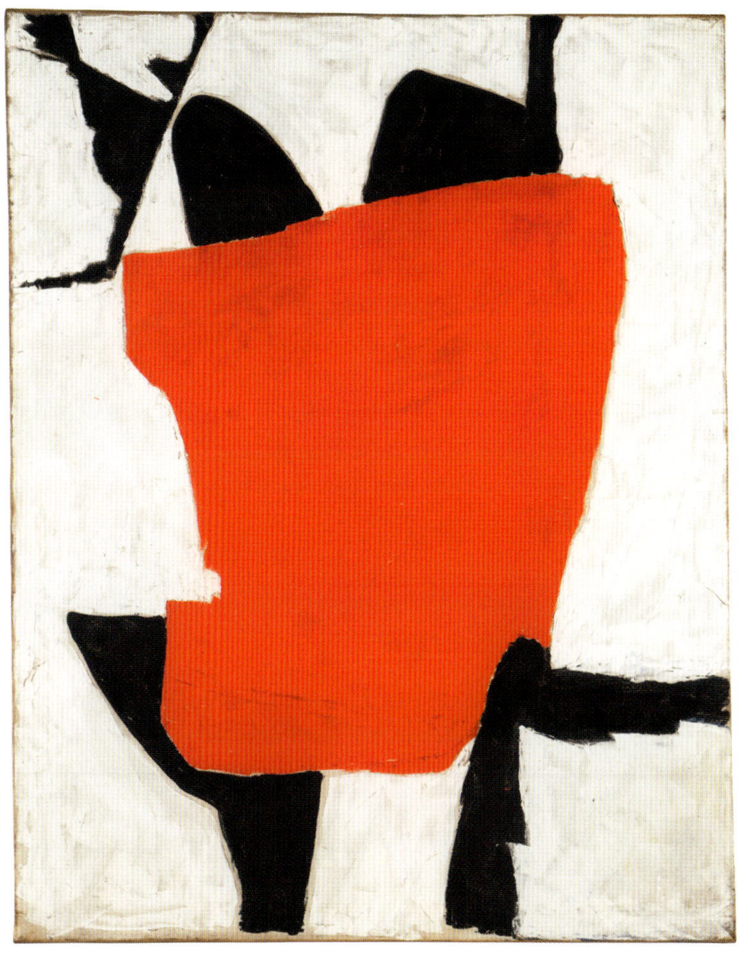

23 Roger Hilton, *February 1954*, oil on canvas, 127 × 101.6 cm, Tate

value as imagination on the painter's part – the power to render significant intuition into critically significant illusion and decoration – would be inconceivable were metaphorical forms of connection not central to its procedures. It is therefore an impoverished and inadequate search for unconscious content that stops at the finding of half-hidden figures or scrambled landscapes. Whatever direction it takes, interpretation needs to be adequate to the entire form of the painting, not simply to its pictorial content. It would not be accurate, or not sufficient, to say that Hilton's typical works of the mid- to late 1950s invite reading as pictures of landscapes or of figures. Rather what they do is set in play in the spectator those processes of recognition and discrimination by which significant modalities in the natural world and in forms of human encounter are felt for and assessed. In so far as these are active and critical processes, they are inconsistent with adherence to conservative conventions of recognition and representation. Though such a manner of proceeding may go against the normal habits of 'reading', we shall often be better employed in exploring what it is that Hilton's paintings make us feel, and in trying to see how it is that they make us feel it, than in puzzling at what it is that they picture and at how it is that that picturing is done.

## DRAWING AND EXPRESSION

As suggested earlier, the quality of Hilton's drawing is crucial in establishing the expressive character of his work. We can connect the principal functions of drawing to the two forms of reading that I have suggested Hilton's work both elicits and requires us to supersede. To whatever decorative ends they may be employed in abstract or figurative forms of art, the habits of drawing are learned either as means to model or to modulate solid forms (a face or a breast or a thigh, a jug or a hill) or to establish the edges of planes (the corner of a house, the vertical face of a screen wall, the curve of an eyebrow, the edge of a table). In relating one form of drawing to the other – call them modelling and delineating – an artist will develop certain habits. These are among the principal identifying characteristics of a personal style. It may be that an artist will tend to settle for a given range of motifs in part because they enable certain manners of modelling and delineating to be related to best advantage. By this means the artist may learn to establish a personal style while camouflaging its actual limitations. It is no coincidence that the

English neo-romantic painting of the 1940s and 1950s is particularly rich in examples of artists who succeeded by doing just this, John Piper and Graham Sutherland most prominent among them.

What we are considering are the very terms on which figure–ground relations are established and complicated in painting. These relations are crucial. A style of drawing is both a means of learning and a means of expression of a person's knowledge and thought about the world. It follows that how an artist relates line to plane, detail to mass and so forth will be both a function and a condition of that artist's capacity to engage with the terms of the larger culture: with how it is that one thing is customarily singled out from another; on what basis discrimination is established; how it is that something becomes an object of thought or attention; how we establish our patterns of isolation and integration, of touching and of separation.

Hilton's work seems at first sight to be relatively limited in its repertoire. This is to say that his hand can be recognised without difficulty in certain idiosyncratic forms of arrangement and combinations of effects. Yet it is easy to forget, in the presence of these paintings, how very few painters of Hilton's generation were able to maintain the intensity of their work without restricting themselves to a far narrower range of motifs and formats than he actually employed. In fact, if the semi-abstract form of Hilton's work serves to identify him with a widespread group of painters of like age, the distinctive emotional range of that work marks him out as one of his generation's most interesting representatives. And underlying that emotional range, furnishing its practical base, is the intelligence and variety of his drawing. The measure of that intelligence and variety is to be found in the figure–ground relations of the work, and in the richly expressive modes of their animation.

Hilton's consistent tendency is to suspend the fixing of an identity or the formalization of a contact. He renders figure–ground relations as reciprocal as they can be made to be within the achievable state of painting, leaving the terms of identification as open as possible within the context of certain clearly established quiddities and evocations. In the painting *March 1961* (fig. 24), for example, an opaque red figure projects upward from the bottom edge of the canvas to make contact

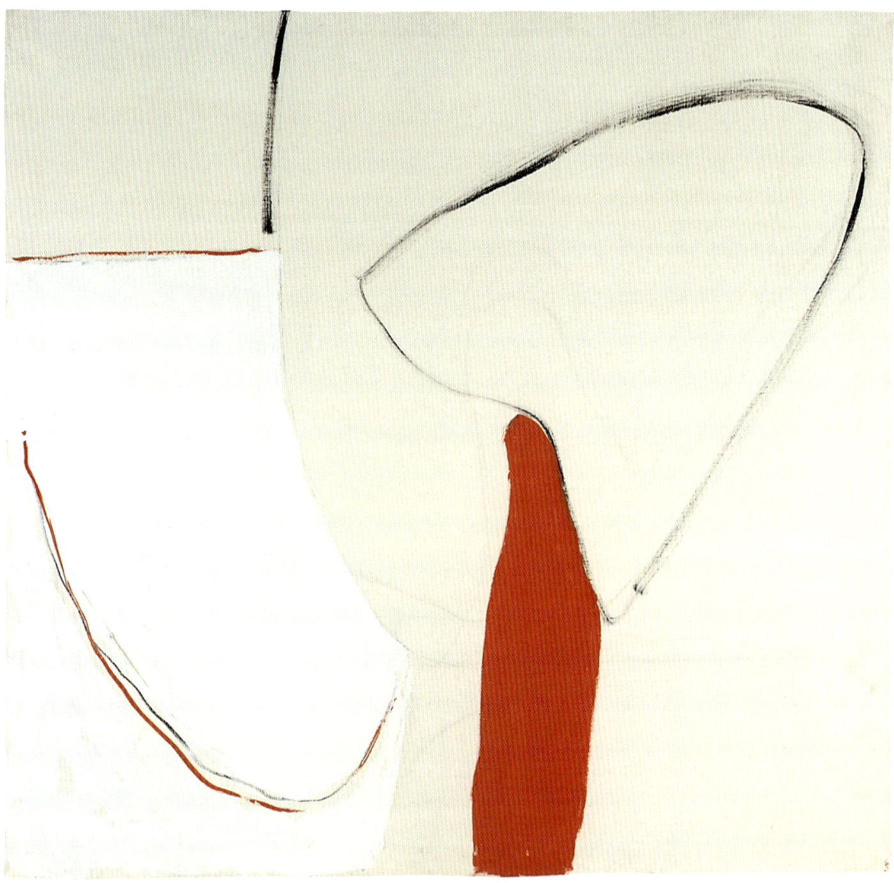

24 Roger Hilton, *March 1961*, oil and charcoal on canvas, 132 × 140 cm, private collection

with a larger form that occupies the upper right portion of the composition. Unlike the red figure, this latter form is so lightly outlined and sketched that it barely dissociates itself from the spatial ground. Yet where these two components meet they seem to touch on the same plane. To be more precise, the nature of the edge between them is so rendered as to suggest contact of a specific kind and quality, in which there is reciprocity in spite of difference. It would be inaccurate to say that our response to this contact is a matter of seeing it in a certain way, since it is a condition of our responding that we are endowed with other organs of sense besides our eyes. Whatever else occurs on the surface occurs as it were in the context of this meeting and as a further qualification of the complex sensations it evokes.

It is a kind of truism that we cannot translate such sensations without loss. It has been a problem for the late development of Modernism that the idea of art's independence from language has become a cliché, available in support of art that all too clearly plays out the antecedently described or the easily describable. Yet it remains the case that in crediting some art with originality we are in effect admitting its power to bring home to us the limits of our language. Originality of expression could not be conceived as a durable and significant value were it not associated both with sense and with intention. In art, that which we value for its originality we also value as something meant – but meant in ways we cannot properly register without the full engagement of our senses. Thus, while we conceive of 'looking' at painting, the experience of art is one to which all our faculties are relevant.

This is after all how we proceed in the conduct of our other relationships. We test for sincerity not simply by assessing the truth-value of a speaker's words. We listen for tone and timbre, note how the speaker stands, moves and looks, and in doing so we draw on our own forms of bodily self-consciousness. There are times when what we mean is what cannot be said in literal terms. At such times a speaker may extend the limits of language by recourse to inventive metaphor. But there are also occasions when to resort to words at all would be to commit a form of insincerity, as it were to withhold or to reserve something of oneself. The ensuing unvoiced extension of the self towards the other is a paradigm of expression. Our sense of the value of expression in art and in music owes much to the power of this paradigm. But it is not always easy to distinguish acts of expression from those forms of behaviour through which we seek to coerce others, to impose silence on them, or to render them accountable for our own failure or inability to articulate. Yet it is crucial to the ethical conduct of our social lives that we are able to distinguish forms of expression from forms of imposition.

Music and painting rehearse us in some of the relevant skills of discrimination. The difference as they make it manifest is a difference in aesthetic power. Perhaps this is just what we mean by aesthetic virtue: this enabling of discrimination through the senses. Hilton painted as if to be always at the point at which words will not do, when the real measure of what is meant is an action directed towards another. 'I see art as an instrument of truth', he wrote in 1961, 'or it is nothing.'[18]

## POSTSCRIPT: THE LATE GOUACHES

Hilton's late works in gouache and charcoal are the strategic products of a kind of enforced incompetence (see fig. 38). They are for the most part drawn with the right hand by an artist who was normally left-handed, but who at the time could not comfortably use his left hand, being confined to bed with peripheral nephritis. I suggested earlier that Hilton's paintings typically advertise a procedure that involves progression from tentative exploration, through deliberative revision, to decisive spontaneity. In his final years he was committed to act out the last of these stages without apparent practical preliminaries, not simply as a consequence of the loss of certain forms of fine control, but rather because such preliminaries are inappropriate to the gouache medium he chose, favouring as this does the impression of a childlike directness of touch. In other words Hilton exploited his physical disadvantage in furtherance of expressive ends. To be more precise, he transformed an enforced incompetence, which had at times become a necessary condition of working at all, into the enabling condition of an expressive power by which all his late work was enlivened.

The gouaches were produced when he was bedridden at the end of his life, between Christmas 1972 and February 1975. They constitute a virtual genre of their own, albeit one in which various of modern art's traditional investments find revival: childlike and 'primitive' forms of expression valued as models of authenticity and, as a corollary of this valuation, polite notions of competence and sophistication disparaged; the accidental embraced as a condition of fertility in composition, at the expense of those forms of prejudice that would equate aesthetic achievement with planning; the decorative advanced as a virtue supervening over the interests of narrative. These investments were revived by Hilton as it were to be spent on paper with an insouciant prodigality.

It is tempting to consider these works as forms of reaffirmation of the equation of realism with Modernism. Produced at a time when Modernism itself had been widely though falsely proclaimed a dead issue, they serve to revitalise that combination of festiveness with irony that has been a constant though by no means widespread virtue in the modern tradition of painting. To recapture a theme from discussion of the earlier paintings, in face of a structure of habitual dichotomies established in our language, they serve to maintain a sense of complex value in ordinary experience. They are humorous in a way that fine art is not generally supposed to be, vulgar in a fashion not generally allowed to high culture, delicate but also robust, generous but also acidulous. They treat themes of animal vitality and human mortality and render them alike flagrantly decorative. They may give some indication of the emotional range of those materials that are worked into more inscrutable forms in some of the earlier paintings.

Given the circumstances of their production, it would be surprising if these gouaches were all deserving of sustained attention. It was anyway in the nature of his procedures from an early stage that Hilton would be an uneven painter. These late works are consistent, however, in the disposition to which they attest and which they in turn serve to encourage. It is one impatient of self-serving superficiality and contemptuous of sentimental gravity. They thus continue the struggle against forms of antinomy institutionalised in culture. In doing so they do what art must do to be modern, and they do it with what seems a defiant delight.

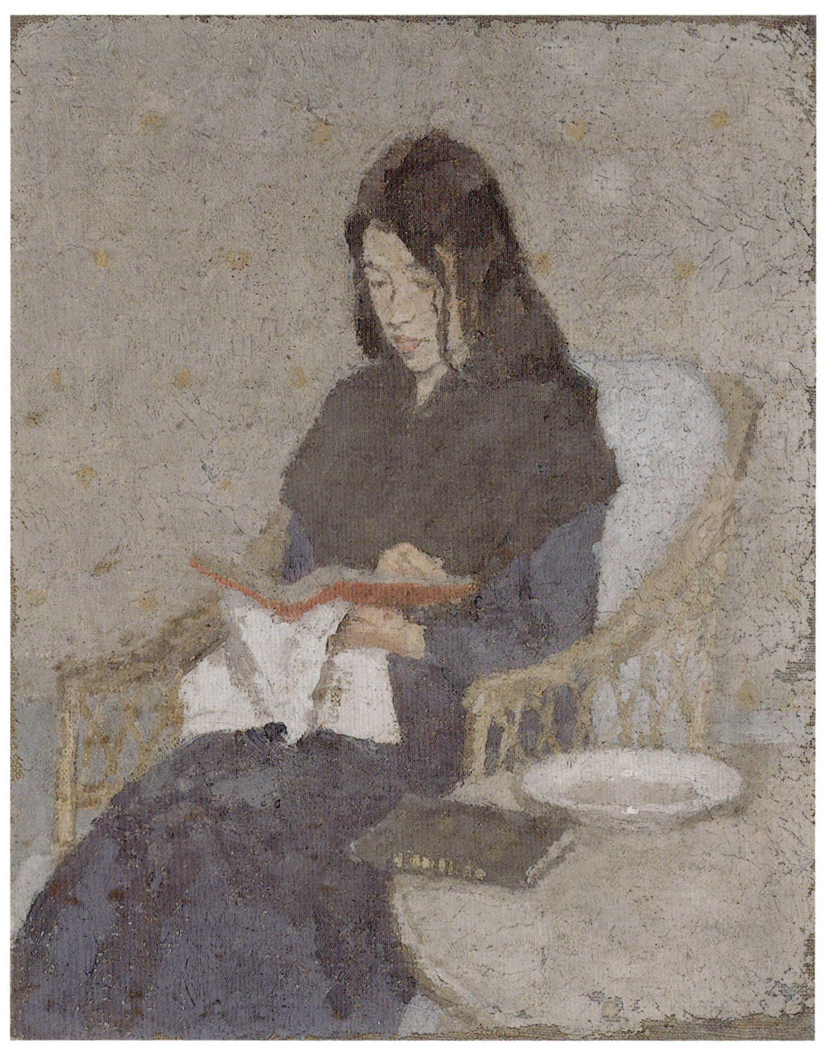

25 Gwen John, *Seated Woman (The Precious Book)*, c.1919–20, oil on canvas, 27.2 × 22.5 cm, Ferens Art Gallery, Hull

# 5 'ENGLISHNESS' AND 'MODERNISM' REVISITED

In its original form this essay was written as an opening address to the conference 'Rethinking Englishness: English Art 1880–1940', held at the University of York in 1997, in association with the Henry Moore Institute. It was delivered with the title 'Leaving go and Going on'. For reasons given in note 2 to the text, it was not printed in the proceedings of the conference. A revised version was published with the present title in the journal *Modernism/Modernity* in January 1999. It has been further revised for the present publication.

In announcing an agenda for the conference, the organisers referred to an admonition that I published in 1981 in the preface to a book called *English Art and Modernism 1900–1939*: 'There is a need for a study of this period of art which is not subject to the traditional closures on art-historical writing.'[1] The organisers' implication was that the need still existed, and that the project in question was one to which the conference should attend. I assume that I was invited to provide an opening address in view of the prominence that my admonition was given.

I accepted the invitation with some trepidation, conscious that in the course of the past near-twenty years, I alone among those likely to attend had conducted no significant research into the English art of the period under review. (Since the time my book was first published there has been a massive growth in studies of the subject.) At the time of my acceptance I tried the patience of a friend by describing the difficulty I anticipated in contributing to the rethinking of Englishness. 'Well,' he suggested, 'imagine that someone has a gun to your head and you've got to come up with a series of lectures on early twentieth-century English art. What are you going to say?' The answer came easily enough: 'I'd say pull the trigger.'

And yet, of course I felt obliged to answer to the statement to which I had put my name some sixteen years before. The results are represented in the essay that follows: an attempt to make some sense both of the retrospect to which the use of the quotation seemed to commit me, and of my present sense of distance from the enterprise to which the quoted statement was originally addressed.[2] I make no pretence to an overview of the present state of scholarship regarding early twentieth-century English art. As a form of individual testimony, this essay stands or falls by its relevance to the more general study of modern art, and by its bearing on conditions by which those engaged in comparable areas of study are variously if sometimes unwittingly affected.

In its original context my admonition was followed by a necessary disclaimer: my book, I said, was not the project that I had prescribed. By including that disclaimer I meant in part to acknowledge my inability – and indeed my disinclination – to provide the kind of detailed social history that seemed then to be required. My task as I saw it was simply to review the terms on which the modern in English art had been singled out, and in the process to work for a more sophisticated understanding of the nature of Modernism in general. It certainly surprised me that the book was seen as 'Marxist' by some of its English reviewers and by all of the few Americans who noticed it. But it was certainly not so seen by T. J. Clark, whose identification with the Marxist intellectual tradition was more properly earned, and who supplied a generous testimonial which the publishers in their wisdom declined to print. Why was I so sure, then, that it was by a detailed social history that the traditional closures on art-historical writing might be opened?

To answer that question I need to provide some background. The work on which *English Art and Modernism* was largely based was done in the 1960s and it was driven by two primary motives. On the one hand I wished to discharge a hopelessly untheorised sense of identification with the modern in art; on the other I meant to establish some intellectual distance from what was at the time the dominant mode of modern art history in the English-speaking countries, which I saw as a form of unquestioning modernist liberalism resting uneasily on a base of snobbish antiquarianism. At the outset, I assumed that these motives were complementary and self-supporting. But during the long period over which I tried actually to write the book, that assumption was subject to drastic revision. I was alerted to the uncomfortable truth by friends I made among the artists of the Art & Language group at the very end of the 1960s: an untheorised identification with the modern in art is virtually *indistinguishable* from unquestioning modernist liberalism. It followed that an enthusiasm for the modern could be worth little unless the culture of that enthusiasm were itself opened to inquiry and to explanation.

In the original preface to my book, I represented this lesson to myself in terms of a barely veiled reference to Clive Bell, who had suggested that works of art speak for themselves to those who have ears to hear – which is to say to those sufficiently sensitive to 'formal qualities'.[3] If there were any readers who still wished to persist with this notion, I implied, my book would disappoint them. In the spirit of this declaration, Clark wrote that my book would 'begin the process of rescuing modern art from its admirers'. Ironically, it was probably just that verdict that alarmed the original publishers, who, since the book was to include pictures, could only conceive of it as a kind of coffee-table item directed explicitly at the admirers in question.

The simple explanation for my sense of the need for social-historical detail, then, is that it was the standard counter to what has been represented as modernist formalism, which, like many others at the time, I tended mistakenly to conflate with the culture of art appreciation. If Bell and others claimed that art spoke to those who had ears to hear, then the riposte would be that the constituency he had in view was more effectively picked out in sociological terms than on grounds of any criterion like sensitivity. Those who had ears to hear, in other words, had actually been identified as such in advance of any demonstration of their actual competence as interpreters or explainers of art – or of art, at least, that was not pre-selected for its congeniality to their world-views and self-images. They were that social section already active in France by the mid-nineteenth century as the self-appointed proprietors of modernist culture and arbiters of aesthetic virtue: the advanced section of the *haute bourgeoisie* or hereditary middle class; that class's semi-autonomous avant-garde in a historically significant struggle for power with the rising commercial bourgeoisie or lower middle class. In explanation of any cultural item favoured by the members of this avant-garde, the claim that the artist did his work out of some inner necessity must always be asserted in the face of the vulgar 'He did it for the money' – to quote a formula used in the journal *Art-Language* in the late 1970s.[4] Bell described artists as people who 'do not work to live but live to work', thus strategically putting them outside the human species as defined from a historical-materialistic perspective, since from within that perspective it is precisely the need to provide the means of subsistence that defines humans as historical beings.[5] If the likes of Bell could be made adequately to represent the English culture of Modernism, it followed that the appropriate tool for the critical and oppositional job must be some form of historical-materialist explanation: the social-historical scenario of *everyone* doing it for the money – or doing it, at least, in accordance with some commensurable material determination.

On the rare occasions when I can now bear to open my book, it is the resulting untidy joins and conflicts and contradictions that tend unfailingly to catch my eye. Attempts at a form of historical-materialist criticism sit side by side with statements about individual works of art that presuppose a form of autonomy both for the compositional aspects of those works and for the responses these avail. So the simple explanation for my assertion of the need for a social history of English art was that I meant to acknowledge the incompleteness of my own scepticism regarding the values that works of art had been supposed to enshrine. Perhaps *English Art and Modernism* might have been more coherent had it been finished earlier and before I began to have 'doubts'. I could then have more easily put it behind me and tried to become a full-blooded social historian or social anthropologist.

This conjecture raises an alternative possibility. Might it have been possible to sort out the contradictions in more positive fashion had the publication been delayed even longer? The question itself goes to a non-disconfirmable hypothesis and is no doubt fruitless to pursue. What can be said, however, is that I was contracted to write a sequel on the art of the following forty years, that I made various attempts to do so throughout the 1980s, and that the more I wrote the worse it got.

There were many reasons for the difficulties I experienced, and of course some of them are personal and irrelevant to the matter in hand.

But my principal problem was one that may have some bearing on the possible agenda for a 'rethinking' of 'Englishness'. The truth is that it seemed ever harder to treat English art as a case study of the character and development of Modernism without adopting one or other of two contrasting modes: it would be possible to contain the subject and thus to maintain its integrity, so long as a nationalistic interest was allowed to control what came up for the count as modern; or alternatively I could maintain a larger sense of proportion, but at the risk of a kind of continual and unpatriotic carping at small achievements.

Of course neither of these modes needed to be problematic, so long as the issue of purely aesthetic merit could be kept at bay. Yet there were two reasons why this was impossible. The first was that aesthetic merit is never pure or uncontingent – for all that some modernists are supposed to believe that it is – so that aesthetic considerations tend to insinuate themselves even into those texts from which they have been most determinedly banished. The second problem was that if the question of aesthetic value *could* somehow be relegated to a second-order discourse – such as a social-historical discourse about the mechanisms of fixing of value – then there would be nothing left to distinguish and to contain Art History as an intellectual discipline; nothing, that is, apart from professional self-interest and bad faith.[6]

There seemed, then, to be two equally unattractive alternatives to consider: a social history of late twentieth-century English art which would effectively be a form of broad socio-economic history crippled by the weakness of its examples and the evasiveness of its judgements; or an analysis of the aesthetic character of late Modernism – in all its impurity and contingency – in which a few English artists might just get walk-on parts. In fact the nature of the dichotomy was already clear enough by the time my first book was finally published. The artist Tom Phillips was among those who reviewed *English Art and Modernism 1900–1939*. He complained that I had not said enough to establish a sense of proportion: to make clear, for instance, that the best of Vorticism was not up to the best of Cubism. I published a snotty letter in response advertising my projected sequel and assuring Phillips that I would properly delineate the confines of the pond in which he swam, 'lest the brilliance of his own splashings be lost to view'.[7] I felt smug about my riposte at the time but of course it was my own dilemma I was really exposing. That I would somehow have to locate Tom Phillips and his ilk in my art-historical tableau was one of the many reasons I could not proceed with my text.

It took me a very long time to silence the voice of what I came in the end to recognise as a repressive conscience, and to admit to myself that the sequel was a book I was never going to write. The admission was liberating when it finally came. My conclusion was that a social history of English art might well be written, albeit not by me; but that there could be no viable study of the modern, whether in English art or in art at large, without some non-sociological grounds on which to determine what is and is not deserving of attention. And by non-sociological I mean adequately theorised in aesthetic or formal or, let us say, Greenbergian terms – a requirement which seemed to rule out any use of Englishness as a criterion.

It was not entirely coincidental that my appearance at the conference on 'Rethinking Englishness' came as an interruption in teaching at a summer school of the Open University, to which I was obliged to return as soon as my paper was read. In the year-long course on modern art of which this summer school formed a part, there was no discussion whatsoever of English art as such.[8] If selection is to be made from the period 1880–1940, how many works of English art are likely to be treated as exemplary in teaching students about art – not about art history but about art, for that is what most of the Open University's students come to learn about? The simple answer is that it is the negative cases that come most easily to mind. There are certainly didactic points that can be made by reference to John Byam Shaw, to Stanley Spencer, to Henry Moore at his worst. But we should be suspicious, I think, of the very usefulness of such work to the task of connecting art history to the local concerns of more popular disciplines: literature or history or sociology or psychology. If we rely on them too much, how are we to interest our students in the work of Van Gogh or Matisse or David Smith, difficult as it can be to connect such work to anything at all without lapsing into irrelevance?

So far as art is concerned, then, it now seems hard to see an interest in Englishness *per se* as other than inauspicious. It is less clear that the social history of English art is an endemically unpromising project, but it may well be. Of course the idea that works of art 'speak for themselves' is still deserving of examination. There is a continuing need to trace those works back into the complex conditions of their production, and to demonstrate that historical accounts of those conditions may be – indeed must be – various and mutually inconsistent. Yet over the past twenty years, works of English art seem to have discovered plenty of people to speak for them and to interpret them as the products of a history. Social-historical exegesis does indeed have the capacity to render any object apparently vivid so long as it can embed it in a ramified discourse, or otherwise build a sufficient human context around it. I say *apparently* vivid, however, because the price of this ramification is often to render the work in question effectively irrelevant to the larger concerns of the discourse. The harder task, it seems, is to extract from the work of art as an intensional object that light that reveals its own specific ramifications – harder because these ramifications may not be such as to confirm any well-established set of historical generalisations or any well-supported account of the surrounding culture. It follows that the more the art is complex in any critically significant sense, the more it matters that one stay with it and not bury it in anecdote. There is no denying, though, that this demand runs counter to the prevailing professional tendency of modern art history, which is to position the work of art according to what are now seen as the defining complexities of the discipline. Through such positioning we advertise a degree of intellectual and methodological sophistication. This may be all very well but it is not necessarily the same as facing up to the complexities and opacities that art itself may present.

This lesson was brought home to me at about the time when *English Art and Modernism* was first published, when Art & Language's engagement with the art of painting made me both a witness and a contributor to inescapable acts of discrimination in the studio – acts of discrimination which tended to start with some form of the question 'What is this thing we have made?' The realisation that it was Modernism and not 'Englishness' that I was interested in thus coincided with a conclusion of a slightly different kind: that what really distinguishes art from other cultural materials is its aspect as something made, and made to be regarded as intentional under some description – the point being that the description in question will be more or less otiose or irrelevant to the making unless it poses problems for available historical generalisations and cultural theories and self-images. Surely, it is just this power to pose problems that we recognise in calling a work modern. For Modernism is itself a form of criticism, and a far more complex one than many critiques of modernist art history or modernist art criticism have been able to allow. So much for the supposed conflation of Modernism with mindless art appreciation.

It seems then, that I need to reinterpret the admonition that was borrowed in announcement of the agenda of 'Rethinking Englishness'. If the inhibiting closures on art-historical writing are not such as to be opened by social history, just what was the failing to which my statement was meant to call attention? I can best explore this question by means of a kind of case study. In the process I will aim to fill out what I intend in referring to Modernism as a form of criticism.

The culminating moment in the narrative of *English Art and Modernism* was the avant-garde phase of the mid-1930s, when Ben Nicholson and Barbara Hepworth pursued a highly refined form of abstract art. Looking back to this moment as an earnest researcher in the 1960s I saw it as the point at which Englishness became successfully merged, however briefly, with cosmopolitan Modernism. In fact to talk of merging is to fail to catch the value I then associated with that moment. For me, the particular virtue of Nicholson's white reliefs and of Hepworth's abstract carvings was that they represented the very extinction of Englishness – of Englishness, at least, as an attribute that might be indexed with any real critical effect to their formal and stylistic properties. It was clear enough from comments published at the time that this was how those works were seen by some of their contemporary viewers. It was also clear that this extinction was felt to be dangerous – somehow totalitarian and inhuman – and by none so much as the articulate British representatives of a more moderate and more domesticated modern art; people like Geoffrey Grigson, Myfanwy Piper and, later, Robin Ironside, each of whom wrote with some sense of responsibility and even proprietorship with respect to the values of the national culture.[9] I have argued elsewhere that the sophisticated *littérateurs* had turned the critical climate against modernist abstract art in England even before the Second World War came to replenish the reserves of insularity.[10] The more reason for my admiration of the artists' enterprise. Not only were they working against odds to bring the native artistic tributary into the international mainstream, but in the process they were also struggling against the inhibiting cultural power of the literary, and against the desires of those anxious to secure the natural world in the image of their own values. I am grateful to the art historian David Masters for allowing me to borrow a quote that he elicited from Myfanwy Piper. Denying that her eclectic anthology *The Painter's Object* of 1937 was in any sense intended to make it better for the national culture in face of the publication of *Circle* – the determinedly *inter*national '*Survey of Constructive Art*' published in the same year – she claimed that she would have invited Nicholson and Hepworth to contribute had they only been 'better writers'.[11]

I do not now mean to withdraw my assessment either of the singularity of the artists' work or of the repressive nature of the writers' recourse to insular and primarily literary values. But it seems to me that the point may now be of limited critical interest. From our present perspective, we look back over a different gap, to the moment of the late 1960s and early 1970s, and to another avant-garde, also determinedly anti-literary, for all its preoccupation with the relations of art and language. The pursuit of the modern in art has become associated with different kinds of critical enterprise. For my own part I recall how involvement in the Art & Language indexing project of 1972–4 seemed gradually but decisively to transform the practical grounds of thought, and in particular of thought about the relations between history and modernity and between art and criticism.[12] More generally the study of art history has become accommodated to critiques of modernist historicism, to forms of recuperation of the previously marginalised, to a dissolution of the containing boundaries between art works and the world, and to an extensive questioning of concepts of medium, canon, mainstream and so on. From this changed perspective it would not be hard to represent Nicholson's white reliefs (fig. 26) as late and bureaucratised forms of a historicistic Modernist culture which had already been shown

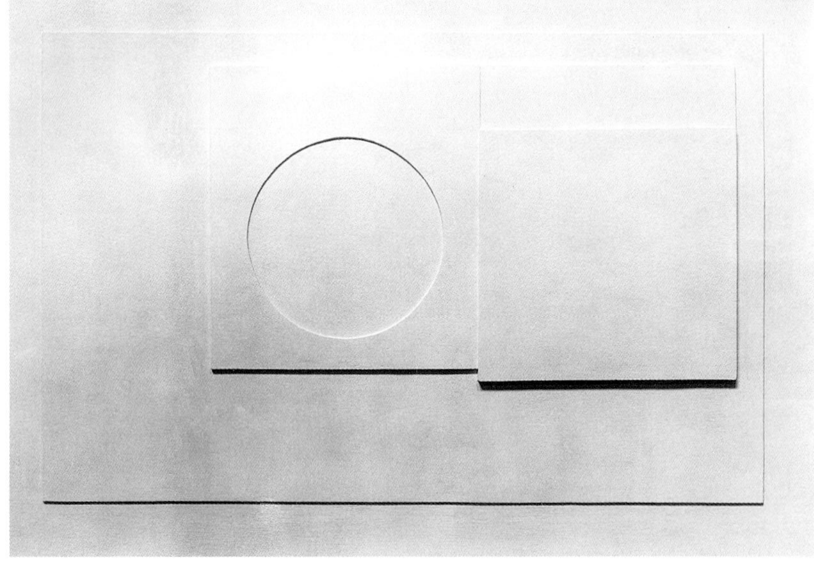

26 Ben Nicholson, *1935 (white relief)*, oil on carved board, 73.5 × 79 cm, British Council Collection

up as unrealistic in its international and utopian pretensions. When set against the self-interested temporising of the *littérateurs* in the mid- to late 1930s, the idea that the European Modern Movement represented authentic mainstream culture might still seem attractive. The derogation of Nicholson's principled abstraction to the advantage of John Piper's topographical whimsies must remain an irredeemably conservative and provincial gambit, which is to say that it could never be justifed on aesthetic grounds. But we have now learned to look behind the supposedly authentic for the unsightly material it serves to occlude – and in the case of Nicholson's white reliefs the occluded material seems to cover all and any trace of biological determination on psychological life. In contrast, what now seems to distinguish such works as Hepworth's *Three Forms in White Marble* of 1935 (fig. 27) is less its Modern Movement austerity than its quasi-metaphorical identity as a trio of individuals conceived in terms of physical touch and containment.[13] This may turn out to be

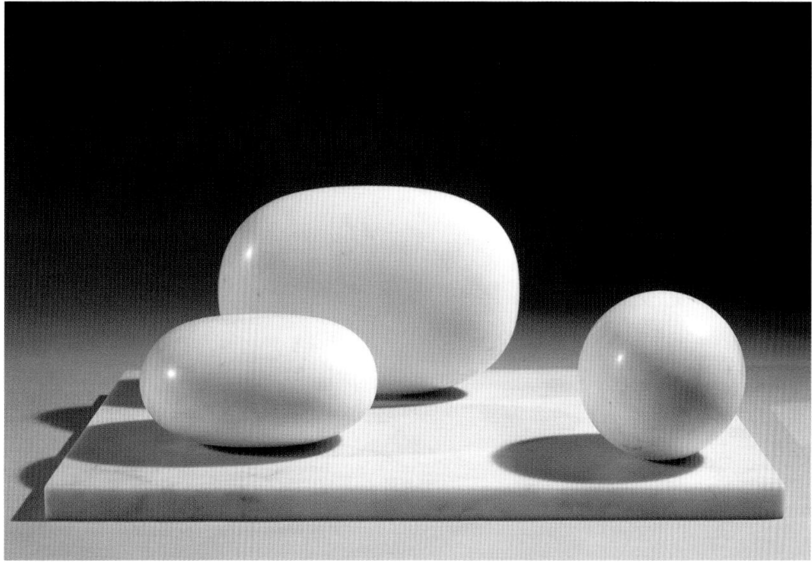

27 Barbara Hepworth, *Three Forms in White Marble*, 1935, Seravezza marble, h. 18 cm, Tate

a sentimental assessment of Hepworth's work and thus one in the end irrelevant to the matter of its aesthetic interest. But however we decide on that issue, Modern Movement claims for the universality of abstract art are unlikely now to recover their credibility.

Let me come clean, though I risk a certain loss of face in doing so. An interest in the art of Ben Nicholson was the principal motivating force for the work that led to *English Art and Modernism*. He played a central role in the story it was written to tell. The painter Gwen John, on the other hand, is not even mentioned in the book. Yet if I were now required to choose a work by one or the other – let us say to live with – it is the picture by Gwen John that I would take (fig. 25). Of course, such statements of preference tend to combine rhetorical effectiveness with theoretical emptiness. In this case, who is to decide whether I am guilty of that form of intellectual fashion by means of which a born-again anti-Modernism gets to parade in the clothes of the post-modern;

whether my eyes have been opened by a desperate need for the approval of my feminist colleagues; or whether there's no more to be made of my decision than that the Gwen John would go better with the wallpaper?

In fact I have to allow each of these potential explanations to be a kind of half truth. On the first count, as the hope of socialism sinks ever further beneath the horizon, it would indeed be vain to look for stability in the relations between Modernism, conservatism and Englishness. On the second count, it would be equally vain to deny the work done by women working in the field of art history not simply to draw new attention to the art of derogated women artists, but also to render insecure many common assumptions about how and with what interests we look and about how we represent that looking to ourselves. And on the last count, while there may actually be no wallpaper in my home for the Gwen John to chime with, my reluctance to give imaginary house room to Nicholson's work is based on the not entirely unfounded expectation that it would sooner or later disappear without remainder into any congenial scheme of décor – as I suspect a Mondrian or a Rothko would not.

I had better try to explain myself. In the 1960s it seemed appropriate and necessary to identify Modernism first and foremost with the critique of insularity, and with the search for some broader basis for self-criticism and for stylistic development than the native culture on its own could furnish. In part, no doubt, this was because there were parallels to be drawn between the significance of the European Modern Movement to the English art of the 1930s, and the significance of American Modernism to the English art of the 1960s. But of course new kinds of critical material were carried within the later developments and some of these, as they filtered down into art-critical and art-historical practice, were such as to require revision of the principles on which those practices conducted their own forms of self-criticism. One clear change was that the concept of art as exemplary design for a better world came to be replaced by a view of art as necessarily resistant to the priorities of design. It is precisely the lack of this resistance that now makes Nicholson's work look relatively meagre in its credentials as art. I think of a passage from a letter written by Mark Rothko in 1945: 'If previous abstractions paralleled the scientific and objective preoccupations of our time, ours are finding a pictorial equivalent for man's new knowledge and consciousness of his more complex inner self.'[14] All too often now, design history acts as the mere lubricant that smoothes the descent of art history into cultural studies, where Nicholson's work remains exemplary of a certain taste, but where work such as Rothko's could hardly expect to meet with that combination of need and spirit that he looked for in his audience.[15]

Let me make clear what I am *not* saying. I am not saying that works of art have no stable and intrinsic properties. That they do have intrinsic properties and that these do not change without physical decline or intervention seems to me to be precisely what ensures their abiding value. There may be a tendency over time for judgements to converge with regard to this value. It is this tendency that the likes of Clement Greenberg had in mind in claiming objectivity for the consensus of taste.[16] It does not follow, however, that our views are likely to converge on some one true account of the properties by which that value is established. Why should they? To paraphrase Barry Barnes, while we may allow the work of art to be the final arbiter of any account of it, there is no reason to suppose any tendency to convergence either in our interpretations or in the reasons we give for our judgements.[17] On the contrary, how we perceive and understand the work of art is a matter which is subject to continual change in accordance with shifts in our knowledge, interests, cognitive capacities and material circumstances, however banal. I am saying neither that Nicholson's work has somehow got worse nor that my judgement has got better. I am saying that as the projective political implications of that work have come to seem less interesting, it has become harder to ignore those aspects that were always present as signs of its psychological conservatism. By the same token it has become easier to perceive the relative technical and psychological sophistication of Gwen John's work, and to connect that sophistication to a renewed sense of Modernism.

Specifically, her work may be associated with a current of concerns by which painting was animated from the 1860s for about fifty years (for instance in the work of Manet, Degas, Cézanne, Bonnard and Matisse), which was then broken and remained largely marginal until the 1940s, but which seems to have been recapitulated first in some American Modernist painting (notably Rothko's) and subsequently in the painted work of Gerhard Richter and Art & Language over the past twenty years.[18] What I have in mind is the use of the opaque picture plane as a kind of frontier across which self-critical imaginative exchanges are conducted between the absorbed and self-exerting spectator on this side and whatever may be contained or connoted by an evoked or illusionary depth on the other. It is a distinctive feature of the surfaces in question that they are not so much the containers of mimetic worlds as scripts for imaginative self-transformations, among them transformations of time and place, of class and even of gender. (What is it like for a man to be the fully imaginative, fully absorbed spectator of a self-portrait by a woman?[19] Simply to ask that question is to bring to self-consciousness all that has customarily been assumed in the interpretation of self-portraits by men.)

Of course the traditional form of these imaginative exchanges was established in paintings containing depicted figures. Gwen John's paintings are thoroughly traditional in this sense. But at a certain point the presence of the figure proved unnecessary – and possibly even inimical – to the business of modernisation of the scripts in question. It was at this point, I think, that the second major phase of abstract painting was initiated.[20] The important point here is that the characteristic work of this second phase had more in common with certain earlier figurative painting than it did with the abstract art of the first phase, to the latter part of which Nicholson's work remained irrevocably attached. This is the sense, then, in which Gwen John's work now appears more readily assimilated to the critical aspect of Modernism than does Nicholson's. And that is why she may now appear the more plausible artist.

So what is the point of this lengthy case study? What does it have to say about the traditional closures on art-historical writing and about the means by which they might be opened, if not by social-historical work? My principal point is that it is in the practice of art that reasons are discovered for rethinking the history of art. The damaging closures in art-historical writing are thus not now those that divide it from economics or from sociology or from social anthropology. They are those forms of professional and intellectual decorum that serve as hedges against the inflations and deflations of criticism in practice, changing as these latter do in response to other currents than those that flow through the academy. The more effectively that decorum rules on the one hand, and the more elusive and unstable is the critical potential of art on the other, the more insistent will be the attempts to protect the decorum with such predicates as prove negotiable within academic discourses – predicates like 'Englishness'.

This, then, is the justification I offer for my sense of distance from the enterprise of rethinking Englishness. It is from modernity in the practice of art that motivation to intellectual work most fruitfully comes. When I commenced my study of English art I told myself that I was engaged on a significant critical enterprise: that attention to local detail would serve to expose Modernism as a form of globalising and bureacratic abstraction. But it was always a mistake to confuse Modernism with the ideological pretensions of capitalism, or to treat modernist theory as if it offered a complete system of speculative logic. It is one of the most secure findings of modern philosophy that there is no such complete system. Nevertheless, we need to account to ourselves for the processes whereby we make a kind of sense of the world, including the world of art. What we call Modernism is a form of this accounting. To say that Modernism is a form of criticism, however, is to acknowledge that this making sense has continually to be revised, given that there is no fixed measure of its adequacy. The practice of art furnishes empirical – though not systematic – grounds for the revisions in question. In other words, the intelligibility of art or of anything else is a matter of its being continually thought about in a manner productive of self-consciousness – of its being reflected on and reflected from. The necessity and continuity of this self-consciousness is also what Modernism means. It is not to be foreclosed – in the name of 'Englishness' or anything else – without loss of critical and cognitive vitality. It follows that there can be no end to the project of modernity, once the process of self-questioning has been initiated and internalised, for Modernism is itself the end of epochality.

If we are to look for the *social* bases of a modern art, they will be discovered in the uses to which that art is put by those in search of other self-conscious agents, and of forms of reconciliation with them. To concern oneself in the course of this search with a value such as Englishness would be to behave as if there might be adequate measures of the validity of our representations, or secure and local points of reference for the intelligible world – possibilities which the condition of modernity will not admit.

To be methodologically modern, then, is to generate that which must necessarily be deflated. In this sense the likes of Clive Bell and Clement Greenberg stand not as figures of the failure of Modernism but as kinds of guarantor of its continuity as a critical project. It seems appropriate, therefore, to conclude by retrieving two of their more distinctive contributions to that project. Bell claimed, notoriously, that 'To understand art we need know nothing whatever about history'.[21] He also proposed, however, that history might be read 'in the light of aesthetic judgements', and even that the history of art might be 'an index to the spiritual history of the race'.[22] Greenberg said that 'Art has its history as a sheer phenomenon and it also has its history as quality';[23] but he also said of Mondrian's most pared-down abstract compositions that when they are good there is a whole world of experience in them, and that this is not a matter of accident.[24] These are powerful and interesting hypotheses. One speaks of the human race, another of a whole world. If either were made to bear on questions of national culture and national characteristics, however, it could only be to note the limiting effect. With these hypotheses in mind, it can at least be said of both Ben Nicholson and Gwen John, as of my friends in Art & Language, that it was not an English art that they were working to produce.

# 6 THE POWER OF MODERNISM

This essay derives from a paper written for the conference 'Art and Ideology', held in Zagreb in 1999. In the initial announcement of the conference it was declared that one aim was to consider 'Art as a Means of Manipulation in the relations between the United States and Western Europe during the 1950s'. It was to this agenda that I was invited to speak. The text has not previously been published.

The theme proposed for this essay calls to mind a now all too familiar narrative of the Cold War years. That narrative concerns a gradual change in the value accorded to modern art in America, a change associated on the one hand with the recognition of artistic achievement, or 'triumph', on the other with the instrumentalisation of that achievement in the pursuit of political goals. Each end of the narrative can be marked by an appropriate text. The first of these was intended for a domestic audience. The speaker is George Dondero. He is addressing his fellow American congressmen in the summer of 1949. His argument is that while the Russian art sponsored for home consumption is realistic and propagandist, what Communism exports is the form of avant-garde art which had been 'used . . . to destroy the Czarist Government'.

> The art of the isms, the weapon of the Russian Revolution, is the art which has been transplanted to America, and today, having infiltrated and saturated many of our art centers, threatens to overawe, override and overpower the fine art of our tradition and inheritance. So-called modern or contemporary art in our own beloved country contains all the isms of depravity, decadence and destruction . . .[1]

The second text comes from a decade later. The speaker is the art critic Clement Greenberg, reading from his essay 'Modernist Painting' in the spring of 1960.[2] The medium is the Voice of America, a radio channel congenial to the CIA, serving the ends of American foreign policy and addressed as it were to the world at large. In his introduction to Greenberg's collected essays John O'Brian notes that the Voice of America reached 'between 30 and 50 million listeners each day in Europe, the Soviet Union, the Middle East, Africa, South Asia, the Far East and Latin America' – though of course we should not equate being 'reached' by a broadcast with actually attending to it, let alone understanding it as theory.[3] This is Greenberg:

> Modernism includes more than just art and literature. By now it includes almost the whole of what is truly alive in our culture . . . The essence of Modernism lies, as I see it, in the use of the characteristic methods of a discipline to criticize the discipline itself. . . . [The development of Modernism meant that] the task of self-criticism became to eliminate from the effects of each art any and every effect that might conceivably be borrowed from or by the medium of any other art. Thereby each art would be rendered 'pure', and in its 'purity' find the guarantee of its standards of quality as well as of its independence . . . Modernist art belongs to the same historical and cultural tendency as modern science . . .[4]

Between these two texts lies a history of the 1950s in which two themes are dominant. The first concerns the development of painting in America. In the same year that Dondero was speaking, Mark Rothko established the format by which his mature work was to be characterised. He was the last to do so of the five major painters of his generation; the others – Clyfford Still, Barnett Newman, Willem de Kooning and Jackson Pollock – had each reached an equivalent point between 1944 and 1948. During the 1950s the work of the so-called Abstract Expressionists was to attract both market interest and critical attention. It came, in fact, to define more effectively than any other art form from any other culture on the globe just what it meant for an art to be modern. Modernism is a term that can mean and has meant different things – different forms of art and different historical and cultural moments – in different national cultures and languages. But with American painting viewed as the end point of an art-historical trajectory, and with Greenberg as its expositor, a particular interpretation of Modernism became at once theoretically coherent and hegemonic. If *modernismo* meant Gaudí to the Spanish, or if *modernisme* meant Duchamp to the French, then so much the worse for their prospects of claiming a seat at the high table of modern high art.

The second theme serving to link these two texts is the ascendancy of the business liberals in American planning for the post-war years.[5] By the mid-1950s this wealthy and cosmopolitan faction had gained the initiative in American foreign policy, in the cultural enterprises which supported that policy and in the more or less covert operations by which both were pursued. Among their ranks were to be found discriminating collectors and supporters of European modern art, served by a rising breed of scholars and curators. As the interest of the business liberals was aroused by the emergence of a distinctly American modern art in the 1940s, our two themes became intertwined. By the mid-1950s the old-guard isolationists like Dondero had become clear liabilities, their anti-modernist rhetoric all too close to totalitarian forms of philistinism from the 1930s. Much better to export an image of American experimentalism and individualism. Far from conceiving of Modernism as a threat, the business liberals seem to have perceived that it could be used as an ideological motor driving international trade and advertising American values. (Some interesting detail on the actual problems involved is provided in the work of Michael Leja.) My immediate concern, however, is with the cultural power of certain political stereotypes. In the world in which these stereotypes were to be effective, what more appropriate vehicle with which to oppose the politicised culture of Socialist Realism than a dynamic modern art driven by the demands of 'art itself' and thus somehow 'beyond politics'? It has become a convention of art history that this was the perception which lay behind the famous overseas tour of the exhibition *Modern Art in the United States* in 1955–6. Organised by the Museum of Modern Art in New York under its International Programme, the show received economic support and additional loans of work from the Rockefeller family. It opened at the Musée d'Art Moderne in Paris and travelled in triumphal progress to Zurich, Barcelona, Frankfurt, London, The Hague, Vienna and Belgrade.

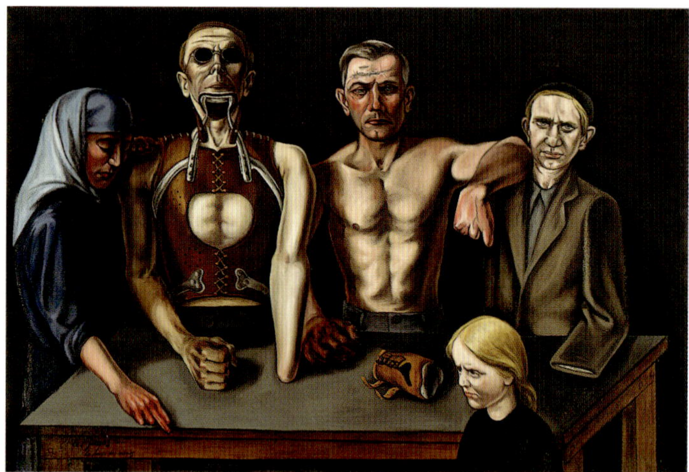

28 André Fougeron, *Les Juges, le pays des mines*, 1950, oil on canvas, 195 × 130 cm, Musée nationale d'art moderne, Centre Georges Pompidou, Paris

Given the timing of the show and the enthusiasm of its reception it is easy to forget how small and how partial was the representation of the Abstract Expressionists – confined in London to a single concluding room. Three years later, however, the account was filled out by a second exhibition. This was devoted entirely to *The New American Painting* and included a far higher proportion of abstract work. The evidence is that *European* enthusiasm for the most recent work shown in the first exhibition served to strengthen domestic support for American Modernism, thus easing the way for a much wider exposure in the second.

So much for the familiar narrative itself. In what remains of this paper I mean to consider three of its effects. The first is the structure of illustrative contrasts which the narrative tends to propose. The second is the growth of a revisionist art history apparently dedicated to the rewriting of the narrative and the re-examination of the structure of contrasts. And the third is the legacy of problems left both by the narrative and by the forms of its revision – problems which I suspect must lie at the heart of any discussion of art and ideology which looks back to the 1950s across the ruins of the Berlin Wall.

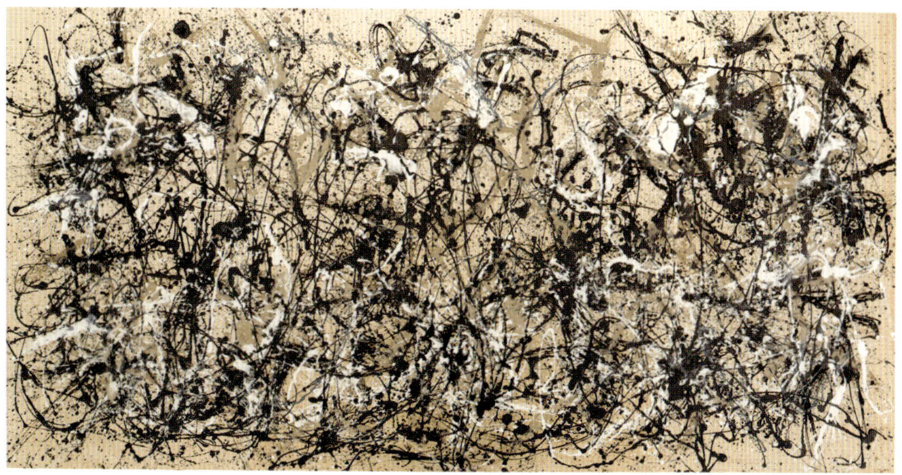

29 Jackson Pollock, *Autumn Rhythm (Number 30)*, 1950; enamel on canvas, 266.7 × 525.8 cm, 1950, The Metropolitan Museum of Art, New York, George A. Hearn Fund, 1957 (57.92)

First, then, for the illustrations. The spectacle which our narrative immediately produces is staged as a series of binary oppositions. The culture of Socialist Realism – whether from Russia itself or in the hands of adherents from further west – is projected into competition with a distinctly American form of Modernism: the outward-facing iconography of dictatorship (Gerasimov, Shurpin) is confronted by surfaces inviting to emotional intimacy and exchange (Rothko); spurious collectivity (Vasilev) is contrasted with uncompromising individuality (Newman); the dogmatic appeal to correct sentiment (Fougeron) is answered by an apparently restless and risky improvisation (Pollock). I would like to dwell for a moment on this last juxtaposition: André Fougeron's *Les Juges* (fig. 28) contrasted with Jackson Pollock's *Autumn Rhythm* (fig. 29), both pictures painted at the very beginning of the decade, in 1950. Fougeron's is a figurative work with its heart in the right place, painted on behalf of the oppressed French mining industry during the period of post-war reconstruction and clearly designed to draw attention to the price being exacted in human terms. In Pollock's work the possibility of figuration seems ruled out by the nature of the process, and with it any trace of explicit human content. A few years ago, when Fougeron's painting was unearthed for an exhibition about Paris in the 1950s, it was still in the possession of the artist. Pollock's painting hangs in the collection of the Metropolitan Museum in New York – in company not simply with other canonical works of the modern Western tradition but with the treasures of all the world's cultures from earliest times. There is no denying the power of these contrasts: on the one hand the fascination which the idea of proletarian revolution still exercised over the political conscience of the West in the 1950s and 1960s; on the other the power of Modernist art to show up any representation lacking in self-reflectiveness. Technically, aesthetically, politically even, each work might be seen as the negation of the other.

Yet of course the contrast itself is staged and misleading – at least to the extent that it encourages us to generalise about the relationship between artistic styles and political positions. Given the conclusions to which this comparison tends to lead us, how are we to recover the Jackson Pollock who was attracted to Communism in his youth, who came to New York with the aim of working on public projects in the manner of the revolutionary Mexican muralists? What should we make of Greenberg's unguarded conclusion about his friend, that 'The trouble with Jackson was he was a goddamned Stalinist to the end'?[6] And how are we to reconcile our explanation for Fougeron's stylistic conservatism with the apparent friendship and esteem in which he was held after the war by that arch-Modernist Pablo Picasso, himself another party member at the time?

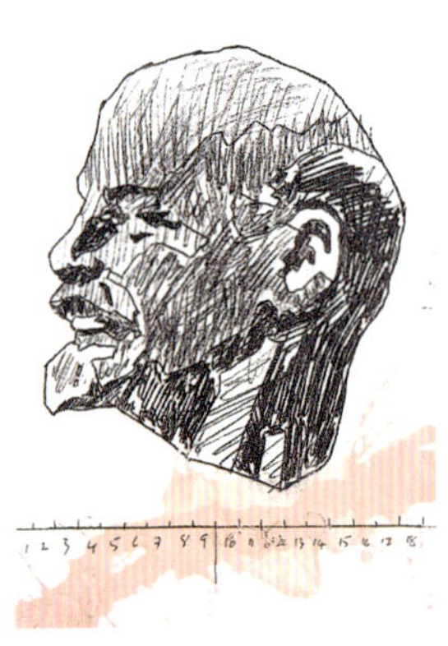

Thirty years after these two paintings were made, the English artists of Art & Language made an ironic theme of this highly charged but misleading confrontation of Modernist abstraction with Socialist Realist figuration, declaring an end to the Cold War which, if it was merely aesthetic, was also wryly prophetic. In their *Portraits of V. I. Lenin in the Style of Jackson Pollock* (1979–80; figs 30 and 31) they brought the two elements into co-existence on a single surface, thus

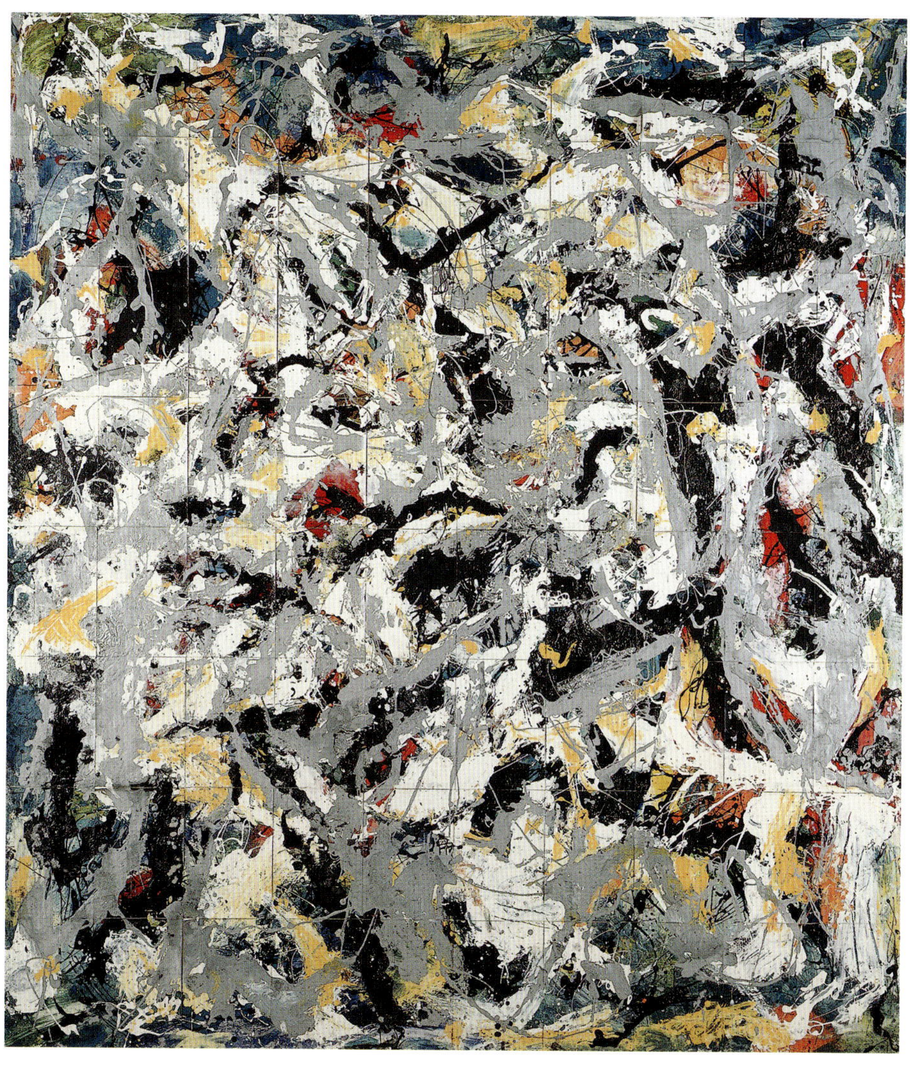

31 Art & Language, *Portrait of V. I. Lenin in the Style of Jackson Pollock*, 1979–80, oil and enamel on paper mounted on canvas, 239 × 210 cm, private collection, Brussels

30 (*facing page*) Art & Language, *Map for Portrait of V. I. Lenin in the Style of Jackson Pollock*, 1979, pencil and watercolour on paper, 23.7 × 20 cm, artists' collection

effecting a 'monstrous stylistic détente' between opposed cultural blocs. Among the intuitions recoverable from these paintings is a sense of the necessity by which Modernism and Socialist Realism, West and East have actually been bound into a system of mutual misrepresentation. Each requires that its account of the other be seen as plausible: Socialist Realism needs Modernist abstraction as a palpable demonstration of the emptiness of individualism, of the tendency to disguise exchange value as spiritual value, of the ultimate self-destructiveness of an avant-gardism restricted to the aesthetic sphere, so that its rhetorical transparency and topicality may signify as virtue by contrast – just as the Soviet empire needed the threat of the Imperialist Aggressor in order to justify its build-up of arms and its iron control over its satellite states. Modernism in turn needs Socialist Realism to be technically conservative, sentimental and politically dogmatic, the better to defend its own unpopular opacity and individualism – just as American liberal capitalism needed Stalinist state capitalism to stand for an aggressive Communism, the better to justify its own arms spending and economic expansionism. In the hall of mirrors which is the Cold War, portraits of V. I. Lenin are technical and ideological conditions which rule against the style of Jackson Pollock. In the style of Jackson Pollock, portraits of V. I. Lenin are a technical and logical impossibility. Except that in the hands of Art & Language they are not.[7]

During the 1980s, the ironic revisionism of Art & Language's paintings found its earnest academic counterpart in a revisionist art history. In 1983, the institution by which I was employed launched an undergraduate course on Modern Art and Modernism.[8] Our explicit aim was to set the valuations of modernist criticism against the explanatory power of Marx's historical materialism; as it were to recover Pollock's socialism from the celebrations of his abstraction, to restore Realism to its central place in the history of the modern, and thus to dissolve the structure of contrasts by which the Cold War narrative was illustrated. Albeit with varying degrees of conviction, those of us who worked on this project saw ourselves as mounting a kind of intellectual resistance to a Modernism conceived as ideological and hegemonic.

The course ran for nine years. I have two memories to recount, one from each end of that period. The first is from the time of the British miners' strike, whose defeat was a thoroughly dishonourable but definitive triumph for the Thatcher government. So long as the outcome of that strike was uncertain, any conversation touching on political matters served rapidly to reveal the polarisation of opinion. The conversations we conducted about the art of the modern period were no exception. There was a dramatic rise in the temperature of debate among both tutors and students. It was not that aesthetic issues were rendered subordinate to political arguments. On the contrary, my memory is that what Greenberg had called the 'challenge to taste' mounted by modernist art came to seem more rather than less urgent, if only because we all felt the more exposed in attempting to face it. It is not only tendentious art that is invigorated by political practice.

The second memory is taken from near the end of the course's life, in the early 1990s. A student approached me with some colour photographs of paintings on which he wanted my opinion. They must have been painted in the 1950s. I told him they looked like worthy but incompetent semi-abstracts, insignificant examples of a vulgar provincial Modernism. Of course, I apologised for the disappointment this assessment must cause. But it turned out that I had told him just what he wanted to hear. The photographs had been taken in some outpost of the rapidly disintegrating Soviet Union. His appearance as a student was a kind of masquerade. His more substantial identity, it transpired, was as companion to one of that avant-garde army of Western art dealers which was already busy pillaging for merchandise behind the rubble of the Berlin Wall. In those early years of the great collapse there was a market for *anything* that could be made to testify to a heroic modernist resistance – as it were to give the betrayal of Socialism a vivid cultural history. In a terrible parody of the early history of Modernism itself, the very incompetence of the pictures waved under my nose would be represented as a measure of their virtue to buyers only too willing to invest them with an unspeakable sentimentality. There is a warning here for any of us who may be engaged – wittingly or unwittingly – in the dignification of late and provincial Modernism.

Since then, however, the trade has matured. Authentic examples of Socialist Realism now command even higher prices than the pathetic remnants of *samizdat* Modernism, and that, of course, within metropolitan Modernism's own markets. Perhaps the pseudo-student was more typical than I wanted to admit of those we were in a position to enlighten. No doubt his sponsor did indeed send him to learn. For it comes to seem, depressingly, that it is the dealers and their ilk who have profited most from the kind of revisionist art history we were concerned to teach. Everything now gets to be good of its kind. In the global triumph of liberal capitalism the Modernist succession is assured: we are already in the era of the 'post-'. And as for the culture of Socialism, it has run its course and its tokens have become rare and precious commodities, for there will be no more of them.

Now, in the world of post-modern 'choice', one hears the empowered and the disempowered alike speaking, absurdly, of 'my ideology', meaning not some system of beliefs which identifies them as members of a certain social section, but rather the set of desires and attitudes which they see as their personal stylistic property and thus as the very measure of their difference. The managing of difference, we are told, is the defining political task of the post-modern era. When each of us speaks from within the world of our individual interests, preference supplants judgement and all preferences claim equal respect. Everyone gets to be good of their kind. No plausible political discourse can any longer be founded on an assumed community of interests. The idea of collective action becomes an irrelevance, and Management surveys an uninterrupted terrain – the fulfilment of its unspeakable dream.

But this is just another narrative – a narrative of the 1980s and early 1990s positioned between the punctuating effects of a pair of anecdotes, as the earlier narrative was positioned between texts. It is not my aim to persuade readers of the truth of either narrative. I merely wish to extract some general conclusions relevant to the overall theme of this essay – that is, to the conjunction of 'Art' and 'Ideology'. It seems that there are two modes in which the relationship has normally been conceived, one connected to a travesty of socialist collectivity, the other to a travesty of modernist individualism. In the first mode art is regarded, for better or worse, as included in ideology and as incapable of escape from its determining effects. To see art as standing somehow apart from or outside ideology is to indulge in idealism or essentialism. To someone conceiving of art and ideology along these lines, we can justifiably ask how and why the one might be distinguished from the other: if art is not to be reduced to equivalence with all and any other signifying practices, what are the grounds of its difference? In the second mode art is regarded for better or worse as a manner of practice or expression bearing critically on ideology and resistant to its effects. In this case we may ask what is the mechanism by which the spectator somehow positioned within ideology is alerted to this distance or difference from it?

The answer in both cases must surely be found in some capacity the work of art possesses to resist those interpretative statements which are addressed to it. And that capacity in turn must be connected to its being *made*, of certain materials, by certain techniques, within a certain tradition and so on. Wittgenstein spoke somewhere of 'the body's resistance to ideology'. There are circumstances under which we simply cannot adjust ourselves – or cannot be made to adjust – to the mode of life a given system of beliefs may presuppose. Perhaps it is the same with those things we make which we think of as works of art. If so, however, the resistance in question will be a function of the *made objects* themselves. It will be associated somehow with their qualitative character or relative aesthetic power. But it may well be quite unrecoverable from any reproduction or other representation of them.

The implication of Abstract Expressionist painting in the politics of the Cold War may have had some effect on how it looks. The nature of that effect is a matter for conjecture. A further matter for conjecture is whether the use of Abstract Expressionist painting as cultural propaganda was or was not a form of abuse of that painting. There is much to be said about the role of the American Council on Foreign Relations or of the International Council of the Museum of Modern Art in the circulation of exhibitions of Abstract Expressionist painting. And what is to be said is certainly relevant to the subject of art and its ideological manipulation. But if we are to talk of art as a *means* of manipulation, we need to be clear about what it is that we are referring to. There is not much point in treating 'Art' and 'Ideology' as separate terms unless we can allow the work of art to be possibly at odds with the work of its interpretation and distribution.

On occasions such as this, the normal tendency of art historians is to advance a historical theory and then to ask how effectively it serves to interpret some relevant work of art. In the event that the theory fails to match the established characteristics of the work, the assumption is that the theory should be abandoned. But would it not be better to adopt an alternative procedure: to ask how well the work of art serves to exemplify the historical theory? In the event that the painting failed to match, we could simply abandon it, leaving it free to lead its different life while we pursue the serious men's work of historical study. The difference in question could then be allowed to be its own property; a difference *from* ourselves and from the ideological world in which we do our work of interpretation.

Rothko once wrote that 'History is not demonstrated by pictures, nor should pictures be demonstrated by history.'[9] He and his friends also suggested that the meaning of their work was not to be explained by any 'possible set of notes', but that it must come 'out of a consummated experience between picture and onlooker'.[10] Consummation entails mutual and unconditional exchange between separate individuals – the very reverse of manipulation, and indeed of management. This is not to say that the work of these artists was itself immune from being managed and manipulated. But unless we are prepared to look through the manipulative projections of culture, to register the signs of *unmanageable* difference, we might as well come clean and admit that it is not really art that we are interested in.

# 7 FEELING THE EARTH MOVE

This essay had its origins in a workshop and conference on 'Art History and Criticism', held at the Sterling and Francine Clark Art Institute, Williamstown, Mass., and the Getty Research Institute, Los Angeles, in October 2001 and February 2002, respectively. A subsequent version was printed in French in the collection *Sans Commune Mésure: image et texte dans l'art actuel,* published by Editions Leo Scheer, Paris, in September 2002. The present, much expanded version was delivered as a keynote address to the postgraduate symposium 'Drawing Disciplinary Lines?' at the School of Fine Art, History of Art & Cultural Studies, University of Leeds, in May 2004. It is concerned with the changes to the priorities of criticism that attended on and followed the crisis of Modernism in the late 1960s. The text has not previously been published in this form.

The purpose of this essay is to connect a number of themes with regard to a particular moment in the history of art: the moment of Modernism's supposed disestablishment in the transatlantic art world of the late 1960s and early 1970s. My particular concern is with the apparent decline in the status and potential of abstract art, with the coincident emergence of an art that employed language as its medium and with the implications of both for the practices of art history and art criticism.

I claim no originality for the thesis that the decline of modernist abstract art coincided with a crisis in art criticism, and particularly in the relations between art criticism and art history. More than thirty years ago, when Rosalind Krauss argued that modernist criticism had come to be unreflectively dependent on its art-historical assumptions, she did so in the context of Michael Fried's claims for the abstract work of Stella, Olitski and Noland.[1] I shall give the thesis a small inflection, however. I mean to associate an apparent loss of direction in art criticism on the one hand with the playing out of the potential of abstract art in general, and on the other with the problem of writing as art, or art as writing –

a problem dramatised by the Conceptual Art movement of the late 1960s and early 1970s, though neither wholly identified with that movement nor exhausted by it.

I suspect that most of those professionally interested in the history of recent art have tended to fix on certain autobiographical moments by means of which to connect remembered changes of purpose and self-image to what appear with hindsight as larger cultural and historical developments. Viewed in the self-enchanting light of retrospect, these are our cherished moments of involuntary realism.

The moment I have often tended to refer back to occurred in the spring of 1969. I was then 27 years old and working part-time as Assistant Editor on the magazine *Studio International*. Having finally abandoned my graduate studies in art history for the more exciting world of art journalism, I found myself in front of a painting by the American artist Morris Louis in a gallery in London – a work from 1962 (fig. 32), the year of the artist's death. It consists of a column of stripes painted in bright acrylic dyes on unprimed cotton canvas. I was due to write a review of a forthcoming one-person show and I had gone for a preview. My presence before this work was somewhat overdetermined. Substantial claims for Louis's painting had been made by Clement Greenberg and Michael Fried, who were by then the writers with whom I most wanted to engage. I aspired to be a serious critic like them. One way to draw attention to yourself as a critic, I had learned, is to match your judgements in print against the verdicts of authoritative judges, particularly where these concern work that other artists are curious about, as my English artist friends of the time were curious about Louis. If it seems a bit odd to have regarded Louis as a still controversial figure in 1969, I can only plead that this was England and that, having spent much of the previous half-dozen years studying art history, I still had some catching up to do. And in 1969 there was a lot to catch up with.

So I stood in front of the painting, tried to empty my mind of all circumstantial considerations – and really looked. If the quality was there, and if I looked hard enough, I ought to feel it. After all, 'To appreciate fully a work of art we require nothing but sensibility. To those that can hear Art speaks for itself' (Clive Bell, 1914);[2] works such as Louis's stand

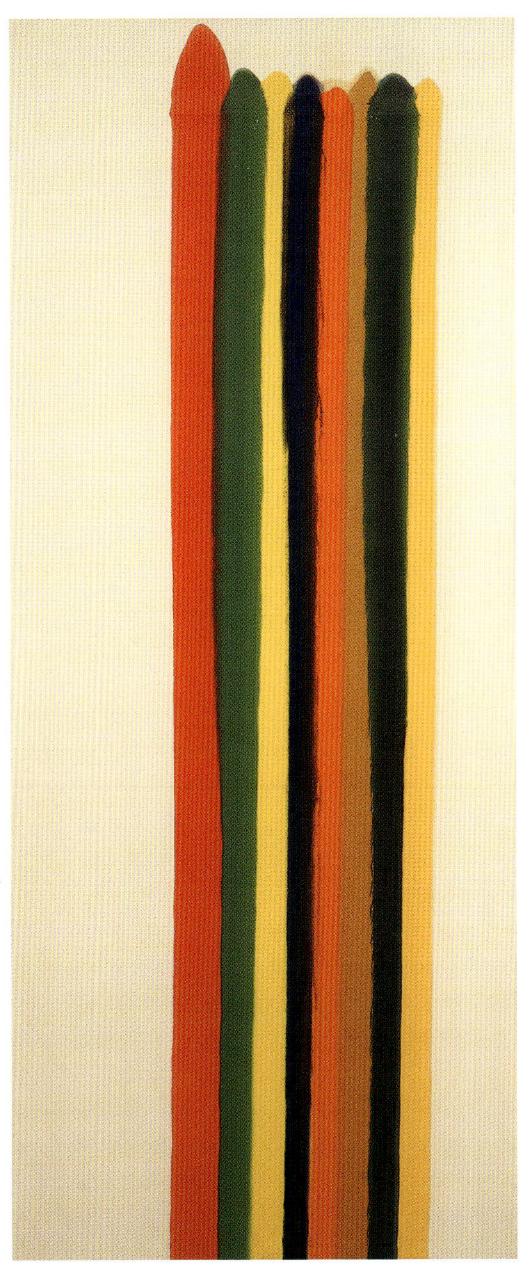

32 Morris Louis,
*Red Go*, 1962,
acrylic on canvas,
203.2 × 76.2 cm,
courtesy Waddington
Galleries, London

or fall 'as vehicles and expressions of feeling' (Clement Greenberg, 1963);[3] and 'Aesthetic judgement coincides with the immediate experience of art; it is not arrived at afterwards through reflection or thought' (Clement Greenberg, 1967).[4] So I looked and, sure enough, I felt the earth move. I went home and wrote up my article: a little biographical information, some brief reference to what Greenberg and Fried had written, some speculation about technique, a formal analysis and finally, the money shot, the value judgement. Given suitable literary dressing, this was to the effect that Louis was not just a major painter, he was a great one.

While my article was in press I went for the first time to New York. I wanted to meet Greenberg and to see more American art on its home ground. I was also very inquisitive about the apparent rift in the landscape of American Modernism that had been made explicit in *Artforum* some eighteen months previously with the publication of a special issue on American sculpture.[5] It should be borne in mind that no single work by any artist associated with the Minimalist tendency had been shown in England at that point. I saw an exhibition of Carl Andre's work at John Weber's Gallery and was very impressed by it, and I visited Greenberg, who was courteous and helpful. He wondered, though, how someone who could see the virtue in Louis's work could possibly be taken in by Andre's. There was a show of Louis's 'bronze veils' currently running at Emmerich's, he told me, and I should be sure to see it (fig. 33). By the time I finally got to the show I had been in New York for about ten days and I was beginning to feel thoroughly provincial – not just provincial but somehow pathetically European. I had the wrong clothes and not enough money and whenever I went into a deli to buy a sandwich the bloke behind the counter would give up on me long before I could work out the combinations. The gallery looked forbiddingly classy and the large paintings were hung round the walls each with its carefully tuned soft lighting – and I could not see them as art at all. Far from serving as vehicles and expressions of feeling, they had the aspect of wallpapered money, dissolving without remainder into a culture I was feeling put down by. What I had thought I had found in Louis's work was an internal integrity sufficient to render any considerations of context more or less irrelevant; now what I was faced with was a context

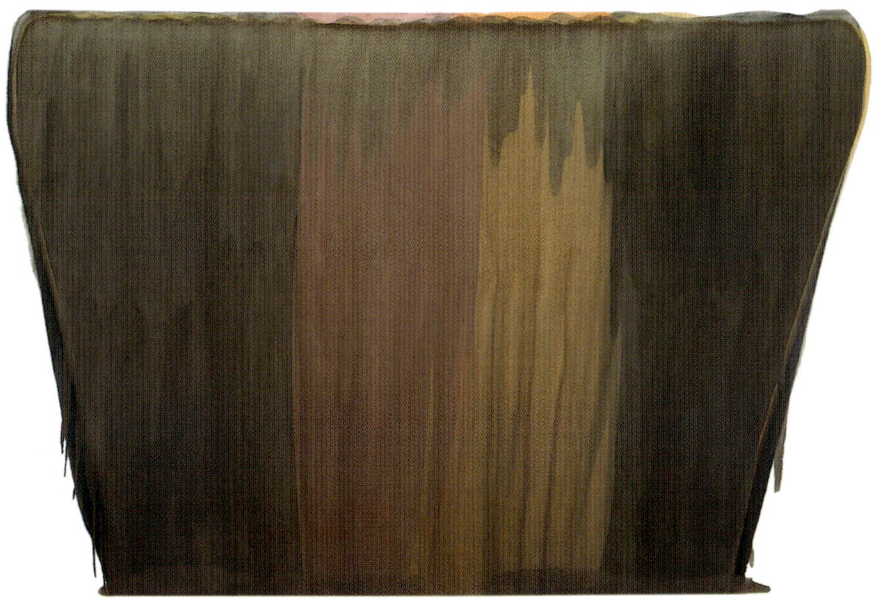

33 Morris Louis, *Dalet Beth*, 1958, acrylic on canvas, 231.2 × 362.1 cm, Baltimore Museum of Art

by which that work appeared to be wholly represented. I could not get out fast enough. But I paused just long enough to cast an eye over the customary apparatus of publicity laid out on a table at the entrance. And there, given pride of place, having just appeared in New York, was my article; a nice double-page spread with colour plates, announcing the judgement of which I had been so proud.[6]

This was a humiliating and confusing experience – and the beginning of the end of my intended career as a critic. It was not that I was sure I had been wrong about Louis. The point was that I could no longer be sure that the work itself had been responsible for my conviction of its value. If that conviction was so easily destabilised by circumstance, maybe all my writing had really done was to reproduce a certain culture of appreciation so as to establish my membership among those with sensibility. And if I could not resolve that issue, then I had no business putting judgements of taste into print. So I was out of a job.

This was by no means an unprecedented insight. On the contrary. The point is that both my discomfiture and my reaction were symptomatic of a larger state of affairs – a widespread loss of faith in two connected ideas: that works of art can be the real occasions of transcendental emotions; and that spectators can be capable of disinterested responses. At the time the best diagnosis on offer as regards my personal situation was the one that was given in class terms. I had learned to reproduce a certain emotivist language – one where 'This is good' effectively reduces to the injunction 'Like what I like'. Emotivism works fine while it is those to whom art speaks for itself that are doing the talking and so long as you can see yourself as one of them. But when you find yourself on the receiving end – as I certainly was during my first trip to New York – then your own injunctions tend simply to rebound on you as though they were being uttered by someone else.

I do not mean to suggest that the scales had suddenly fallen from my eyes or from anyone else's. There had always been opposition to the kinds of modernist theory that accompanied the development of art in the twentieth century. In fact we might say that the period of effective dominance of that theory was very short, given that the determined assault on its authority began shortly after its clearest articulation in Greenberg's publications of the early 1960s. By the time of my big moment in front of Louis's stripe painting, the authority of modernist protocols to regulate responses to art had already been on the wane for a few years. But I think you would find widespread agreement among artists and art historians of my generation that the period of the Conceptual Art movement – say between 1965 and 1972 – can be associated with significant change in the broad culture of art, and that one of the symptoms of that change was an unwillingness to conceive of art as either self-justifying or self-sufficient. Benjamin Buchloh, for instance, refers to an entire 'mid-1960s generation that had recognised the historical failure of the modernist concepts of autonomy and visual pleasure'.[7] I question whether a concept can actually 'fail' in quite the manner Buchloh suggests. What can be said, though, is that it seemed at the time as though the sole purpose of the Greenbergian injunction to concentrate on the pictorial surface had been to conceal the social conditions of art's production, and to block all traffic with other areas of practice and knowledge. Now there just did not seem to be enough there on the surface to do the distracting job. It was as though everyone was looking round the edges of art works to see what was concealed behind them, or to see what they were actually made of, both in material and in cultural terms.

It took a little while for me to sort out the implications, and I had a difficult couple of years while I tried to fool myself that I could get round the problem by sponsoring a different kind of art. I was fortunate during that time in the contacts and friendships I made with a slightly different generation of artists, people for whom the merit of such work as Louis's was simply not an issue, or not an issue, at least, that was of interest independently of the case that had been made for it in the better sort of criticism – or in any event in criticism that was better than mine. But when I tried to write about their work the same problem tended to recur. The reason, I now understand, was that the problem lay in the language itself – and in the assumptions that were built into it concerning the division of cultural labour. To conceive of criticism as a literary practice distinct from the self-criticism of the studio was to assume that some justifiable difference in function served to insulate writing about art from making it. By the end of the 1960s, this assumption seemed no longer to be tenable. And to ask why was to confront an assumption operating at a deeper level: the assumption, fundamental to modernist theory, that art and language are related in a dichotomous hierarchy.

In fact it is not so much within the wider sense of Modernism that these assumptions necessarily operate. Rather, they have a specific bearing on the case made for abstract art during the twentieth century. On the one hand, given its sheer difficulty and unpopularity, abstract art had required an advocacy that would lead to justification outside the immediate contexts of its production. On the other, that justification had tended to stress abstract art's radically un-language-like properties – and none so much as its tendency to abjure that concern for the rootedness and vividness of descriptions that figurative art had previously shared with language.

So what had happened to put these assumptions in question and thus to destabilise the writing of criticism? In a wide view we should obviously take account of the growing awareness of American imperial ambitions at the time of the Vietnam War and the concomitant disenchantment with the consumer culture that the U.S. had been exporting to Europe since the end of the war. Another factor to bear in mind is the long-term effect of the post-war de-Stalinisation of the Marxist intellectual tradition, and its consequent reinvigoration in the student generation of the 1960s. For all that Modernism might once have been identified with the idealism of a largely socialist avant-garde, it was now looking suspiciously like the cultural face of capital.

There was a further factor internal to the modernist critical discourse itself. Though I could not have formulated this at the time, I think what the evidence was pointing to was that the great twentieth-century adventure of abstract art was finally over. It was not that abstract art had become impossible or necessarily uninteresting. It was simply that the best of it was by then already in the past. In fact I would now say that by 1969 it had been past for almost a decade. Given that there could now be no non-conservative return to figuration, it might be said that painting and subsequently sculpture were finally left confronting that prospect of their own redundancy that had first been raised in the second decade of the twentieth century, and that the long experiment with abstraction had simply served to postpone. Support for such a thesis might be found in the revival of Marcel Duchamp's reputation among the post-Abstract Expressionist generation in America, and in the renewed currency of the ready-made in the art of the late 1960s and early 1970s. Hence the hiatus. On the one hand abstract painting had come to be the paradigm art of Modernism; on the other there was only so far that painting could go once it abjured description. Three-dimensional forms of abstract art perhaps had a slightly longer lease of life but not for long. The question that now recurred was how the practice of art was to be distinguished from other cultural or intellectual pursuits if neither frames nor pedestals could be counted on to separate its outcomes from the rest of the world as signifying stuff.

In other words, once a certain limit was reached, art could no longer be insulated against language without becoming Byzantine or conservative or nostalgic or all three. And one clear consequence of that was that the professional separation of criticism and practical self-criticism, of writing and art, was no longer subject to the same necessity or justification. To maintain that separation on now questionable grounds was to condemn one's own practice to conservatism.

Of course, this is rationalisation offered in the light of hindsight. All I personally knew at the time was that what I had formerly regarded as the first-order culture of art – the culture of art as ineffable effect – seemed simply to have been evacuated, at least so far as concerned the useful purposes of criticism. It was indicative of this evacuation that such categories as 'feeling', 'sensibility' and 'experience' could no longer be plausibly cited in justification of the work of art. Under these conditions an art history that was uninformed by social history was liable to be denounced as arid at best and callous at worst.

The same could be said of aesthetic theory unengaged with social theory. An institutional theory of aesthetics had been virtually required by Duchamp's first unassisted ready-made in 1915 (fig. 34), but in fact it was not until 1964 that one was actually formulated. The occasion that prompted it was the first exhibition of Warhol's *Brillo Boxes* (fig. 35), and the author was Arthur Danto. In Danto's view there was nothing intended to distinguish Warhol's *Brillo Box* from the

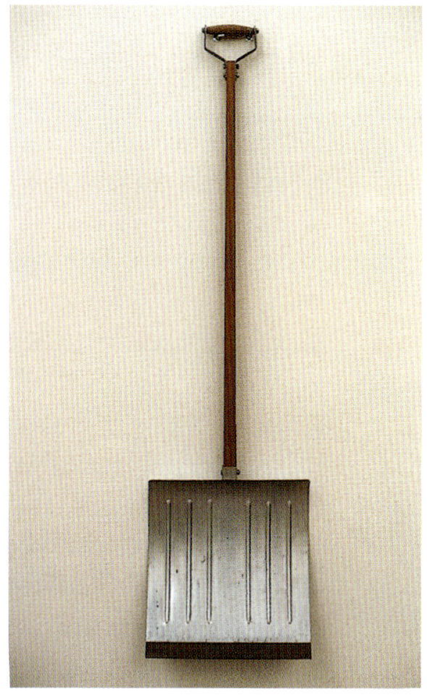

34 Marcel Duchamp, *In Advance of the Broken Arm*, 1915, ready-made snow shovel, wood and galvanised iron, 121.3 cm, replica, Philadelphia Museum of Art

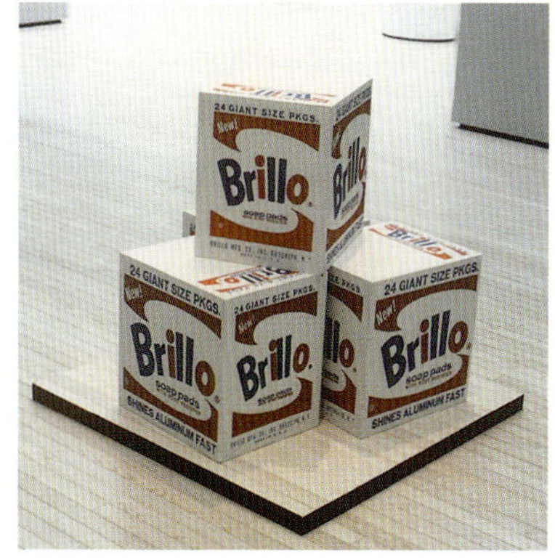


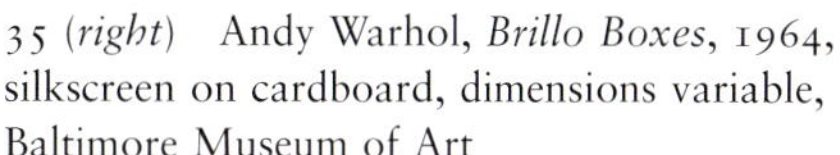
35 (*right*) Andy Warhol, *Brillo Boxes*, 1964, silkscreen on cardboard, dimensions variable, Baltimore Museum of Art

one on the supermarket shelf, *except* for the all-important fact that one was art and the other was not. What this appeared to him to demonstrate was that art could not be defined in terms either of the intrinsic or of the manifest properties of specific works; it could not be decided by what the viewer sees or feels in front of it. Rather it must depend on some factor 'outside' the work; in other words on its being the object of a theory of art developed by some relevant community. 'To see something as art', Danto wrote, 'requires something the eye cannot descry – an atmosphere of artistic theory, a knowledge of the history of art: an art-world.'[8] So much for the idea that works of art were to be identified either by the intensity of one's feelings in front of them, or by their empirically discernible similarity to other works of art.

The institutional theory was subsequently developed by George Dickie, whose article of 1969 was developed into a book five years later.[9] By the early 1970s a demotic version of that theory was spreading apace through the graduate departments of American universities. Within a few years it was commonly assumed among advanced students of art and art history that the entire modernist tradition of criticism could be dispensed with – along with the theory of aesthetic autonomy that that tradition had supported. For Greenberg, relevance in the discussion of art meant relevance to the quality of effect; purposeful self-criticism in the practice of art would be directed at intensification of this effect. Since the mid-1970s, on the other hand, there has been virtually no limit on what is considered relevant in writing about art, and thus no restriction on the conjunctions or admixtures that may be proposed between art and anything else. As might be expected, art-educational regimes designed under these circumstances tended to direct their critical attention to those questions of cultural legitimacy and legitimation that institutional theories were designed to address.

The naturalisation of institutional theory proceeded with an equivalent rapidity through the avant-garde sectors of the international art-world. Among those artists who gave it their endorsement Hans Haacke was particularly explicit. The following encapsulation is from a statement published in 1974:

> Products which are considered 'works of art' have been singled out as culturally significant objects by those who at any given time and social stratum wield the power to confer the predicate 'work of art' unto them; they cannot elevate themselves from the host of man-made objects simply on the basis of some inherent qualities . . . In order to gain some insight into the forces that elevate certain products to the level of 'works of art' it is helpful . . . to look into the economic and political underpinnings of the institutions, individuals and groups who share in the control of cultural power.[10]

Haacke was not alone in scenting an opportunity. 'Strategies might be developed for performing this task in ways that its manifestations are liable to be considered "works of art" in their own right.'[11] Here perhaps was a solution to the problem of art's apparent loss of its traditional media following the exhaustion of abstract art. All that was needed was for artists to reconceive themselves as kinds of radical systems analysts within the institutions of the art-world. With the development of computer technologies in view, there was also much talk at the time of art abandoning hardware for software. One mode of Conceptual Art involved the design of 'aesthetic systems . . . capable of generating objects, rather than individual objects themselves.' Those are the words of Victor Burgin.[12] An exhibition with the title *Software* was organised by Jack Burnham in New York in 1970. That which was once conceived of as an avant-garde medium is now running the world in the interests of capital.

We might say, then, that by the early 1970s it was already quite possible to conceive of art in terms of a systems-based interface with science, or technology or economics or whatever. That model has had a long life. This is perhaps not surprising. In the eyes of those anxious about the matter of art's relevance and effectiveness, one clear advantage of the model has been that it seems to endow avant-garde practice with a certain renewed potential for breadth of content. This is Mary Kelly, interviewed as late as 1986: 'Art isn't confined to speaking about art, it can refer to things outside itself, it can have what you would call "social purpose".'[13] If Buchloh is to be believed, this remarkable realisation that there is no necessary prohibition on external reference in art was due to the 'complex set of aesthetic strategies' initiated by Haacke.[14]

The assumption at work in such enterprises, of course, is that the relevant artistic purpose is virtuously oppositional. For all the Brechtian talk about 'Difficulties in Writing the Truth',[15] the career of the systems interventionist is sustained by a romantic view of the artistic individual – as someone significantly free from institutionalisation. How else could he or she intervene within any given system as a constructively critical agent? It is also worth noting that, for all the disparagement of 'modernist concepts of autonomy', the avowedly post-modernist art work tends to rely heavily on the operation of some individuating mechanism to describe its effective boundaries, whether this be furnished through curatorial compact, installed by means of a stipulative text, or flagged as the relevant component in an adjacent theoretical discourse. After all, without the accompaniment of a framing mechanism it might be that the world would do just as well.

My purpose in describing my moment of confusion in front of Louis's paintings in Emmerich's Gallery was to suggest that it might be explained at least in part in terms of the changes I have been describing. Whether or not I was able to formulate it for myself at the time, the question I was left with was just how criticism was now to proceed. Of course, this was not really my own private problem. In fact it could be said that criticism simply failed to proceed at all. I think it could be argued that no one substantial critical voice has emerged since the late 1960s – at least if what we expect from criticism is the presentation of forthright judgements made on the basis of articulate descriptions. Rather, a kind of broad anti-modernist consensus has emerged in the art-writing of the past thirty-odd years. It follows, I think, from the assumption that the meaning of the work of art is not, or is not now, to be uncovered as a function of its intentionality or implicit self-description. The paradigm work of art is no longer conceived as a thing whose semantic energies are concentrated within its formal boundaries. Instead, the art work functions as a kind of vivid signpost, directing attention to significant aspects of the social and cultural world. Its meaning is to be read out of an intersecting network of interests. The task of the art-writer is to follow the signpost into the social context, to gather references and background information and to draw out the resulting material as an account of the work. In so far as the value of the work is matter for consideration, it will be decided according to its success in living up to those issues by which the moral content of social life is thought to be decided.

I suppose I might well have responded to my second experience of Louis's work by adopting some such model of criticism, as a replacement for the one that had led me to make so public a fool of myself. After all, had I not received an object lesson in the importance of social context where the establishment of meaning and value was concerned? I certainly came to feel that I needed to learn a great deal more about how the art-world works if I was to go on trying to put judgements into print. With the benefit of hindsight, I would say that whatever case there may be for treating art as a highly specialised business, it does not follow that there are valid reasons for allowing the work of art to hide the world that makes it. To put the point more forcefully, there is no good argument to be made for the autonomy of art that justifies ignorance of *anything*. In accordance with this conclusion, it might seem that the shift in the priorities of criticism that I have described must have been thoroughly positive, in so far as it has led to the breaching of disciplinary boundaries and to the consequent expansion of artistic culture into 'all areas of society'.

But there is one point forcefully made by the writers of modernist criticism that deserves reiteration. This is that works of art are not necessarily interpretable by reference to social or historical events; they are events requiring interpretation in their own right. To put the point another way, if what we expect of works of art is that they provide vivid testimony to the character of social life, we risk failing to register their potential status as exceptions; not simply as critical anomalies vis-à-vis the systems to which they refer, but as entities whose systematic character is of a different order altogether – an order that may in the last resort be *only* aesthetic but, for all that, none the less vivid in intellectual or sociological terms.

I suppose I learned this lesson myself a year or so after my debacle in New York, when I first tried seriously to come to terms with the early

The initial assertion is that a wall between 26 and 25 Sunnybank <u>is</u> an art object. Now the possible outcomes of what's going on include the building of a wall between those two houses; such a wall is an art object.

This raises the possibly jejune question whether any vestige of the formal properties of identity is to be salvaged. And this question is asked not necessarily from the point of view of 'essentialism'. The point that it looks as if one is individuating something as an art object, but what he appears to individuate it as may in some sense determine what's singled out, but any connection with a principle of individuation is, to say the least, tenuous. And even the postulation of surrogate contemporary objects of future ones doesn't hold singling-out on the rails for long. It looks as if it will have to be shown how the singling out is done if an essentialistic view is to be supported. It's worthwhile making at least a glossy survey of these problems (and others) so as to propound the efficacy of developing a theory of the esthetic domain. And this also to show that such a theory is not inevitably committed to revisionary metaphysics or circumlocuted by the novel. And if identity has no place in the domain of art objects then there is every reason to show that it has none.

Now, the possible outcomes of what's going-on don't include the starting to exist of an individual individuated as 'the wall between 26 and 25 Sunnybank.' Those outcomes do include the possibility that there shall be an individual built, etc. and that it will be singled

36 Art & Language, *Sunnybank*, 1968, first page of a 28-page typescript, private collection, Brussels

work of Art & Language (fig. 36). This was work in textual form – Conceptual Art of a kind – that could neither have been readily assimilated in positive terms to a modernist account of the development of art, nor approved by a representative modernist criticism. It was also interdisciplinary in a certain sense. As Michael Baldwin has suggested, 'It was art in case it was taken to be philosophy, and philosophy in case it was taken to be art.'[16] But it was as rigorously focused on the problems and paradoxes of self-description as any modernist abstract painting. In fact it might be said that what the work did was to adopt those problems and paradoxes and rework them in the form of linguistic texts. It was as though a kind of open-ended conceptual analysis had come to replace the empirical criteria by which art works had traditionally been verified as such. I found these texts both fascinating and very hard to understand. I thought I might understand them better if I devoted some time to the study of analytical philosophy; as a result I perhaps became a slightly more competent reader of the texts. But I could not say that the texts themselves became any clearer. Rather than delivering understanding, they became more vividly problematic. They were explicit enough about what they were made of, both practically and intellectually. It was *what* was made that was difficult to grasp. They were like things that talked to themselves, or talked among themselves, trying on descriptions and *façons de parler*. But it was just this discursive activity internal to the work-as-text, I think, that secured a dialectical relationship to the painting it had displaced – and that made that text appear to be art.

For all the irrelevance of their physical properties, and however improbable it may seem, these early works of Conceptual Art had one significant property in common with the stripe painting by Morris Louis on which I had exercised my premature judgement – and perhaps in common with all paintings produced as art. They were not hanging about the art-world waiting to have the status of art conferred on them and thus, as it were, to discover where their boundaries fell. They were in a sense indifferent to the mechanisms of that conferral. But that very indifference – an indifference, if you like, to the various little knowledges that are forms of power – was the condition of a kind of aesthetic distinctness and integrity – the condition, in other words, of their being art. In so far as that condition seemed to be established independently of any conferring or curating institution, these texts seemed surprisingly to have more in common with paintings – which are works of art whatever an institutional theory may make of them – than they did with Snow Shovels and Brillo Boxes. I suspect it was no coincidence that without trespassing much on the topical subject matter of the sciences, they also drew here and there on the principles and problems and possibilities of logical and scientific inquiry.

This is all explanation in the light of hindsight. Yet in the period between 1969 and 1971, while I was trying to come to terms with the impossibility of the career I had proposed for myself, it was some such intuition of the interesting strangeness of Art & Language's practice that saw me through. For many artists in the late 1960s and early 1970s, the breakdown in the authority of modernist protocols was an opportunity, to be exploited with claims to artistic status on behalf of a wide range of novel and exotic objects. For Art & Language, the crisis of Modernism was a context of problems to be worked on and worked through, where the workings themselves might or might not count as works of art. My conclusion was that it was in association with this practice that I was most likely to be able to learn.

At the outset, around 1966–7, texts advanced into the sphere of art lived with insecurity and absurdity. Much of this initial absurdity attached to claims that the works in question – if they were works at all – were kinds of abstract art, or were colonising the space that abstract art itself had claimed. Michael Baldwin has suggested that his first moves into text not conceived as writing – or as 'literature' – 'departed from the thought that text (a sort of figure-ground based entity) could occupy a dimensional space more interestingly than a stripe'. The viewer would have to work hard *not* to read lines of type as text. 'But *not* reading them as text was the cultural/psychological challenge.'[17] At the same time, however, the fact that the lines were lines of text would provide resistance to the degeneration of claims for artistic status into a mere aesthetics of design – a degeneration entailed by the attenuation of abstract art.

There were also texts that described hard-to-imagine imaginary objects – columns of air, air-conditioned spaces, geographical areas – it being left uncertain whether the artistic claim was for the text that did the describing or for the exotic object described. The text functioned as a kind of 'signpost' pointing to the object in question. 'The "signpost" sits in the place of painting (or ?) and shows the way out – out being the place where what was to count as a work of art is located – located but not imagined, for it is imagined there and then. But the signpost is not what it points to. The text is not "the work" and "the work" is not present. But "the work" nevertheless is attended to in the specific location of the text.'[18] The possibility which it seemed Conceptual Art had to sustain at all costs was that a precarious kind of medium specificity might be made out of the slippage between something's being a text and its being an image: that however exotic the form of any art object proposed, it was in that gap that the critical *work* of art was both to be discovered and to be done.

It should not need saying that if Conceptual Art were to issue in practical modes capable of sustaining some better than trivial connection to traditional artistic genres, then it would have at some point to give rise to something other than Conceptual Art. In the case of Art & Language one crucial consequence of the concept of art as writing was that it tended to install or to reinstate conversational exchange at the heart of the practice of art. The principal public outcome of this tendency was the work *Index 01* (fig. 37), exhibited at *Documenta 5* in 1972. This was a work that included a large body of text, but which seemed in the end to reduce its readable contents to a mere remainder of the indexing system applied. The text was, as it were, pushed back to a moment in the genesis of the work so that its disappearance was necessary. And that very disappearance was the condition of reconnection to a kind of tradition – one in which the possibility of painting could in the end be once again conceived as an issue in practice and not just in theory. I associate the commencement of Art & Language's indexing project with the closing out of a transitional phase that Conceptual Art had represented. By then it seemed clear enough, however, that no artistic images deserving of the name could any longer dissociate themselves from the texts

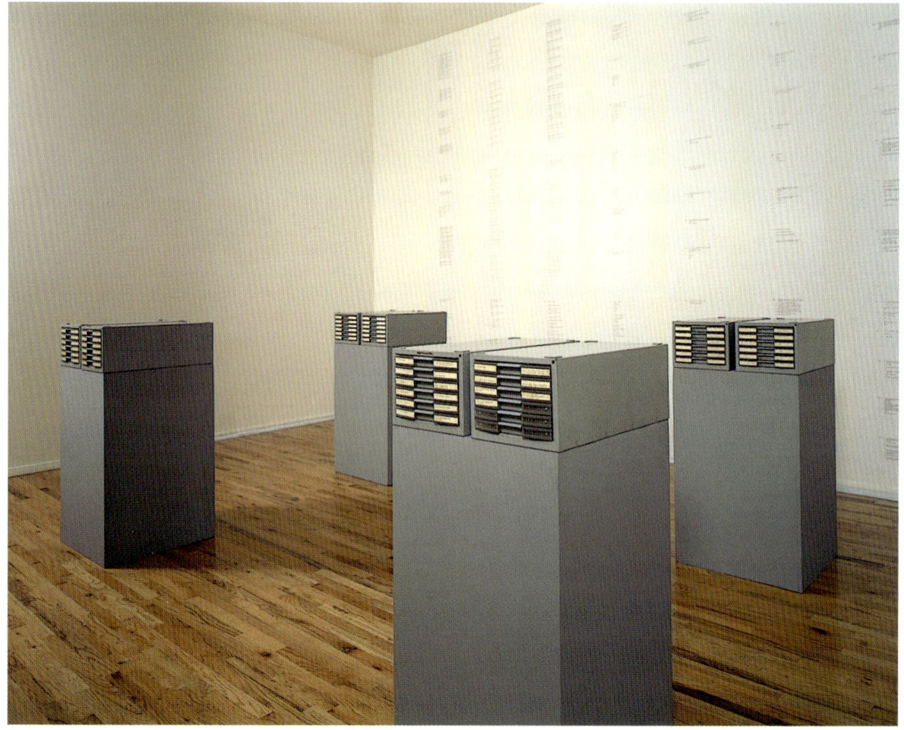

37 Art & Language, *Index 01*, 1972, 8 metal filing cabinets with texts, four plinths, Photostat wall display, dimensions variable, Daros Collection, Zurich

buried in their memories, or lurking in their margins, or lying in wait for them in the future.

None of this could have been very clear to me at the time in question – say during the three years from 1969 to 1972. My aim is merely to explain with the benefit of hindsight why I found it so hard to keep my balance in the attempt to find words for art. I am reminded of an observation made by Delacroix in 1857, at the supposed beginning of the long phase of modernist art: 'This new world, good or bad, which is trying to reach the light across our ruins, is like a volcano under our feet, and lets no one catch his breath again.'[19] So much for my self-important little frisson in front of the Morris Louis. The earth really had moved, and it was not just me that was out of a job.

I do not mean to suggest that the exercise of critical faculties had in itself become either impossible or redundant. Quite the reverse. I suppose what it means to see yourself as a critic rather than a historian is that you get stuck with the textual evidence of your intuitions. And if the embarrassing evacuation of meaning from my own prose was what had brought home to me the insecurity of my response to Morris Louis, it was the fascination I felt for some art as writing, or writing as art, that served to suggest the reasons for that insecurity. The problem I was left with was just what to make of that fascination in practical terms: quite simply, how to find employment.

This was the point, I think, at which a possible shift in the relations of art history and criticism seemed as though it might be the answer. Just as criticism in a modernist vein was becoming unsustainable, art history was finally coming to terms with Modernism as a theoretical concept. For lapsed modernists with academic qualifications there were thus careers to be made in teaching. Rather than continuing to contemplate the sensitivity of our responses before paintings and sculptures of decreasing plausibility, hoping to save ourselves by *writing* on the grounds that it is on its writing that art criticism will be allowed to stand, maybe we could address ourselves to the cultural and historical mechanisms by which values had been constituted and attributed, and try to insure ourselves by *knowing* – on the grounds that knowingness is what art history is supposed to be good for. For some writers of my generation, myself included, a progressive art history did indeed seem to offer a viable alternative to pursuit of an art criticism that tended inescapably to conservatism. In turn, some artist savants cultivated the company of art historians as a sign of their indifference to criticism in a modernist vein.

During the 1970s, then, it looked as though there might be grounds for convergence between an art history interested in radical interpretation and those artistic practices that were concerned with the aftermath of abstraction. I have to say, though, that little encouragement was in the end to be drawn from the products of this convergence. Over the past two decades the centre-stage of the art-world has been largely occupied by a species of academically supported Conceptualism in which Cultural Studies is practised at the level of the illustrative vignette. And when we examine the relations between the art in question and its characteristic literary support, it is clear that something very like the modernist division of labour has been restored with a vengeance, though with the writer's part now discharged in much less readable prose.

So however much of my own time and energy I might occasionally have expended in trying to make it work, I do not think a move into academic art history was any kind of long-term solution to the problems of criticism in the last third of the century. If I now go back to that moment – the brief moment of Conceptual Art as I envisage it, lasting a mere five years or so between 1967 and 1972 – then it seems that so far as the possibility of criticism was concerned, the really productive effect of art as writing and of writing as art was that it made holes in the barriers that had come to separate the self-criticism of practice from the practice of criticism – a separation that had left each holding on to a different part of the narrative. And the holes were made from both sides. However difficult art history's larger story might have become, perhaps it might now be possible to bring the different components of present practice back into some kind of alignment. The more promising move for criticism, then, was not towards art history but towards art work.

In my own case this involved an explicit association with the practice of Art & Language. No security followed from this. The practice constantly shifts. The division between words and pictures gets demolished and reshaped as a distinction internal to the practice. The words are part of a self-description – a mechanism of re-engagement or re-entry that has constantly to be renegotiated. But to speak of internal distinctions and of self-description is not to imply that the larger story has to be ignored. Sometimes it is the puzzling at new work in the studio that makes a wider art history interesting and available, and that makes different words available with which to reanimate it.

# 8 A PLACE OF WORK: CONCEPTUAL ART AS REALIST PRACTICE?

This essay was originally written for a panel on 'Realism in the Art of the 1970s', held at the College Art Association conference, 2005, in Atlanta, Georgia. It considers alternative accounts of the legacy of the Conceptual Art movement. It has not previously been published.

As I understand it, the concern of the panel on 'Realism' is with the new art that emerged in the late 1960s and early 1970s, which is to say with the moment at which artists from my own generation constituted an avant-garde. I find myself caught between the spurious authenticity of anecdotal reminiscence and the equally spurious objectivity of art-historical overview. I will do my best to steer a course at a distance from both. In fact in so far as I have a coherent view of the period in question it is subject to constant revision. It may be that the best I can do is to address such representations as have already been put forward.

I will start with the grounds on which the panel was proposed. They assume significant contrast between a dialectical Modernism, associated with the writings of Clement Greenberg and Michael Fried, and a variety of putatively realist practices that flourished around 1970. These are seen as non-dialectical in so far as they are independent of the self-critical historical tendency that Greenberg saw as definitive of Modernism. The following are named as 'possible subjects':[1] Vito Hannibal Acconci, Carl Andre, Jo Baer, Mel Bochner, John Chamberlain, Chuck Close, Arthur Danto, Dan Flavin, Dan Graham, Hans Hofmann, Albert Jensen, Jasper Johns, Don Judd, Allan Kaprow, Joseph Kosuth, Annette Michelson, Barnett Newman, Claes Oldenburg, Barbara Reise, Barbara Rose, Harold Rosenberg, Richard Serra, Frank Stella, Andy Warhol and John Wesley. The character of this list of artists and writers is best caught by reference to its omissions: no Jules Olitski or Kenneth Noland or Anthony Caro, in fact no artist or writer of whom Greenberg approved, with the strange exception of Hans Hofmann (Barnett Newman's work being by 1970 well beyond the Greenbergian pale); and no artist or writer who is not an American.

It will be an incidental function of this paper to suggest that realism in the face of Modernism is incommensurable with chauvinism. If realism entails some notion of social truth, as it presumably must, and if Modernism is a projectively cosmopolitan value, as it has always been taken to be, then to conjoin the two terms is to counter the partiality that a concentration on particular schools and national groupings tends to naturalise. The apparent partiality in this case is the more troubling in so far as it masks a significant critical point. It could reasonably be said firstly that late high Modernism was vulnerable to criticism precisely on account of its restrictively American character, and secondly that one significant effect of the Conceptual Art movement which succeeded it was to render the development of modern art once again a significantly international matter.

Before proceeding we need to loosen the connection between Greenberg's modernist theory and the notion of art as dialectical. On the one hand we should not assume that what the theory catches in the art it surveys is all that is there to be caught; on the other we should not accept that whatever art got pushed into a marginal category because Greenberg happened not to like it was necessarily produced independently of some dialectical process – some engagement with antecedent theory and belief about art – whether modernist or not. Greenberg was notoriously hostile to the work of Robert Morris and Don Judd, but there have been few artists so art-historically self-conscious as Morris, while it seems clear that Judd's eventual bitterness at his reception by Greenberg and Fried[2] was due in large part to his belief that his art was unimpeachably modernist – as indeed it was. In fact if the term Minimal Art means anything that matters, what it designates is that point in American art when the Greenbergian dialectic was absorbed so thoroughly and was so literally interpreted that it began to look as though the theory was making the art. The irony in this circumstance is that Greenberg was bound to disapprove, since it was his declared and disingenuous belief that no artist could work successfully in conscious awareness of the self-critical tendency of Modernism. Artists had somehow not to know the rules while nevertheless obeying them.

The problem had been brewing since the early 1960s – we might say since the first printing of Greenberg's 'Modernist Painting' was closely followed by the publication of his collected reviews and essays in *Art and Culture*. We have become so thoroughly accustomed to thinking of Modernism as a tendency in artistic culture persisting over the course of at least a century that it is easy to forget how very short was the period of effective hegemony of Greenbergian theory in the criticism of art. To all intents and purposes it had ended by the summer of 1967. The publication of *Artforum*'s special issue on American sculpture provides a convenient marker, shortly followed as it was by the printing of Greenberg's defensive 'Complaints of an Art Critic' in the same journal in October 1967. No sooner had Modernism been given a coherent and graspable value in the discourse of the art-world than a hectic competition had opened to exemplify what would in due course be labelled post-modernism. If it was indeed the case, as Greenberg had argued, that the self-criticism of modernist art could only be carried on in 'a spontaneous and subliminal way',[3] then the art of the post-modernist would be clearly recognisable by its manifest knowingness, its mannerism and its self-consciousness.

These were among the identifying characteristics of work in the Conceptual Art movement. Conceptual Art as I understand it emerged in the mid- to late 1960s partly out of the confusions of Minimalism, and partly in response to Minimalism's apparent dissolution of the painting/sculpture dichotomy on which certain aspects of modernist theory had depended. This dissolution may in turn be seen as a long-term consequence of the twentieth-century investment in abstract art. As has been observed by others, Greenberg's modernist theory had done a more than adequate job of accounting for the development of abstract art and of formulating an appropriately unsentimental technical vocabulary; but by virtue of its teleological and reductive aspect it had also framed the crisis by which its own currency would be restricted. In fact that crisis had already occurred by the time 'Modernist Painting' was published. The crucial point was reached when the minimal conditions of pictorial illusion were established on the blank canvas – the alternative of a return to figuration being ruled out by the prohibitions built into the theory itself. No wonder Greenberg could not warm to the work of Frank Stella. No other artist did quite so early or so thorough a job of reflecting the critic's version of Modernism back as a set of virtual rules and prescriptions. For the rest of the 1960s the idea of the art work as quasi-object was to be a focus for horrified or eager fascination to critics, curators and artists alike.

During this period realism was not a value of much practical interest to avant-garde artists, nor was it one much debated on either side of the divide that opened up in American criticism. In the continuing cultural climate of the Cold War, the modernist critique of figuration had been effectively conscripted so as to ensure the association of realism with socialist dogmatism and both with technical conservatism. The legacy of this cultural circumstance was to be travestied in Art & Language's series of *Portraits of V. I. Lenin in the Style of Jackson Pollock*, painted in England in 1979–80 (see fig. 31). But in the late 1960s in New York, instead of an engagement with the question of realism, what developed was a concern with the relations of abstraction and literalism, and a preoccupation with the idea of the 'real': real paint on real surfaces, real objects in real spaces, real piles of stuff resulting from the application of real processes, real marks on real bodies and so on.

In 1969 a showpiece collection of art from the 1950s and 1960s was toured by the Museum of Modern Art in New York as *The Art of the Real*, encouraging an interpretation of Abstract Expressionist painting as proto-literalism, and providing English audiences with their first actual sight of the work of Morris, Judd and Carl Andre alongside such improbables as Paul Feeley and Georgia O'Keefe. Though the 'real' may briefly have served as a curatorial rubric under which to extend the critical life of American art, the notion of reality in play was both confused and primitive. It was only to be expected that the resulting categorisations would prove altogether incoherent.

The arrival of the *Attitudes* show in London that same autumn brought matters more abruptly up to date (see figs 11 and 12).[4] Originally shown at the Kunsthalle in Berne, Switzerland, *When Attitudes become Form* was the first large survey of a new and loosely connected international avant-garde – a precursor to the Museum of Modern Art's *Information*, which was staged the following year. The members of this avant-garde were united by nothing so much as their lack of belief in the immediate potential of painting and sculpture as construed in the kind of modernist theory represented by Greenberg and Fried. It does not follow, however, that the work exhibited was without significant antecedence in Modernism as more broadly conceived. If American high Modernism was widely identified with the advanced culture of capital at the time of the Vietnam War, components of the new avant-garde aspired variously to revive modern art's earlier connections to socialist and anarchist theory and practice. For a brief moment at the end of the 1960s, the sense of dissent from Greenbergian Modernism provided the illusion of a common platform which late Minimalist anti-formalists and Conceptual artists from New York could occupy alongside late late Surrealists and neo-Dadaists from France and Belgium, advocates of Arte Povera from north Italy, disciples of Joseph Beuys from Düsseldorf and selected graduates of the St Martin's sculpture course in London.

Realism was not evidently a property by which any of this work was distinguished – unless we allow the label realism to that strain of romantic materialism which was prevalent at the time, but which Carl Andre alone was able to pursue in his work without descending into archness and sentimentality. It has to be said that even Andre was guilty of extraordinary tweeness in his written and spoken pronouncements. The generally hippie flavour of much of the work in the *Attitudes* show was conveyed by the injunction 'Live in your head' that was printed on the cover of the catalogue.[5] The introduction by Grégoire Muller is also representative of the euphoric spirit by which some of the new movement's contributors and supporters were possessed: 'For all those polemicists who, from the point of view of the sociology of art, fight against the traditional concepts of the museum, the gallery, the work of art . . . this movement is a godsend . . . With this new movement art is liberated from all its fetters.'[6]

The utopian moment was short-lived, of course. In the larger scheme of things the hoped-for revaluation of values was realised during the

1970s not in a progressive cultural transformation but by the insidious ramification of management practices and by a rapidly accelerating swing to the right in the political economies of the transatlantic alliance. In the more incidental world of art the semblance of a common front dissolved as differences in practical and theoretical commitments hardened into different career paths, and as cultural power passed increasingly into the hands of curators and self-curators. To put the matter simply, if 'major art' could no longer be identified as such by reference to the technical and ontological limits of specific media, and if formally based notions of style were no longer appropriate to decide matters of characterisation, then questions of definition would bear down with a vengeance on any candidate enterprise. And in how one defined what one was doing two crucial factors were at issue. The first was how one understood the Greenbergian account of Modernism: in particular its critique of literariness, transparency and sentimentality, which is effectively a critique of spurious realism. This issue touched on the epistemological character of one's enterprise. The second factor concerned the nature of the claim that one made regarding the 'social truth' – realism – of one's own practice. This issue touched on the projective aspect of that enterprise. It was over these issues that the Conceptual Art movement split around 1970 – whether into two or three separate strands is a matter open to debate.

According to one defence of the movement, the fallibility of the Greenbergian account of Modernism lies in its inclination to construct its narratives in terms of the reductive tendencies of painting and sculpture, conceived as distinct and dominant media. In Joseph Kosuth's much-quoted 'Art after Philosophy' this inclination is corrected in favour of a narrative of art as a generic concept – a narrative in which Marcel Duchamp is the founding figure.[7] The self-critical logic which Greenberg associated specifically with the development of painting is applied to the evolving definition of art itself. In so far as a claim to social truth can be made on behalf of Conceptual Art as thus conceived, it has to be secondary to an autonomy claim more extreme than any advanced by Greenberg himself.

A second strand of the Conceptual Art movement issues in what has come to be known as 'institutional critique'. Its aesthetic justification is largely to be found in institutional theories of aesthetics. Originally developed by Arthur Danto and George Dickie between 1964 and 1970, by the early 1970s these had been widely adopted as conventional wisdom in graduate art and art history departments and in areas of the American art world. In a statement of 1974, Hans Haacke quoted Brecht on 'Difficulties in Writing the Truth'. These are the need for 'the courage to write the truth, although it is being suppressed; the intelligence to recognize it . . . the judgement to choose those in whose hands it becomes effective; the cunning to spread it among them'.[8] Institutional critique is typically achieved through exposure of the operations of real-life social and economic and curatorial systems, and in the more performance-oriented aspects of the avant-garde by means of a kind of institutional theatre. The exemplification of social truths is its vaunted stock in trade, which is to say that its claim to realism is more or less explicit.

What renders this tendency vulnerable is the weakness of its epistemological grasp on the artistic culture it purports to supplant. At the heart of the modernist enterprise, from its origins in the mid-nineteenth century until the early 1960s, lies a critique of sentimentality in all forms of representation. The power of the modernist aesthetic lies in its unresponsiveness to those questions of moral or political virtue that sentimental criticism has always tended to read out of art's figurative motifs. It is this aspect of Modernism that is most successfully rendered in Greenberg's criticism. In case it needs stating, unresponsiveness does not entail sheer indifference to the moral and the political. The point is that the aesthete as conceived in modernist theory will only acknowledge moral or political content in so far as it is inseparable from the formal properties of whatever is presented to view – that is to say only when its intentional character is involuntary and automatistic. The problem with art conceived as institutional critique is that however unimpeachable its political credentials may be, it runs the risk of buying its effectiveness at the price of transparency – and thus of sentimentality in its interpretation if not in its conception. And it is part of the ineradicable legacy of Modernism that transparency and sentimentality are incommensurable with realism. Art just is highly mediated. Transparency is an illusion and a mystification. If the production of journalistic emotion is not its objective, it is surely its predictable consequence.

The third strand of the Conceptual Art movement, then, while pursuing a social critique of high Modernism as class culture, seeks to preserve the spirit of the Greenbergian critique of transparency and sentimentality. Its potential claim to social truth lies in its demonstration that reflexivity is a condition of realism. What is meant by reflexivity in this context is acknowledgement on the part of the practice in question of where that practice is itself situated historically and culturally, of what it is that the work is made – what resources and materials – and of how it is that the work takes the form that it does. I have in mind particularly the extensive indexing project that Art & Language pursued between 1972 and 1975 (see fig. 37), and that provided me among others with a kind of place of work – and a position in a set of determinate relations of production. I think that that project may be seen as an attempt both to pursue and to map out a continuing critical conversation regarding the problems of definition entailed by the collapse of high Modernism. There seemed at the time no secure means by which the limits of those problems might be established. At a late stage in the indexing project a tag was borrowed from the young Georg Lukács and inserted in modified form in the printed text of an exhibited work. He had written, 'The icy finality of criticism in the dialectic is only the margin of our soul contents', which became, 'The icy finality of criticism in the dialectic is only the margin of our index contents.' This was certainly realism of a kind.

# 9 DRAWING: COMPETENCE AND INCOMPETENCE

This text was written for the conference 'Drawing Viewpoints', held at the University of Gloucestershire, in 2006. It is concerned with the division of generations marked by the moment of the late 1960s as this bears specifically on artists' drawings. It has not previously been published.

For the purposes of this essay, my interest in notions of competence and incompetence is driven by two practical episodes from the art of the final third of the twentieth century. The first of these occurred in the work of the painter Roger Hilton, one of the so-called Middle Generation of English artists, whose emergence was associated with the spread of informal, semi-abstract styles throughout Europe in the 1950s. Between 1972 and 1975, during the last three years of his life, Hilton was confined to bed with peripheral nephritis. Although he was left-handed, he found it most comfortable to lie on his left side. The drawings and gouaches he produced during this period were therefore made with his technically incompetent right hand. Figure 38 reproduces one of the results: a drawing in charcoal of an artist and nude female model in the studio.

The second episode occurred in the early 1980s in the work of Michael Baldwin and Mel Ramsden, the artists with whom I collaborate in the practice known as Art & Language. Active a full generation later than Hilton, Art & Language had its origins in the Conceptual Art movement of the late 1960s and early 1970s, when a kind of irresponsible and often home-made competence in theory and criticism was deployed by a small number of artists against the failing studio protocols of a decadent 'fine art' culture. Until the late 1970s the work of Art & Language mostly took textual and diagrammatic form. But the conditions of work changed

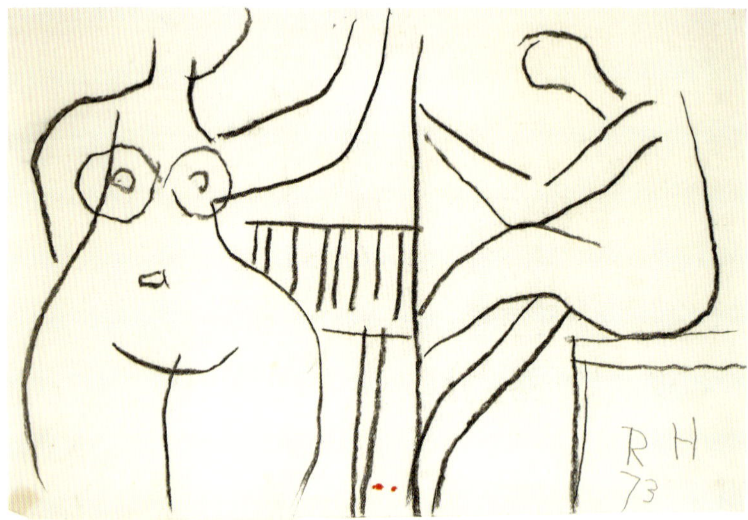


38 Roger Hilton, *Painter and Model*, 1973, charcoal on paper, 37.5 × 55.9 cm, author's collection

during the late 1970s as Conceptual Art became academicised and institutionalised. At the same time, various types of neo-expressionist figurative painting began to emerge in Germany, in Italy and in Glasgow, restoring the briefly severed connection between art, painting and masculine aggression, to the great relief and hysterical acclaim of the international art market. During the three years from 1980 to 1983 Baldwin and Ramsden made two series of pictures, each based on a number of complex drawings. The first series featured female nudes shown as the victims of acts of violence (see, for instance, *Attacked by an Unknown Man in a City Park, a Dying Woman; Drawn and Painted by Mouth*, 1980, ink and crayon on paper mounted on canvas, private collection, France). The second – with which I am concerned here – was devoted to the theme of the Artists' Studio. Both sets of works were largely drawn and painted by mouth – that is, with pencils and brushes held in the artists' teeth. Where Hilton's potential handicap was more or less imposed on him by his illness, Art & Language's was self-inflicted and strategic.

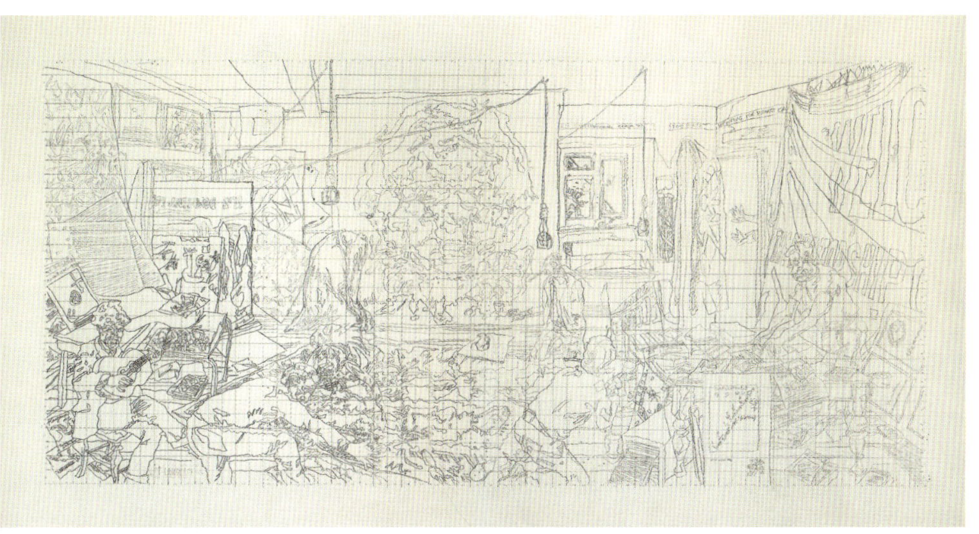

39 Art & Language, *Index: The Studio at 3 Wesley Place Painted by Mouth I (ii)*, 1982, crayon on paper, 93 × 174 cm, author's collection

In the case of the Studio composition, a large initial maquette was made by relatively conventional means, with detailed drawings in pencil and ink incorporated into an overall composition (Art & Language, *Index: the Studio at 3 Wesley Place; Drawing (i)*, 1982, pencil, ink, watercolour and collage on paper, Tate). This was then copied by mouth in order to produce a degree of automatic and pseudo-expressionist distortion (fig. 39). The resulting second drawing was squared up and copied by hand onto a sheet of paper some three and a half metres high and seven and a quarter long. This was coloured in by hand, then painted over in black ink by mouth. The finished work bears the title *Index: The Studio at 3 Wesley Place Painted by Mouth I*. A second version of the composition was then made to the same dimensions. This time the by-mouth copy of the original maquette was copied in black ink without squaring-up, and with brushes held in the mouth (*Index: The Studio at 3 Wesley Place Painted by Mouth II*, 1982, ink on paper mounted on canvas, private collection, Paris). Painting with their heads close to the surface, Baldwin and Ramsden had to navigate by dead-reckoning across the large sheet of paper unrolled on the studio floor. The scale of distortion increased dramatically. The two pictures were shown together at *Documenta 7* in Kassel in 1982.

For all their evident dissimilarity, these works by Hilton and Art & Language have in common not only their submission to a kind of physical handicap, but also their address to the well-established genre of the Artist's Studio, which has the theme of artist and model as one of its principal subsets. (The nude model in Art & Language's composition appears in the picture of a dying woman on which the actual and fictional persons are shown at work.) In their address to the Studio genre, both Hilton and Art & Language would have been able to refer to a rich resource of precedents, including remarkable pictures by Velázquez, Rembrandt and Vermeer in the seventeenth century, by Subleyras in the eighteenth, by Courbet in the nineteenth and by Picasso and Matisse in the twentieth. It is a distinctive feature of the genre that it has served more vividly than any other to represent the practices and processes and materials of art itself, and thus to further art's processes of self-examination over the longer period of the modern. In both cases here the artists are shown drawing, while what is drawn is also shown. Using these two works as starting points, I mean to consider certain changes in the way competence in drawing has been regarded, both over the wider course of the modern period and more specifically in the latter part of the twentieth century.

Notwithstanding the common resource in the studio genre, these episodes in the work of Hilton and Art & Language stand on either side of a kind of fault line that runs through the historical landscape of late modern art, marking the before and after of a crisis in theory and criticism by which the respective generations were divided. For Hilton, the most convincing of England's modernist painters, the function of art was to express, and what was to be expressed was truth. 'Art is an instrument of truth or it is nothing', he wrote in 1961.[1] As long as it served a sincere artistic drive, the potential clumsiness of his picture of artist and nude model would do nothing to hinder its expressiveness, so the clumsiness would not actually equate with incompetence. Indeed, it could be said that the hamfistedness served all the better to highlight a certain urgency and authenticity in the drawing. From the perspective of Art & Language on the other hand, claims for the expressiveness of art, like claims for the authenticity of the artist, served as potential mystifications within a culture of Modernism that had become hegemonic. For all that their pictures of the Artists' Studio were apparently of the moment in the expressiveness of their treatment, they were produced by means that were intentionally bathetic and, in that sense, inauthentic.

Competence is clearly a difficult value to pin down. This is perhaps because it implies not simply some relevant technical ability but also, crucially, a measure of judgement about how and when that ability is to be employed – or withheld, or even negated. How is this combination of ability and judgement to be recognised and assessed? Are there stable criteria to be applied, or is the matter always relative to changing conditions and interests? Is a concern with competence always a sign of conservatism, or is it rather the case that change in the visual arts is merely nugatory unless some grounded distinction between the well and the badly wrought can still be applied to its outcomes? How this last question is answered has considerable bearing on the manner in which one approaches the enterprise of criticism.

I have so far focused on a period in the late twentieth century during what may be thought the closing phase of artistic Modernism. I suggest, however, that the vexed question of competence has lain at the heart of the cultural shifts and critical controversies associated with Modernism since the very emergence of the concept. It is also clear that different ideas about what counts as competence in drawing have been central to disagreements over what is and is not competent in art in general. I therefore propose to make a brief diversion into the art-historical background against which these disagreements developed.

At the level of conversation on the streets we *know* what it means to be able to draw; it means to be able to produce a convincingly lifelike picture through some non-automated graphic medium. In the various circles of modern art's professionals, however, impressively lifelike drawing has tended to be regarded as the devalued currency of the artistic reactionary. For an entire century, the most celebrated of modernist artists were those who appeared to have abandoned naturalistic likeness as an aim in drawing. Now, in the entrepreneurial world of the archly post-modern, it might be thought that the whole issue has been consigned to irrelevance. And yet, still buried in the minds of all but the most doting admirers of the modern artist there lurks a nagging question: yes, but can he or she really draw – meaning could the artist in question produce a convincing likeness if actually required to? What if the rejection of naturalism should turn out to have been merely a self-serving cover for incompetence? Even so impassioned a defender of early Modernism as Roger Fry seems to have needed to reassure his readers on this point:

> Such a picture as Picasso's *Head of a Man* would undoubtedly be ridiculous if, having set out to make a direct imitation of the actual model, he had been incapable of getting a better likeness. But Picasso did nothing of the sort. He has shown . . . that he could do at least as well as anyone if he wished.[2]

That was in 1912. Even now, would we hold the modernist extravagances of Picasso and Matisse in such high esteem if we were not assured that they really could knock out a good likeness if they wanted to? Probably not, though one might not want to admit as much in polite company.

It might seem that matters would be different where abstract art is concerned. But I recall Greenberg in an unguarded moment insisting that Jackson Pollock could draw better from the life after five years of abstract painting than he could before. A kind of double standard seems to operate. For all the critiques of 'visuality' that have been mounted in recent decades, we still retain the idea of visual art as a significant category. We want to celebrate the formal adventures of unbridled avant-gardism, but we also want to be reassured that they rest on just those talents of hand and eye co-ordination and practised skills in descriptive representation that the avant-gardes are supposed to have devalued.

It is perhaps a part of the cultural legacy of Modernism that anxiety about such matters tends to seem historically specific. As Ernst Gombrich once observed, nothing has been quite the same since the critics got it wrong about Impressionism. If the work of such palpable incompetents as Manet and Cézanne could stand the test of time, then maybe all criteria were relative. But the trouble with relativism, as Bertrand Russell memorably pointed out, is that if it is true it is false. It is not only political conservatives who look back to an imagined time when there was a broad if largely unspoken consensus about how one told the good and well made from the bad and incompetent. The timing of the onset of crisis varies according to the kinds of evidence under consideration, but there is a tendency for retrospective views to converge on the second half of the nineteenth century, to associate Modernism with the historical emergence of avant-gardism, and to associate avant-gardism with a previously unheard-of challenge to established taste and principles of judgement. Writing in 1939, Greenberg famously referred to 'the appearance of a new kind of criticism of society . . . becoming a part of the advanced intellectual conscience of the fifth and sixth decades of the nineteenth century'.[3]

If we follow the line of modernist theory as laid down by Greenberg, it is in the work of Manet that the significant shift is made technically manifest. That Greenberg's line is followed even by many of those who have otherwise opposed him may be due to the evidence furnished by commentators contemporary with Manet, who responded with remarkable vehemence to what they saw as the incompetence of his work. A comparison of two drawings from the same collection in Chicago can be used to reconstruct the kinds of judgement that were at issue during the period in question, and to mark the earlier fault-line along which the inception of Modernism may be located, over a century before the possibly terminal crisis I have already referred to. Courbet's study of a model reading in the studio was made in the late 1840s (fig. 40). While there were certainly powerful reasons why the established Parisian critics should have taken exception to Courbet's painted work, it is hard to conceive on this evidence that a strong case could have been mounted against the sheer competence of his drawing. In contrast, what is required to save Manet's red chalk study of the early 1860s (fig. 41) from losing heavily by the comparison is the kind of sympathetic understanding of the modernist enterprise that later critics acquired. It was necessary to learn from experience that a degree of awkwardness in delineation of a pictured figure could be indispensable to the critical effect of a finished

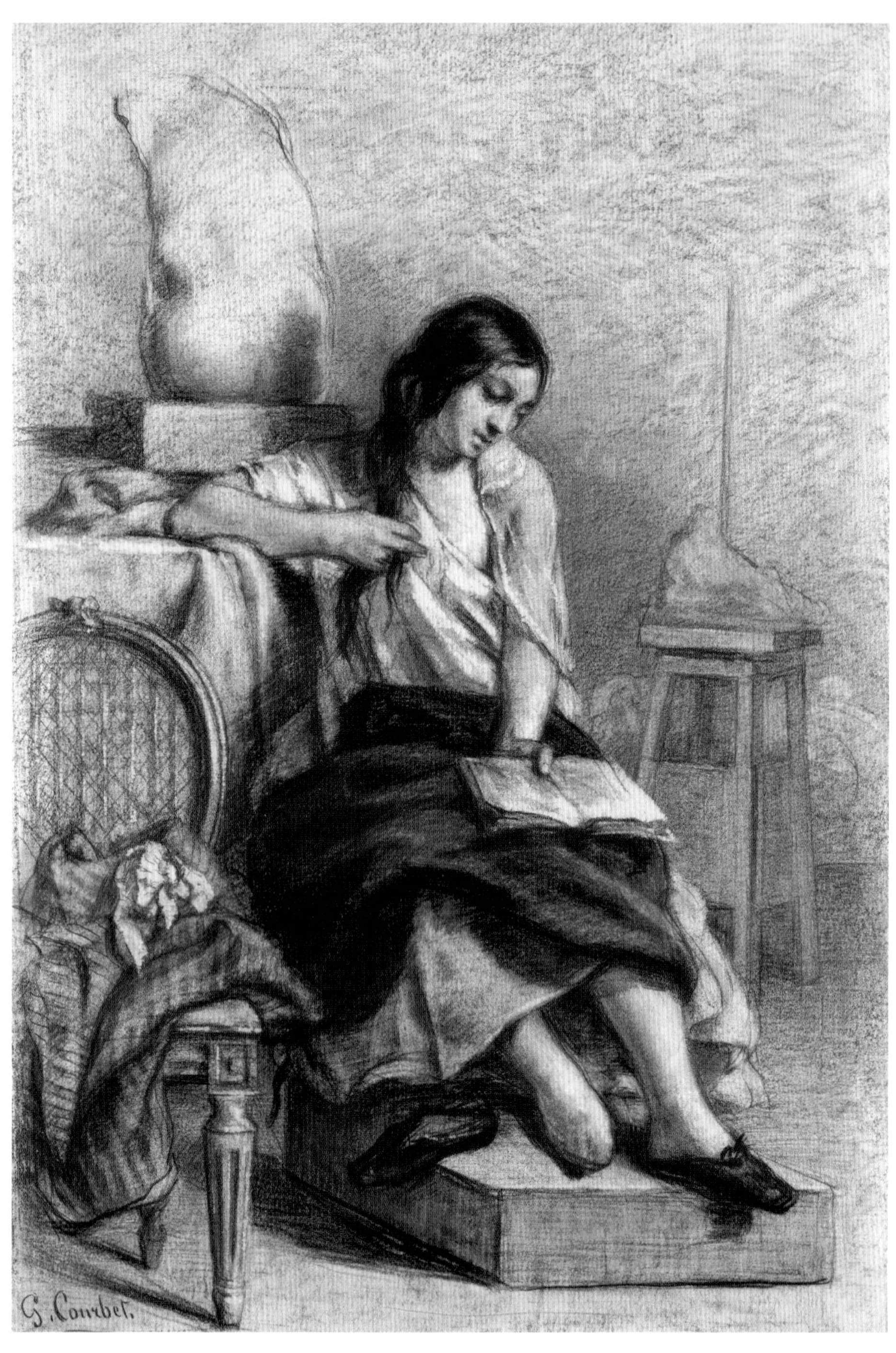


40 Gustave Courbet, *Model Reading in the Studio*, c.1849, black crayon and charcoal with stumping and scraping, on cream wove card, 56.1 × 39 cm, The Art Institute of Chicago

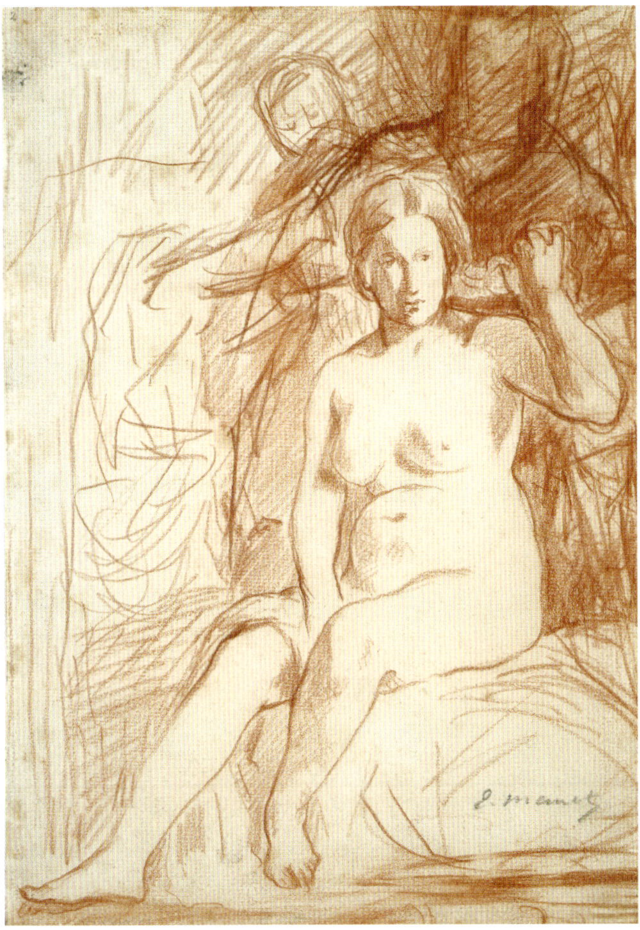

41 Edouard Manet, *Female Nude Study*, early 1860s, red chalk on laid paper, 26.6 × 23 cm, The Art Institute of Chicago

work. To put the point another way, what was required was that established criteria of competence and incompetence be revised, so that certain pictures that had been widely seen as technically inept could be seen as positively challenging, while works that might once have been taken as models of technical accomplishment were derogated for their failure to be modern – a failure that was associated with moral decadence.

It was Tim Clark who first proposed that Manet's *Olympia* might be seen as a painting that 'failed to signify in 1865', asking whether what was being considered was an instance of 'subversive refusal of the established codes' or of 'a simple ineffectiveness'.[4] In a response to Clark published in the name of Art & Language it was suggested that while Manet may not have been an intentional subversive, the significant problem posed by *Olympia* in 1865 may have been its failure to produce the kind of necessary *misrepresentation* of the generating structures that had become the staple fare of academic painting – a failure that was intentional at least in so far as the staple fare was not to Manet's taste.[5] I have argued at some length elsewhere that one significant factor driving this modernist critique of established misrepresentations was the requirement that the technical development of painting be responsive to the matter of how women now looked and were looked at.[6] A positive response to Manet's work, then, implied a measure of realism – that is, an awareness that the kinds of picture that were being generally presented as competent contributions to the dominant culture were actually effective misrepresentations of that culture's real and changing conditions and relations. It implied disenchantment at the least with traditional views as to the kinds of graphic skill on which ambitious painting was supposed to be based, however well those skills might have served a previous generation. Until the early nineteenth century – say around 1830 – it had been possible to base a plausibly disciplined style of painting on a practice of drawing that had the antique constantly in mind and in view. But already by the mid-nineteenth century, a tendency to bathe human relations in the glow of the decadently classical had become one among many signs that the mechanisms of misrepresentation were at work.

It was with the work of Cézanne that the battle of criteria really came to a head. That his critical reputation was assured by the outset of the twentieth century was the clearest of signs that modernist principles had become established in the criticism of the visual arts. Given his present canonical status, it may require a certain exercise of imagination to recover the kind of dismissive response that Cézanne's work (fig. 42) attracted from Salon juries and critics alike in the 1870s and 1880s. But

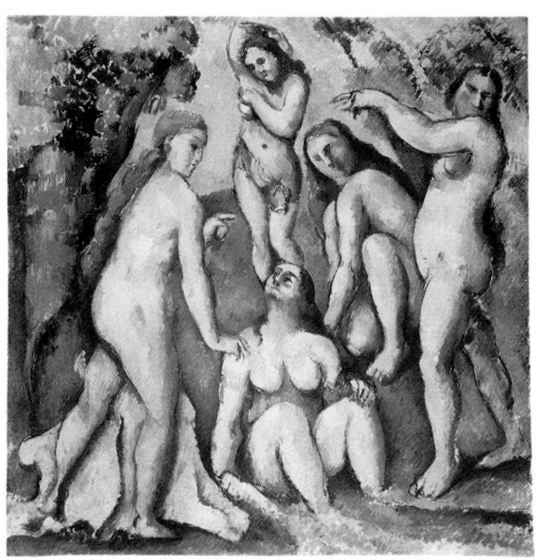

42 Paul Cézanne, *Five Female Bathers*, 1885–87, oil on canvas, 65.5 × 65.5 cm, Kunstmuseum, Basel

if we can adopt in thought the mind-set of those for whom the work of Adolph Bouguereau, say, represented proper professional judgement and ability, it should not be too hard to understand the sense of virtual outrage that greeted Cézanne's submissions. Given the palpable ineptness with which his figures were delineated, how could this Provençal bumpkin possibly conceive that his work was deserving of public exhibition? The assumption underlying such responses, of course, was that the apparent stylistic awkwardness of Cézanne's work, as of Manet's, was an unintentional product of incompetence – that is, its evident difference was not *meant*, but was rather the involuntary result of failure to produce something in the established manner. The point about effects that are unintentional – unmeant – is that they can be dismissed as meaning-*less*.

In Cézanne's case, though, we can be quite sure that the distance from Bouguereau's example was fully intentional. He loathed and despised everything the other painter stood for. Writing to his mother in 1874 he claimed that he had 'to work all the time, [in order] *not* to reach that final perfection which earns the admiration of imbeciles'. He added, 'And this thing which is commonly appreciated so much is merely the effect of craftsmanship and renders all work resulting from it inartistic and common.'[7] What had happened, then, to set craftsmanship and artistic value so decidedly apart, specifically where what was at issue was competence in drawing?

Answers to that question are by now well rehearsed. A very basic account might go like this. The need for satisfaction regarding the craft of depiction was urgent enough where what was practically and commercially at issue in the employment of artists was the expectation of likeness, whether to imagined saints and deities, to patrons and their families or to country estates. But once the development of photography had brought automation and high fidelity to the business of capturing likenesses and recording status, some other justification was required for the hand-made picture if those artists who were not photographers were to stay in business. It is a well-established truism that what followed was a depreciation of art's documentary and descriptive functions and an appreciation of its expressive potential – an appreciation for which the individualism of the Romantics had already prepared some ground. Symptomatic of this depreciation was Clive Bell's flagrantly modernist dictum, 'All that the drawing-master can teach is the craft of imitation.'[8]

The argument I am here representing leads to the following sweeping generalisation concerning the changing priorities of drawing: where traditionally primary attention had been paid to the *image* evoked by a given drawing, and to the vividness of its picturing of some actual or imagined person or object or scene, now what counted most was the character of the assertive mark and the expressive power of the graphic ensemble. Skill in descriptive representation could be tested by matching the results for accuracy against that which was supposed to be being graphically described. This was the skill that Bell derogated as the craft of imitation. But where character and expressiveness were at stake, different expectations came into play – expectations of 'artisticness', whatever that might be. What were now looked for were measures of originality, of authenticity and of sincerity. Though it was not clear just how these measures were to be established, help was at hand from those developing disciplines that were devoted to the study of the human species in general: anthropology, ethnography and psychoanalysis.

There were clear consequences for the establishment of Modernism in drawing. Where competence in the art had been considered in traditional academic practice as a rarefied accomplishment, the amalgam of a set of technical skills that had to be learned and practised according to a curriculum, drawing came increasingly to be thought of as a means of expression that was instinctive and willed, practised to vivid effect not only by Neolithic cave-dwellers and African tribal people, but by children and the insane. In his essay on the art of the Bushmen, published in 1910, Roger Fry wrote of drawing, 'It would seem . . . that it has its origins in several quite distinct instincts of the human race, and it may not be altogether unimportant even for the modern draughtsman to investigate these instincts in their simpler manifestations in order to check and control his own methods.'[9] In other words, the modern draughtsman would be well advised to stay in touch with his inner savage. A dozen years later the German psychiatrist Hanz Prinzhorn published his study *The Artistry of the Mentally Ill*. 'What we seem to lack', he observed, 'is just that primary experience which precedes all knowledge and which alone produces inspired art.' Noticing a convergence between the art of the mentally ill and the work of the avant-garde, he concluded that 'an original configurative instinct intrinsic to all men has been buried in the development of civilisation'.[10] In opposition to right-wing conjectures about the insanity of the avant-garde, what followed was a theorised concept of the artist as someone whose unsuppressed and instinctive will to express was harnessed to a critique of those contingent social conditions that had unleashed it – a critique that entailed dissent from established conventions of depiction.

As this formula implies, in the liberal enlargement of the canons of art that occurred at the turn of the century, it is hard to distinguish cause from effect. On the one hand the modernist critique of academic standards and protocols opened the way for revaluation of the supposedly primitive, from pre-classical Greek statuary and pre-Renaissance Italian painting, to the rock engravings of Africa and the tribal artefacts increasingly appearing in European ports. On the other hand, the growing accessibility of such material in museum collections and in publications served to confirm and to encourage modernist artists and their supporters in associating the practice of art with an avant-garde critique of bourgeois conventions in general. This was the principle that drove the Surrealists' interest in automatic techniques of writing and drawing during the 1920s and 1930s, from the *frottages* of Max Ernst to the collective games of heads-bodies-and-tales, or *cadavre exquise* as they called them. The legacy of these ideas shows in Mark Rothko's assertion, made in 1947, that 'The familiar identity of things has to be pulverized in order to destroy the finite associations with which our society increasingly enshrouds every aspect of our environment.'[11] The modernist strain of romanticised anthropology similarly finds distinctive expression in Barnett Newman's essay 'The First Man was an Artist', published in 1948: 'Man's hand traced the stick through the mud to make a line before he learned to throw the stick as a javelin.'[12] With his own primordial line, the artist would imitate the first maker of worlds.

This, then, is the broad modernist tendency at the end of which Roger Hilton's drawing can now be more thoroughly located. At one level it plays in a highly sophisticated manner on that potential for productive confusion between artist and spectator that is a fertile aspect of the modernised genres of artist and model and artist's studio. We see the artist drawing. We also see a woman's nude torso. But if we make the imaginative substitution of mirror for picture-plane that is always invited by the inclusion of the artist's self-image – and sometimes by its evident exclusion – then the nude is either what the spectator in the imagined person of the artist is seeing and drawing, or it is the reflection of that spectator's own imagined naked form as the artist draws it; or it is somehow both at once, in that shifting back and forth between representation and self-consciousness, and between sexual desire and transsexual empathy, that surfaces as a persistent preoccupation among modernist painters in France from the 1860s until the death of Bonnard.

At another level, however, Hilton's drawing partakes of that enthusiasm for primitive spontaneity and feelingfulness that was central to the modernist critique of sophistication. There is a saving irony to the drawing – as there is to most of Hilton's representative work. But there is no prising loose the sense of obstinate urgency that his line conveys from the modernist stereotypes of masculine creativity to which the composition as a whole perhaps knowingly alludes. Information about Hilton's actual bedridden circumstances and approaching demise cannot save his picture in this respect. The pathos involved in expression-against-the-odds merely serves as an invitation to sentimentality, and thus to further animation of the stereotype.

In fact the more compelling pathos attached to this work concerns its terminal status with regard to a much larger context than the biography of the individual artist. I have said that Hilton's late work stands on the further side of a significant divide – and I meant to imply that it could be seen as marking with distinction and with poignancy the effective end point of the central modernist tendency to which it contributes: that the artist was among the last for whom this combination of traditional figurative content with primitivising graphic style could still produce aesthetically remarkable results.

Exceptions will always be offered to such generalisations, especially where they concern the possible exhaustion of resources of expression. What are the drawings of that unreconstructed expressionist Tracey Emin, for example, if they are not combinations of figurative content with primitivising graphic style? But my main concern is not to rule against any significant trespass across the fault line I have observed. I want rather to consider the nature and effects of the resulting hiatus, with specific reference to the understanding of drawing. The moment I am concerned with may be identified approximately with the decade from 1965 to 1975 – the period of Minimalism and Conceptual Art, the period when the demise of painting, first forecast a century before, was finally announced, and when the 'three-dimensional work' proposed by Don Judd as an alternative to both painting and sculpture was rapidly replaced as an avant-garde medium by art that had no fixed dimensional status at all.

Work such as this was associated with a new retrospect on the history of Modernism. So long as Abstract Expressionism was in the ascendant, the history that had seemed to matter was one that traced the development of Modernism back to a rejection of academic notions of verisimilitude in the nineteenth century, that emphasised the universal nature of the impulse to draw, and that justified an increased emphasis on expressive effects. Now, a new generation of artists and art historians looked back to the early twentieth century, when figurative art was destabilised by the effects of photography and of mechanical reproduction, and what they noticed was a different kind of 'deskilling' – one that involved recourse to geometry, to the ready-made and to semblances of commercial illustration.[13] With this revisionist history of Modernism in mind, what was considered as drawing in the work of the Minimal and Conceptual artists tended to bear more resemblance to the studies and jottings of carpenters or metalworkers or geologists or mathematicians than it did either to the drawings of the old masters or to the inventions of children or so-called primitives.

There were class connotations to this difference. From the first, modernist art's alertness to the social and economic consequences of modernity involved a certain productive conflict with the concept of high art. In the late 1960s this conflict was subsumed into a larger reaction against the political culture of capital, and was both aggravated and complicated by the widespread association of that culture with Modernism itself. The virtue of the Modern Movement had always been supposed to inhere in its oppositional character. Now it seemed that modernist art had become the preferred public endowment and private decoration for a dominant class – one that claimed a universal validity for its own interests. In the ensuing confusion – and in the gadarene rush to establish avant-garde positions that could be claimed as *post*-modernist – the most easily criticised aspects of modernist theory and practice were precisely those that were supposed to be expressive of universal human values. So far as the art of drawing was concerned, the speaking autographic touch became something that those seeking avant-garde credibility tended to avoid like the plague. The look of anonymity was widely cultivated. The previously revealing hand-drawn 'study' was replaced by the authenticating specification or certificate. It is symptomatic of the manner in which this moment has been curated that a scribbled *post-hoc* specification for one of Don Judd's manufactured boxes (fig. 43) is liable to be viewed as more collectable than one of the evocative graphic works of his pre-Minimalist twenties. It is as though what 'drawing' had become was simply a matter of attaching a signature to a logo.

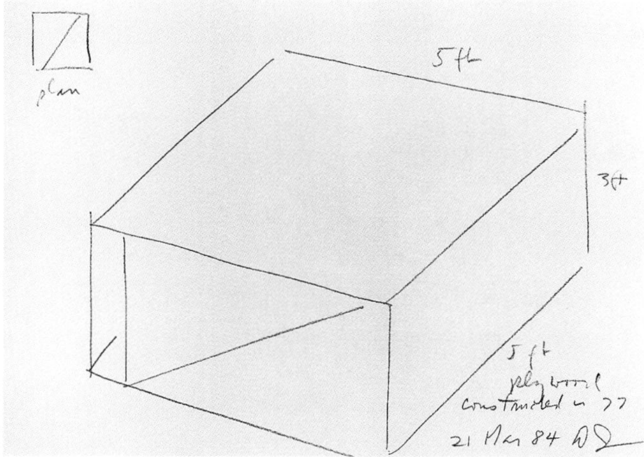


43 Donald Judd, *Drawing for Plywood Constructed in 1977*, 1984, pencil on paper, 24 × 34 cm, Anton and Annick Herbert collection, Ghent

It was all very exciting at the time. There was much talk of the myth of originality and of its exposure, of the transformation of the market, and of the redundancy of the art object. These were the conditions under which Art & Language emerged. Though the practice was largely immune to the utopian strain in the avant-gardism of the late 1960s, it was certainly in the forefront of Conceptual Art's critique of the culture of Modernism – and especially of those stereotypes of artistic personality that conventionally hung on the individual graphic touch. The representative Art & Language work of the time was composed of typed or photocopied or printed sheets, of files and photostats and diagrams. So what changed? How does an artistic practice grounded in the rigorously bland styles and formats of the Minimal and Conceptual Art movements come in the early 1980s to be producing large drawn and painted pictures on the theme of the Artist's Studio?

One way to answer this question is to consider the alternatives that prevailed at the time. As the 1970s ended, as it became clear that the twentieth-century adventure of abstract art was effectively over and as the modernist narrative of modern art's development lost the last of its waning authority, a continuing Conceptual Art found itself competing for the attention of the art-world with the born-again expressionist figuration that I referred to at the outset. Where their graphics were concerned, the response of many of those associated with the avant-garde tendencies of the late 1960s and early 1970s was to remain militantly consistent in the pursuit of an artisanal aesthetic. However resistant the art market may initially be to developments that challenge its validating principles, it seems now capable of commodifying anything that can be associated with avant-garde practice, and it will reward stylistic consistency in the end.

After the mid-1970s, however, stylistic purity was generally bought at a price in critical terms, as the contingent oppositional modes adopted in the struggle against a hegemonic modernist culture became transformed by the passage of time into uniforms worn by veterans. The persistence of Conceptual Art as style also served to harden what had begun as a kind of progressive anti-aesthetic commitment into a new orthodoxy – an expensive taste for graphics without content. As the interests of art history converged with those of the market, and as authentic avant-garde status was established for Conceptual Art, what had once been anarchic ideas on paper that challenged the status of modernist high art came to be enlarged into wall-occupying features in the kinds of white-painted interior that a decade earlier might have been decorated with ambitious modernist abstractions. The mutation of Conceptual Art into Institutional Critique that was overseen in American criticism in the 1980s and 1990s served barely to conceal the fact that the practices in question were themselves already well institutionalised and avidly curated, their politics conscripted to the discourse of a leftish academy, and rendered transparent in the process.

In reinvesting in pictures, Art & Language was aiming to recover some of the productive depth and opacity of content that had traditionally been associated with art. If the potential of modernist abstraction was now exhausted in this respect, then perhaps it would be appropriate to revisit the moment of modern art's original self-differentiation in the mid-nineteenth century – a moment that was coincidentally receiving some attention from art historians. It was Courbet's *Artist's Studio* of 1855 that provided the main point of reference for Art & Language's Studio project, not least in establishing the physical dimensions of the resulting paintings. Courbet's ambition had been to paint 'a moral and physical history of my studio' and to represent 'the whole world coming to me to be painted'.[14] For Art & Language in 1980 these were powerful ideas, invoking expectations of high genre and of the competences such work would require.

There is, of course, one further question that needs to be addressed regarding Art & Language's Studio drawings. Why 'by mouth'? Why having apparently returned to the making of pictures, and to a reconsideration of painting's pre-modernist past, should artists associated with the most intellectually challenging aspects of Conceptual Art have gone to such apparently absurd lengths to frustrate just those competences of hand and eye co-ordination on which the drawing of pictures traditionally depended? Once again a kind of answer may be found through the elimination of alternatives. An obvious first consideration is that, given the challenges that Conceptual Art had mounted to the traditional occupations of the art-school studio, there could be no re-invoking of nineteenth-century notions of artistic procedure and competence unless through some kind of travesty. Nor was there any stepping back across the fault-line of the late 1960s to recover the appearance of late-modernist spontaneity that had invested work such as Hilton's. A final and decisive *via negativa* was furnished by those contemporary styles of figurative picture-making in Europe that I mentioned at the outset. The emergence of these exercises in born-again Expressionism had led to excited curatorial talk of 'a new spirit in painting'; they served coincidentally to satisfy the contingent needs of multi-national dealers to export funds from the U.S. to Europe; and, as I suggested earlier, they promised to restore the connection between art and masculine aggression that Conceptual Art had threatened to sever.[15] Art & Language's enterprise was mounted in deliberate opposition to the tendencies in question.

In fact the original plan for the 'by mouth' project was to sail still closer to this revivalist wind. What was proposed was a series of pictures based on violent, sadomasochistic pornography. In the event, however, the relevant iconography proved too hopelessly suburban and tacky – and simply insupportable as working material for two *patres-*

*familias* with small children. The pictures of damaged women that immediately preceded the Studios were actually based on images from the high art of the immediate pre-modernist period. A second miscalculation concerned the effects of the by-mouth procedure. It was assumed that it would of its own serve to generate an adequate level of distortion – adequate, that is, to produce a false appearance of expressionist urgency and virility. In fact the first studies painted by mouth just looked like bad academic painting. It seems that the results of mouth and eye coordination are only a shallow step down the ladder of competence from the authentic productions of the hand. Hence the need for the pencil studies by mouth, for the enlargement of the resulting small-scale distortions in the first of the Studio paintings, and for the navigation by dead-reckoning that led to the larger-scale distortions of the second.[16]

It was an important consequence of Art & Language's by-mouth procedure that the competences put in question were not just the normal technical abilities of the artists. The established competences of the paradigm 'adequately sensitive, adequately informed spectator'[17] were also rendered insecure, as what looked like the macho 'trans-avantgardism' of the period was revealed as something quite other. If there was any continuing validity to Hilton's belief that art is nothing if not an instrument of truth, then Art & Language's ambitious compositions risked fading into insignificance. If their expressiveness were taken as true – in the sense of sincere and authentic – what was the spectator to do with the apparently deflating claim that these pictures were drawn and painted by mouth? On the other hand, if that claim turned out to be mendacious – as it might well have been – how could one trust any other signifying aspect of the work? Just how was the spectator to know what a proper response might be like?

It seemed that the spectator's experience of these works was inescapably stalked by uncertainty – an uncertainty concerning the competence of the artists that was not to be decided by examining the technical character of the drawing, any more than it had been, in fact, in the case of Hilton's sketch of artist and model. Whatever Hilton understood to be the truth of his work, he cannot have seen it as something reducible to an unfalsifiable statement on the part of the competent spectator. It was his view that 'words and painting don't go together' and that what mattered in art was that 'which intuition alone can grasp'.[18] I suggested earlier that where the identity of the imagined spectator is concerned, Hilton's drawing plays on a potential for confusion between artist and model, and thus between male and female, that is latent in the genre. It is a feature common to these works by Hilton and Art & Language that they evade any easy account of their content, leaving the spectator with some critical and imaginative work to do. In both cases the conditions of that work are bounded as it were on two sides; on the one hand by reference to the terms and potential of a traditional genre; on the other by reference to those contingent technical and stylistic developments in art that serve for better or worse to define a given practical moment.

Perhaps this is what competence really means – this ability practically to negotiate the shifting relationship between tradition and the critical requirements of the present. Charles Baudelaire implied as much almost a century and a half ago in his account of 'The Painter of Modern Life', defining modernity as 'the fugitive, the contingent, the half of art whose other half is the eternal and the immutable'.[19] We might add one further requirement that Baudelaire could probably not have foreseen, though he would certainly have understood it. It seems that the artist who is to stay awake in the present must steer a course between wasteful self-importance and arch triviality. Given the increasing subjection of art to the structural hyperbole of late-capitalist business, the inflation of practice that ambition requires can be critically disastrous unless there is some deflating mechanism at work – some device by means of which a modicum of uncertainty can be insinuated into the processes of consumption; some threat of incompetence, perhaps, . . . like drawing with the wrong hand, or drawing by mouth; some manifest potential for damage to which the art in question must nevertheless prove adequate.

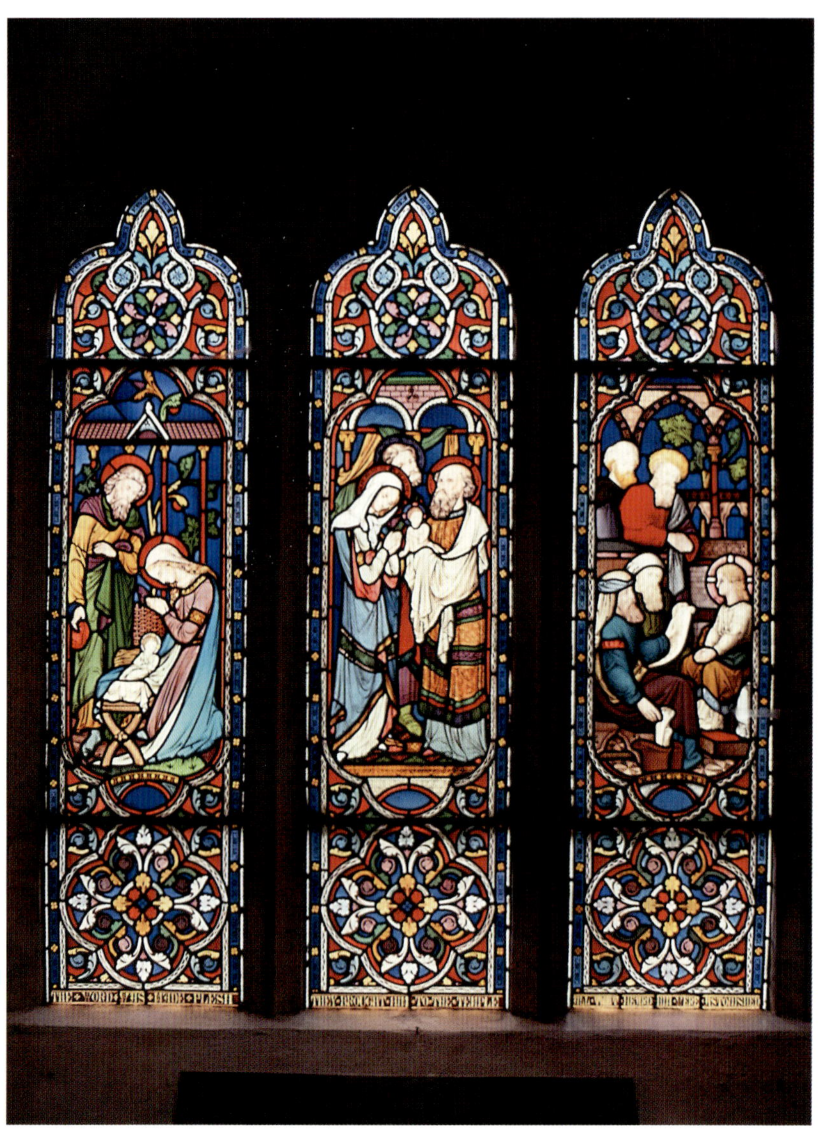

44 Stained-glass window, 1856, Little Tew Church, Oxfordshire

# 10 KEEPING UP

This essay was originally written for the concluding plenary session of the Association of Art Historians' conference in Leeds in 2006. It considers the evidence for shifts in the truth-value of representation and proposes that art tends to descend into sentimentality when these are not acknowledged. It has not previously been published.

What follows has its origins in a funeral service that I attended at the end of last year. An appropriate moment perhaps, on which to try to learn a lesson from history. It was held in the small parish church of Little Tew in the English countryside – an unremarkable building apart from two stained-glass windows with which it was decorated in the nineteenth century. These were commissioned by members of a local family as memorials to their deceased parents, one of whom died in 1856, the other sixteen years later in 1872. I have never been much attracted by the revivalist stained glass of the period. In fact, as part of my induction into the liberal Modernism of my parents' generation, I was encouraged from an early age to look dismissively on the entire corpus of Victorian pictorial and decorative arts. But with the afternoon sun shining through them these windows were hard to ignore, and with some time to pass before the service began, I distracted myself by trying to make something out of a comparison between them.

So far as I could see, the clearest difference between the two lay in the relative consistency of their stylisation, particularly as this bore on the relations between figures and background. In the earlier of the windows (figs 44 and 45), in a side wall, the designers had applied a moderate degree of formalisation overall, in a quasi-medieval style, so that the figures were more or less of a piece with their settings and with the decorative borders. In meeting the demand for religious content, in other words, the craftsmen responsible had not relied entirely on those figures and on the naturalistic representation of emotion in their features. This

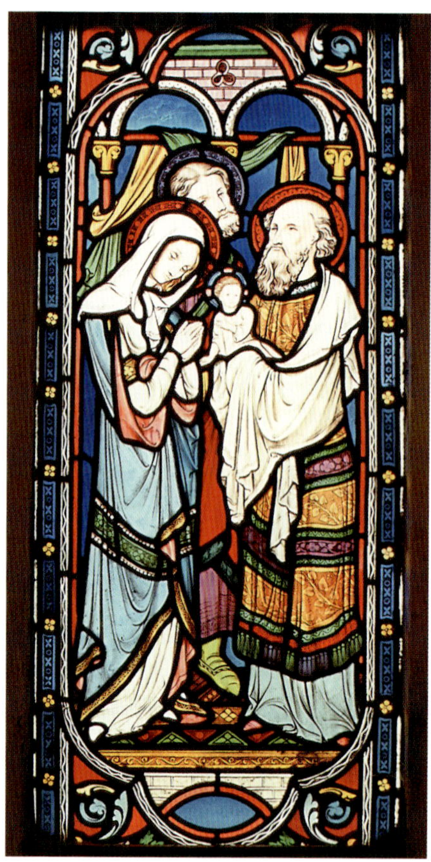

45 Detail of fig. 44

might be seen as an intelligent submission to the traditional tendency of the stained-glass medium – which after all had its big moment well before the onset of humanist naturalism in the Renaissance. In this case, whatever might have been lost in terms of the evocation of sentiment seemed at least to be compensated for by a gain in decorative unity.

The later window was a larger and more ambitious affair, occupying the centre of the west-end wall over the altar (figs 46 and 47). What seemed most distinctive about it in the light of the comparison was the marked stylistic inconsistency between figures and ground. In their depiction of landscape, architecture and vegetation, the designers of this second window had achieved a consistent and attractive formalisation, according an even higher priority to decorative pattern-making than those responsible for the first. But when it came to describing the facial expressions of the figures, they had opted for a degree of naturalism that might be thought of as photographic, were it not that the sentimentality of the emotional content was incompatible with any sense of mimetic realism. In this case the stylistic contrast between figures and ground was so marked it was hard to believe it could have been other than intentional. Yet how could any group of competent Victorian craftsmen working in such a context have knowingly designed something so stylistically heterogeneous and – at least as I saw it – so aesthetically unsatisfactory?

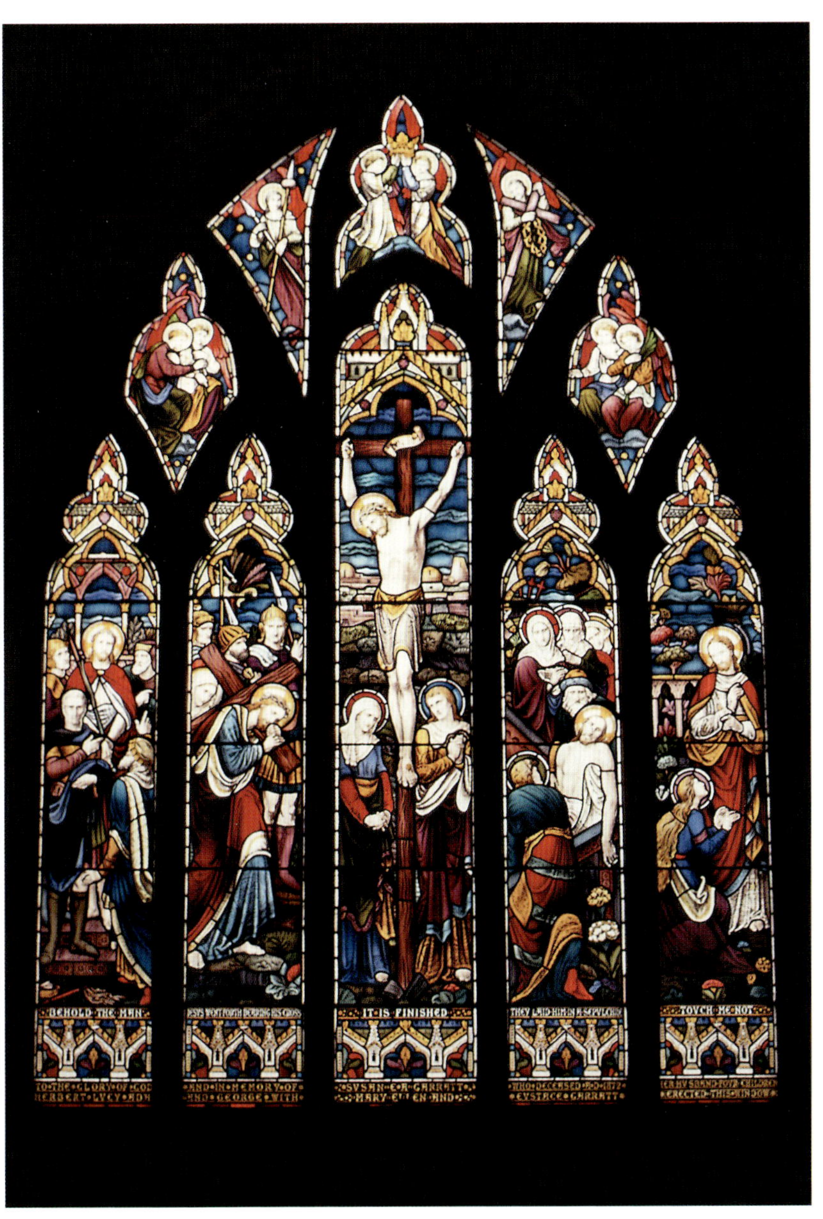


46 Stained-glass window, 1872, Little Tew Church, Oxfordshire

What if one assumed that they simply could not help it; that the kind of unity available to the designers of the first window by recourse to a traditional model was somehow ruled out for the designers of the second, working a couple of decades later; that while the association between decorative integrity and inventive formalisation was pulling picture-making in one direction, the psychological expectations now inescapably attached to representations of the human figure were pulling in another? To see the second window in this light is to accord it a kind of historical representativeness; in other words it is to accord it a kind of content, though this is not content such as the authors could have intended, nor is it the content that for Clement Greenberg was equivalent to aesthetic quality. If we obey Nietzsche's injunction to distinguish in art between the guilty and the innocent, then this is art that might be thought innocently and involuntarily defective, except in so far as it plays to the Victorian sentimental gallery.

It may seem as though I have forgotten that it is English stained glass rather than nineteenth-century French painting that is at issue here. But if we can allow that there may be some fundamental equivalence between representations, we might just consider the stylistic inconsistency of the second window as a kind of failure of Modernism; a failure, let us say, where Edouard Manet might be said to have succeeded. While resort to the kind of decorative stylisation associated with the medieval revival had perhaps now come to seem too explicitly conservative, a mawkish and religiose humanism still stood between the makers of the 1872 window and the different kinds of formality and facticity to which Modernism would conduce. For these craftsmen, we might imagine, the kind of primitivism for which modernist theorists would come to claim an authentic spirituality would have seemed like blasphemy, particularly where the picturing of Christ was involved. Yet here – as in many of those late nineteenth-century paintings in which the demands of Modernism were resisted – the price of seeking to retain a high degree of naturalism of expression was not the maintenance of realism, but an unavoidable descent into soppiness. That Manet was probably the contemporary of the authors of this window serves only to emphasise the distance between them. Of course much of that distance is attributable to the great dis-

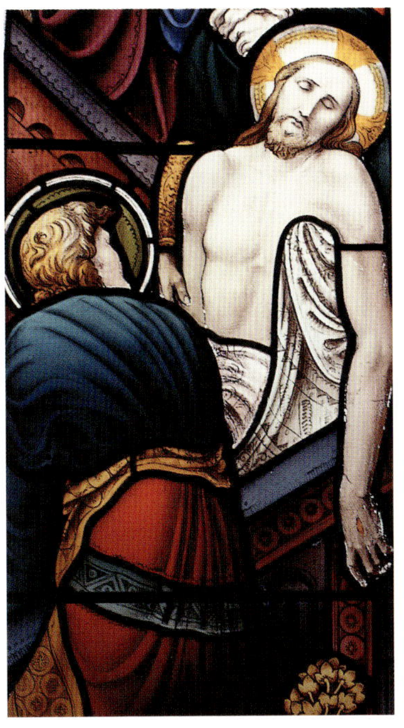

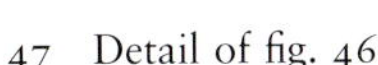

47 Detail of fig. 46

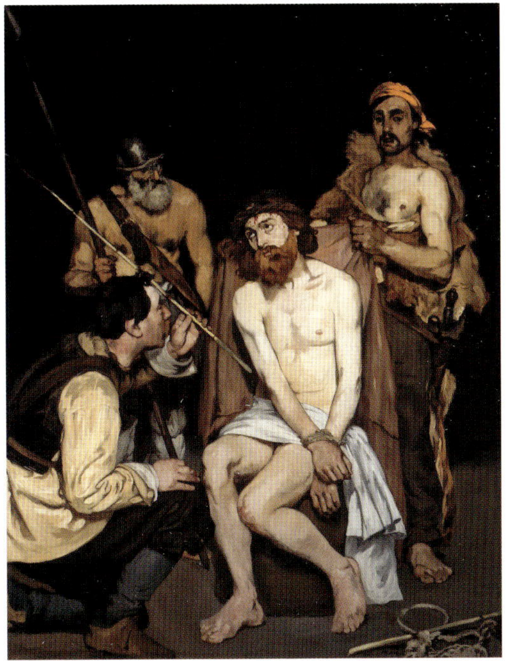

48 Edouard Manet, *Jesus Insulted by the Soldiers*, 1865, oil on canvas, 191 × 147 cm, The Art Institute of Chicago

parities of medium. No doubt the craftsman in stained glass viewed a much more rapidly narrowing horizon of possibilities than the painter, who was after all only the first in the decrepitude of his art. But it is worth recalling that Manet did himself stretch the project of modernist realism to its limits on the two occasions when he exhibited pictures on religious subjects in the French Salon: *Christ with Angels* in 1864 and *Jesus insulted by the Soldiers* (fig. 48) in the following year. If these works were to be seen as sincere, how could they be adequately modern? If they were to be seen as modern, how could they not be dangerously faithless?

∗ ∗ ∗

This is not really intended to be an essay either about stained glass or about the implausibility of religious subject-matter under Modernism – or indeed under any other regime that may be imagined without revulsion. I mean simply to use the example of the windows as illustration for a hypothesis and as staging for a speculation. The hypothesis is this: that what may sometimes be revealed in moments of significant disunity in otherwise competent works is the shifting of historical and cultural ground beneath the practices of art, leading to a separation of previously reconcilable aspects.

I am well aware that this hypothesis is neither original nor surprising. It simply gives abbreviated form to those modes of diagnosis in which formal description and analysis are directed to the ends of social-historical inquiry. In fact I find myself echoing a kind of conclusion I came to almost twenty years ago in discussing Pissarro's *Hoarfrost: The Old Road to Ennery* (fig. 49), a work that is almost exactly contemporary with the second of the two windows. The motivating observation in that case was that Pissarro's modelled and Millet-like peasant appeared as though stuck onto a glassy surface just in front of the surface of the painting. As he was painted, the figure was an event of a different order from the atmospheric moment in the landscape that was otherwise poignantly evoked by the brushwork. In so far as he is there, you are alienated from the accomplished all-over Impressionist surface.

My conclusion in that case was that what Pissarro's painting narrates is 'the divergence of two trajectories: on the one hand those discourses within which rural labour and the identity of the peasantry were possibly realistic topics; on the other hand the developing discourses of artistic modernism, with their emphasis on the autonomy of expression and of pictorial form. [The worthy] Pissarro no doubt wished and intended to hold these discourses together and to articulate them both within one practice. The vivid testimony of the painting is that in 1873 this could no longer be done.'[1] It was left to the pragmatic Monet to solve the problem. Lacking Pissarro's political investments, he simply omitted the peasant – and the rest is history – modernist art history at least. (The coincidence that Thomas Hardy's *Far from the Madding Crowd* was published in the year that *Hoarfrost* was first exhibited provides some

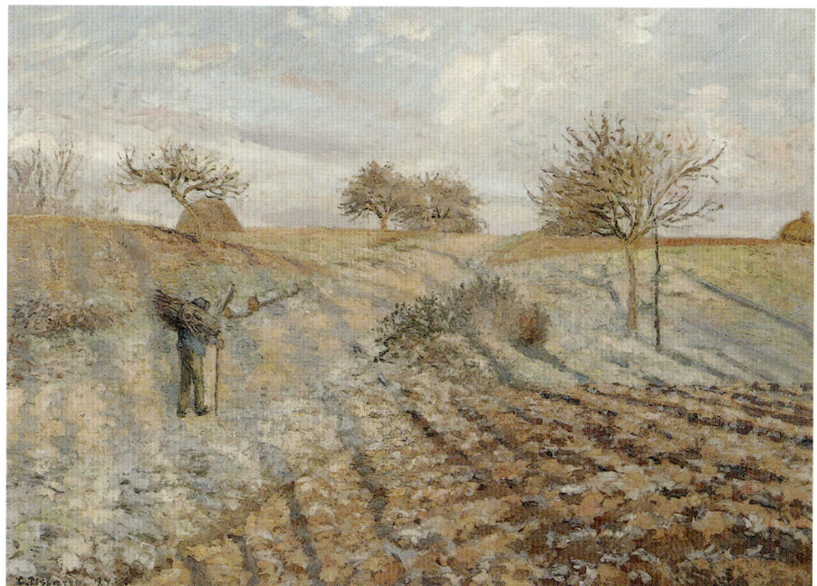

49 Camille Pissarro, *Hoarfrost – the Old Road to Ennery*, 1873, oil on canvas, 65 × 93 cm, Museé d'Orsay, Paris

support for the idea of the possible equivalence of representations, demonstrating as it does a comparable kind of disjunction within the English novel. Hardy's would-be realist account of rural life tends in one direction, the formal and romantic structure of his book in another.)

With the different example of the 1872 stained-glass window in mind, I might now rephrase the conclusion I drew from Pissarro's picture, so as to stress what may be common ground between the two cases. In each instance, let us say, some historically specific conditions bore on the business of picture-making, and did so with relative indifference to the specific tendencies of different media, such that while the urge descriptively to mark out a social world tended to pull in one direction, the need for decorative complexity and unity tended to pull inexorably in another. If the effects of these conditions were not to be crippling to artistic practice, what seemed to be demanded was some sacrifice of emotional investment and cherished belief. From such works as these we may perhaps learn something by inference about the kinds of demand that any would-be realist art might have to meet so as not to be similarly faulted. The implication is that realism is not to be achieved without technical adventure, and that technical adventure is nugatory unless it entails some shift in the truth-value of representation.

Given the uses and abuses to which the term realism is subject, I should offer a kind of definition: for the purposes of this essay, I equate realism with the informed but disenchanted exercise of imagination and with the critique of sentimentality in its many often hidden forms. By sentimentality I understand a tendency to manipulate the appearance of emotion so as to coerce the responses of others, and in the process to evacuate genuine emotional content. Sentimentality is associated with a failure of curiosity, of imagination and of reflexive consciousness. Its typical repertoires can often be distinguished in class terms. It is the natural partner to exploitation and the bosom friend of repressive violence. It is by the inescapable sentimentality of their work that those who failed to keep up in the late nineteenth century tend to be betrayed, however well practised their techniques might have been. On the other hand it is often through some measure of technical strangeness that the most remarkable artists manage to salvage potentially sentimental themes. Luke Fildes's *An Al Fresco Toilette*, and Degas's *Combing the Hair* (figs 50 and 51) were painted within a few years of each other either side of 1890. In fact the vitiating sentimentality of Fildes's work was noted in no uncertain terms by the arch-modernist Clive Bell, writing about his painting *The Doctor* (Tate Britain, London) over a century ago[2] – which observation serves me to point my subject more clearly in the direction of the present proceedings. For of course, it was not only artists who were subject to the polarising effects of Modernism. They also bore down with considerable force on the writing of art criticism and art history. Whatever objections may be raised to Bell's gentlemanly overconfidence, he had a sharp eye for spurious emotional content. It was for the most part in the work of those like him, who were positively put on their mettle by the Modern Movement, that some measure of theoretical turnover was effected in the art history of the early twentieth century – and not only to the advantage of the avant-garde.

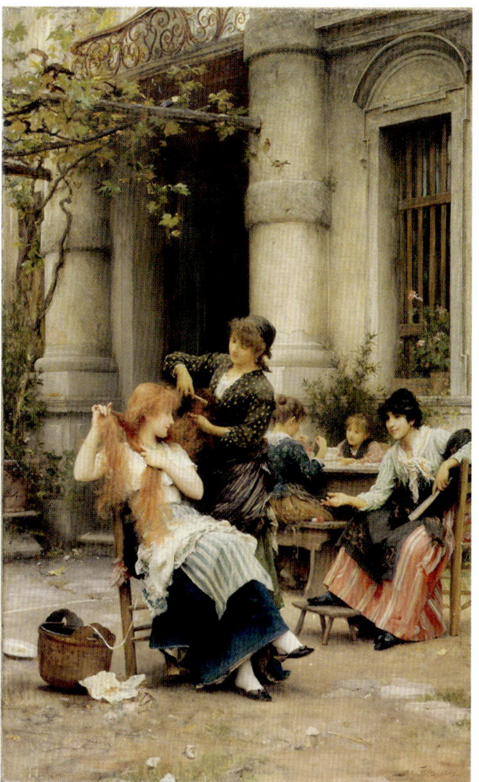

50 Luke Fildes, *An Al Fresco Toilette*, 1889, oil on canvas, 173 × 108 cm, National Museums Liverpool, Lady Lever Art Gallery, Port Sunlight

51 (*below*) Edgar Degas, *Combing the Hair*, *c.*1892–96, oil on canvas, 114 × 146.1 cm, National Gallery, London

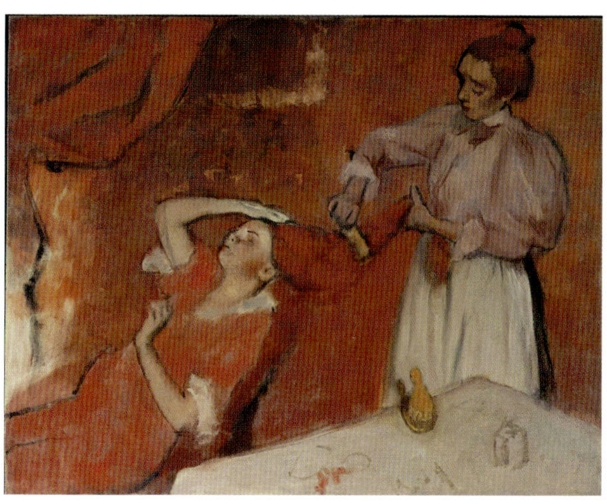

It may seem that this is all ancient history. But in fact the polarising effects lasted a surprisingly long time, through various mutations of modern art and theory. By the mid-twentieth century any Western art historian altogether resistant to that theory was effectively reduced to working as an antiquarian – any art historian younger than Ernst Gombrich at least. The art colleges of the 1960s were bedevilled by them: graduates of the Courtauld Institute on part-time contracts, failing hopelessly to interest art students in a history untransformed by the growth of avant-gardism and the spread of the European Modern Movement – let alone by the Americanisation of modernist theory that was represented in the writings of Clement Greenberg.

Of course, conditions changed eventually. The period from the late 1960s saw increasing dissolution of the association between aesthetic value and medium specificity that had been central to modernist criticism, and with it an end to some absurd protocols and conventions. Art history was then free to expand into the promising market areas of Theory and Cultural Studies. Where the modernist impulse to aesthetic judgement persists at all, it tends to be regarded as an unwanted obstacle to the academic recuperation of the illustrative, the typical and the worthy. But it remains the case that the art that once played the pander reveals its character as ineradicably as it does the paint of which it is constituted. The culture that turns a blind eye to such things is liable to get the art it deserves. If art history is to retain some real intellectual independence, it will depend on there being some mutual entailment between its distance from the sentimental self-images of the age and its critical judgements concerning the art of the past. Without some such reciprocal tension, art history is just so much social grease.

I mentioned earlier that there was a speculation attached to my hypothesis. It concerns the conditions of the present. The speculation is this: supposing that there are instructive parallels to be drawn with the kinds of failure to which the later of the two windows and Pissarro's *Hoarfrost* might be said variously to attest, where in the recent and current practices of art should we expect to find them? What, under the conditions of the decadently post-modern, might be the diverging preoccupations that are only possibly to be reconciled through an increase in scepticism, and a consequent shift in the truth-value of representation? By what early symptoms might a present failure to keep up be betrayed? Where is the sentimentality in our current work?

⁂

These are substantial questions and, however urgent I may believe them to be, I cannot pretend that answers come ready to hand – or, indeed, that I am particularly well qualified to offer critical diagnoses amid the expanding over-production of the present art-world. What I can do is consider some aspects of the art of my own generation about which I am competent to speak – and which seem to me to have implications for the practices of art criticism and art history. My aim will be to build a kind of platform from which to extrapolate.

In fact a connection of sorts was forged for me between the technical concerns of the nineteenth century and those of more recent practice at the time when my attention was first drawn to *Hoarfrost* – though I was certainly not then engaged in the kind of argument I am now trying to construct. Where the history of art is concerned my interests have for a long time now been largely consequent on the work of Art & Language, and they are sustained by the practical activity of the studio. My interest in Pissarro's painting was prompted during the early mid-1980s by a then current group of works by my artist colleagues Michael Baldwin and Mel Ramsden, and by their laconic notion of Impressionism as an uncompleted project – a project that might be revived at some point in the future to haunt modernist painting (or modernist theory at least) with the evidence of its evacuation of historical substance. The formal generic title of the works in question was *Impressionism Returning Sometime in the Future*. But in the argot of the studio they were known as the Snow paintings. The idea was in part provoked by an encounter with Lucas van Valckenborch's *Winter Landscape* (fig. 52) in the Kunsthistorisches Museum in Vienna – one of a late sixteenth-century set of the seasons that must have been carefully painted in order to be heavily snowed on. Each of Art & Language's paintings started out with a surface on which some resonant figurative or textual material had been inscribed. This

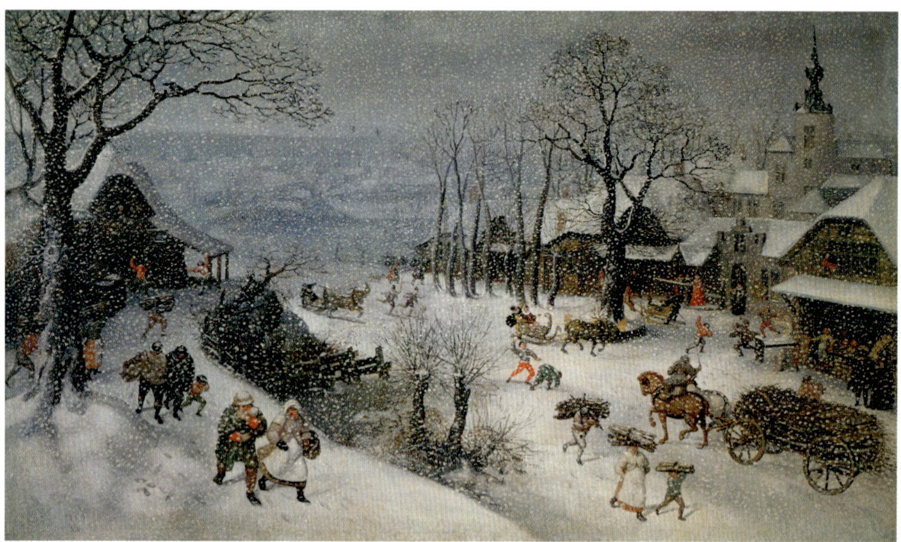

52 Lucas van Valckenborch, *Winter Landscape*, 1585, oil on canvas, 117 × 198 cm, Kunsthistorisches Museum, Vienna

surface was then 'snowed on' with dabs of white paint, so that the image was gradually obscured (fig. 53).

Though a considerable measure of self-consciousness and irony attended on this project from the start, its working-out was a surprisingly exasperating business. In each of a long succession of paintings, there was usually a point in the process when the result appeared interesting and tasteful according to relatively accessible criteria – like an arctic encounter between Pointillism and Cubism. But the game was to continue, and to do so assiduously rather than automatically – to commit in practice to the completion of the surface in intellectual terms, and thus to ruin whatever recoverable content or figurative virtue or aesthetic merit the composition might offer at any interim stage. Working in this manner over the course of about eighteen months, Baldwin and Ramsden generated and overthrew one promising picturesque scenario after another, producing a succession of paintings that they could hardly bear to look at. Few of them survived intact. It was a strange episode –

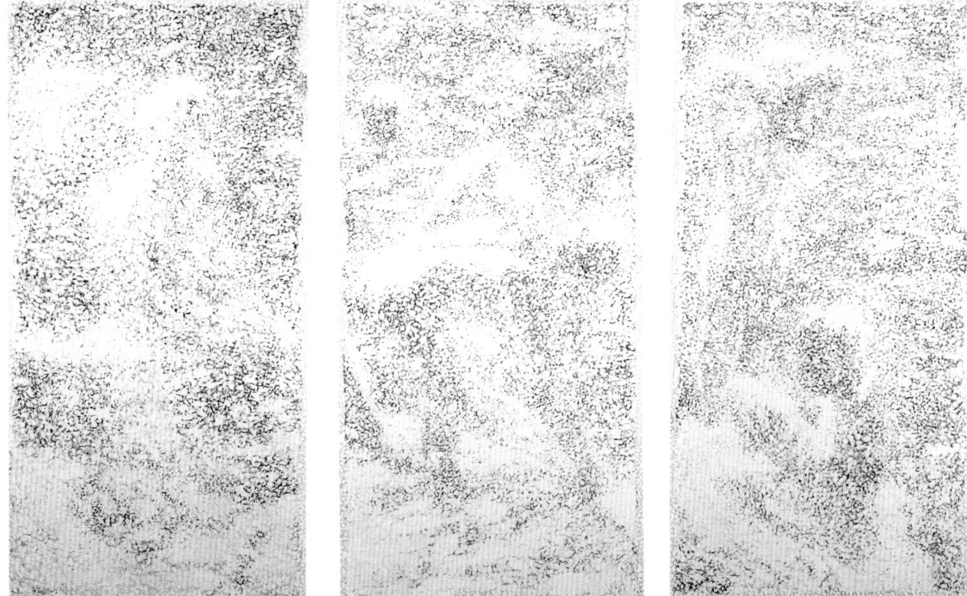

53 Art & Language, *Impressionism Returning some Time in the Future*, 1984, oil on canvas, three sections each 234 × 112 cm, artists' collection

and one that subjected the morale and psychology of the practice to a near-terminal strain.

I was fascinated by this body of work and have remained so ever since. At the time I saw it as a kind of practical examination, both critical and playful, of the avant-garde truism that painting had reached its modernist terminus with the blank canvas. This idea had been skirted in Greenberg's criticism as early as 1962, was revised by Fried five years later and in 1996 was thoroughly ploughed over by Thierry de Duve in his book *Kant after Duchamp*.[3] I am now prompted to connect that perception of the Snow paintings to the hypothesis suggested by the stained-glass window: that is, to see them as enterprises impaled on the horns of a historical dilemma. What these works do is not so much revisit a moment in painting's modernist past as restage the moment in modernist *theory* at which painting's terminal decline was narrated – and then stumble on with nothing. The circumstance to which they bear witness is one in which aesthetic achievement appeared inconsistent with theoretical interest, while consistency in theoretical terms was aesthetically nugatory. It was as though each putative value had become a condition of scepticism about the other. The requirement of realism under these conditions was that neither value should be satisfied – not, at least, under the terms of any possible *oratio recta*.

There is a clear parallel with Art & Language's earlier series of *Portraits of V. I. Lenin in the Style of Jackson Pollock* (see fig. 31), works made in 1979 and 1980 during the closing phase of the Cold War. In that case, the divergent discourses represented were those of a collapsing icon-fixated Realism and a late authenticist Modernism, and the results – in Art & Language's own words – were examples of a 'monstrous stylistic détente' engineered between stereotypically opposed cultural blocs. That the work of art should take responsibility for its own position vis-à-vis modernist art history was a principle that had been made explicit in Frank Stella's work of the late 1950s and in Robert Morris's of a few years later. What Art & Language did was to up the stakes in the game of art-historical self-consciousness by re-installing the facing wall in the Cold War's hall of mirrors.

∗ ∗ ∗

Via the medium of Pissarro's *Hoarfrost*, I seem to have made a kind of connection between Art & Language's Lenin/Pollock and Snow paintings and the stained-glass window of 1872. There is a crucial difference I had better establish. While I believe that Art & Language's works do furnish evidence of the separation of previously reconcilable concerns, they do not do so passively. Rather they *enact* that separation through the intentional processes of their production. Imagine that the makers of the stained-glass window in 1872 had somehow been endowed with self-consciousness about the crippling stylistic inconsistency of their work, and that they had so recast their project as to make that inconsistency a significant part of its reflected content: in other words, that they had somehow effected a coincidence between the work's 'internal' intentional aspect and its 'externally' remarked and crippling historical representativeness. What might that have been like at the time? A bit like a prematurely emergent species of post-modernism perhaps – and no doubt incompatible with the self-imagery of the Victorian church, given that the production of any such thing would have required a high degree of scepticism about the value of piety as a mode of expression. The result might still have taken the form of a stained-glass window, but one now rendered culturally and morally homeless, since to what remained of the audience for such things it could only appear shameful.

In the case of Art & Language's work, however, it is not a mere *Gedankenexperiment* that we have to deal with. The important point about the Lenin/Pollock paintings – and it was one that took some while to emerge – was that they were critically inadequate as mere descriptions, and even as the didactic wall-displays they were initially designed to generate. Despite the knowing impostures involved, they had actually to be made. And despite the inventive character of the procedures involved, it had to appear that the respective and competing techniques – of Socialist Realist picture-making and of drip-and-spatter abstraction – had been properly and intentionally exercised by the artists. Unless they thus ran the risk of failure in technical terms, the paintings would not otherwise be sufficiently troubling to the spectator's customary competences.

With the Snow paintings also, it was the very process of completion that served to demonstrate the suppression or resignation of significance in pursuit of a terminal decorative unity. The possibility they seemed obstinately to address was that there remains a space – infinitessimally small perhaps – in which the painted surface might still somehow retain a measure of decorativeness, spontaneity and authenticity in the face of its alienation from such values and its functioning instead as what Rosalind Krauss has called 'a pure token of sign-exchange'.[4] It was as though they conjured up the kinds of intellectual and aesthetic materials on which art history and art criticism had become accustomed to sharpen their respective competences, only to reduce these materials to a string of empty clichés – the incidental casualties of a droll practical exercise. That there is little I or anyone else can say in valediction of these paintings without sounding pretentious or sentimental tells us something about what they are and are not made of.

In claiming that these works reflect back the contradictory conditions of their production, I do not at all mean to suggest that they were the outcomes of a knowing calculation – unless, that is, one can knowingly calculate one's way into the shit. To say that one might work in conscious engagement with the conditions that normally lead to failure is not to say that one knows how to succeed. It may rather be a case of 'failing again but failing better', to paraphrase Samuel Beckett.

At the time, I regarded these works by Art & Language as highly motivating to art-historical work. In the event, the first exhibitions of the Lenin/Pollock paintings coincided with the period of preparation of the Open University's first serious foray into modern art studies: the course 'A315: Modern Art and Modernism; from Manet to Pollock'. In its first year of presentation in 1983, this course enrolled five hundred students. It also attracted the weasely attention of Sir Keith Joseph's education department and of an anonymous cabal of paranoid right-wing infiltrators who reported to him. The course's avowed and methodologically unexceptionable aim was to set up a more or less orthodox Greenbergian Modernism and to subject this to materialist critique in the guise of the social history of art as Tim Clark and others had worked to reanimate it. I cannot speak for my colleagues on the team responsible for this course, but my own understanding of the task in hand was largely derived from the work of the studio. The overt and somewhat automatic criticism levelled at 'Modern Art and Modernism' was that it was vitiated by 'Marxist bias'. But I do not think that its rather ungainly critique of the principle of disinterest was what really distinguished the course. Rather it was the fact that it rehearsed its students in the dialectic between modernist aesthetics and materialist history that had for some while been central to those developments in the practice of art that had contributed to Modernism's nervous breakdown, and that Art & Language's Lenin/Pollock paintings had played out in imaginative form. In so doing it served to update the more general requirements of scepticism regarding any sort of absolutism in high-cultural values and explanations. In making self-consciousness about the relations of

Modernism and realism a condition of any worthwhile talk about modern art and its history, it drew a firm line under that unreflective, snobbish and sentimental mode of consumption that went by the name of art appreciation.

⁘ ⁘ ⁘

I have singled out two phases of work by Art & Language but it might be said that the reflective working-through of irreconcilables that I associate with the Snow paintings and the Lenin/Pollock pictures is actually characteristic of the practice as a whole. What I have in mind is a more or less consistent tendency to orient projects dialectically towards moments of discontinuity, disjunction and hiatus, and to work as it were with the changing materials of contradiction and dichotomy. Speaking more broadly, a tendency to inhabit the supposed dichotomies of artistic practice can be associated with the collapse of modernist critical authority in the late 1960s and early 1970s, and with the original Conceptual Art movement of that period, in which the practice of Art & Language had its origins.

The claim towards which I am labouring is this. If it was a practical and theoretical commitment to Modernism that served to guard certain artists and writers of the late nineteenth and early twentieth centuries against the crippling effects of what I refer to as sentimentality, it is by its response to the crisis of Modernism in the late 1960s and early 1970s that the art and writing of the last thirty-five years has been similarly polarised. I see the true legacy of the Conceptual Art movement as a much-needed safeguard against that post-modern sentimentality that tends to equate artistic merit with what is now conventionalised as Institutional Critique and with a naively conceived 'radicality', and that reduces the difficult enterprise of formal description to a mere consequence of the approval of tendency – or of content as vulgarly conceived.

This claim needs some refining. Given how diverse the retrospect on Conceptual Art has become, I need to be more precise about those aspects and issues that I see as matters of critical moment to the continuing conduct of art history. Definitions of Conceptual Art tend to rely on one or other or both of two highly schematic art-historical accounts – or travesties. According to the first, a revisionist sense of art-historical tradition gained force during the 1960s and became eventually dominant in the following decade, as the modernist lineage from Manet to Olitski was replaced by another that runs from Duchamp to Institutional Critique, to Site Specificity and to Art-as-artworld-discourse. This replacement was made both necessary and possible by the relative attenuation of the medium of painting and by the collapse of the modernist critical authority by which its definitive status had been upheld. The restraining and autonomising effect of the pictorial frame once removed, art expanded into the enlarged field that included ready-mades, literal objects, installations and performances. It is to such exotica that the label Conceptual Art tends now to be applied more or less indiscriminately in non-professional discourse.

As thus understood, Conceptual Art is a phenomenon of some convenience to the writer on art. The great advantage of an art of literal objects and processes and actions is that it is rarely very challenging to the powers of description or to the powers of analysis that they enable. It might be said, on the contrary, that it is almost hysterically permissive. All that is generally required in writing about such work is an account of its context, followed by a tracing of the path into the culture for which it serves as signpost. In their devotion to this enterprise the theoretically top-heavy art-historical article and the theoretically bankrupt instruments of distribution are usually on common ground.

According to the second account, Conceptual Art involved a storming of the frontier between art and language that modernist theory had formerly policed. Revival of the reputation of Duchamp was an impelling factor in this also. Another factor was the reflexive turn that art had taken in the wake of Abstract Expressionism, with a resulting emphasis on the putatively linguistic character of all modes of expression. A third factor was the so-called 'Dematerialization of Art'.[5] This involved a highly literal interpretation of the reductive tendency of Modernism. It was associated with various hippyish fantasies regarding the ethical character of withdrawal from object-making, and with linguistic nomination or description as alternative modes of presentation of art works. While this second account tends to be preferred by those who have been touched by the Situationist critique of spectacle, the outcome as with the first is that there is very little non-painting and non-sculpture that cannot now be tagged as Conceptual Art.

What I take to be the most substantial implication of Conceptual Art remains unconsidered in either of these accounts, though it takes cognizance both of the weakening of the legacy of the containing frame and of the temporary displacement of pictures by texts. Within the Art & Language community of the late 1960s and 1970s, what started as an interest in art-work-by-textual-nomination developed rapidly if messily under circumstances of conversational exchange into an interest in the theoretical problems involved – a process that led in turn to further conversation and more text, until such formal constraints as had been inherited from painting or from the Minimalist three-dimensional object had been left well behind, along with the stereotypes of authorial individuality and personality that those constraints had supported. What emerged were works in a new and constructively unstable genre. Though their textual content was generally high, these were not literary works. Nor were they works of criticism. They may have been theory of a kind, but if so they were certainly no *less* constitutive of art than were those modernist theoretical texts that the critics of late-modernist paintings had seen as the virtual but necessary content of the paintings themselves. And in this case there was no immaculate 'optical' surface that was supposed somehow to float free of the theory, nor was there any pretence that the 'art' was in any sense 'other' than the text.

What has generally been missed, I think, is the extent to which the development of this new genre has complicated and revised the terms both of medium specificity and of authorship. While much of Art & Language's work since the mid-1970s has involved the application of paint and other stuff to flat surfaces, to call this work painting is to accept that any supporting concept of medium specificity must meet a considerable theoretical demand. This demand is intensified by Art & Language's authorship of a diverse and substantial body of written work, and by the fuzziness of the practical boundaries that separate different activities. No such critical problems are raised by those modes of painting that assume a tradition unbroken by Conceptual Art, or by those other pictorial practices in which reactionary content is given a cutaneous appearance of technical adventure by recourse to photographic techniques.

The late Donald Davidson admonished us that 'A picture is not worth a thousand words, or any other number. Words are the wrong currency to exchange for a picture.'[6] To which Art & Language responds, 'Yes, but what if the picture *is* a thousand words?' Since abstraction was finally exhausted as an avenue of development for painting, it is not only by the pervasive recourse to photography that pictorial art has been transformed. It has also been irrevocably changed by its assimilation to the non-literary ends of the essay, and by the consequent reinvestment of the literal post-Minimal surface with virtual but discursive content of a kind that Modernism had tended to exclude or disparage. It is a feature of Art & Language's works that they serve not only to destabilise the normal distinctions between looking and reading but also to frustrate the habitual protocols each function tends to entrain. In the face of such things, the problems of description return with a vengeance. And it is often through the difficult enterprise of properly describing the other that we uncover the grounds of our sentimentality. It would of course be absurd to claim that Art & Language has been alone in using a wide range of different media over the period in question. On the contrary, it could be said that many of the most successful artistic careers of the period since the late 1960s have been built on the exploitation of a wide range of media (think of Joseph Beuys, Bruce Nauman, Louise Bourgeois, Martin Kippenberger, Damien Hirst). What is at issue is the extent to which some process equivalent to the stringent critique of literary cliché enters into the understanding of authorship.

There is another side to this coin. In a barely ironic paper given to the American College Art Association conference in 2005, Matthew Jackson referred to an 'A & R aesthetic' gathering pace in the practice of art, such that 'distribution, promotion, commentary and display are no longer means to aesthetic ends; they are the media themselves'. The tag is taken from the world of pop music where the 'Artist and Repertoire representative' has been seen as having an undue influence over the commercialisation of production. Prompted by the Jackson Pollock Bar's performance of a script by Art & Language, Matthew Jackson proposed the 'panel discussion as a late modernist medium in the visual arts'.[7] On the one hand the barriers are fast collapsing that formerly served to separate art from fashion, from theatre, from popular culture and from advertising. On the other the writing of art history becomes increasingly professionalised, specialised and unreadable outside the circle of its more earnest devotees. Perhaps this is another incidence of the divergence of once compatible trajectories. In the midst of this mess, the panel discussion conceived as performance retains a precarious and critical autonomy. If so, might it be that just as the unstable and discursive aspect of the essay has served to reinvigorate the genres of art, so we might conceive of a mode of speaking or writing that, while not pretending to the status of theatre or literature, dares at least to be *unsure* about its distance from aesthetic practice.

Let me try to present my point in slightly different terms. The intellectual space that most of us inhabit most of the time is contained within opposing margins. I imagine them defined in the following manner. At the one side there is an art-world where texts are addressed to an endlessly proliferating series of artistic objects and actions, ranging indifferently from the exotic to the mundane. In the language of these texts the sticky phrases of complacent curatorship merge without significant difference into the blandishments of the press release. At the other side there is the academic world, in which the instrumental priorities of a swelling management are increasingly entrenched behind mounting ramparts of procedure. Here the now discredited language that once spoke confidently of qualities is reinstated and co-opted in order to cloak an administrative obsession with quantities. Component texts speak of benchmarks and learning outcomes, of quality audits and research assessments and indicators of esteem. The falsehood to which we are encouraged to subscribe is that it is by steering a politic course between these margins that we will keep ourselves professionally up to date.

Where the field of operation is thus defined, it might not be much easier to conceive of art-historical writing as possibly a practice of art than it could have been to imagine ecclesiastical stained glass as a post-modernist art-form in 1872. But perhaps that is precisely the point. In the miserable isolation of competition, it becomes increasingly hard to imagine the socially positive possibilities of a risky discourse. Yet if art still stands for anything it surely entails impatience with hyperbole and with management. So maybe what we require if we are really to keep up is a practical and shareable resource of scepticism sufficiently bracing to free us from our sentimental delusions both about the vitality of art under free-market capitalism and about the propriety of our academic lives, and to allow each of the opposing margins to be reconceived as the shallow and stagnant ditch it may actually be.

# 11 VIRTUAL ICONOCLASM AND REAL EXPANSION

This text was written for a symposium on 'Art and Anti-Art', held at the Getty Research Institute, Los Angeles, in February 2007, following a workshop on the same theme held the previous autumn at the Sterling and Francine Clark Art Institute, Williamstown, Mass. It is concerned with the relationship between the oppositional tendencies of the Conceptual Art movement and the subsequent expansion in the institutions of the art-world, and is closely related to the essay of September 2007, 'A Place to Work' by Art & Language. It has not previously been published.

The aim of this essay is to pursue a current of thought set in train by the workshop on 'Art and Anti-Art' at the Clark Institute. It was originally provoked by a discussion towards the end of that meeting, when Tom Crow observed that moments of apparent iconoclasm seem often to be followed by periods of significant expansion in art's distributive and marketing activities. As I recall, the observation was prompted in part by consideration of the aftermath of the Conceptual Art movement of the late 1960s and early 1970s, on which I had briefly touched in a presentation to the workshop. In the introduction to his book *The Rise of the Sixties*, Tom wrote of the period that 'the proliferation of dissent and the fragmentation of voices propelled advanced art to new levels of desirability for wealthy individuals, corporations, and great civic museums'.[1] I am not sure about the fragmentation of voices or what would now be allowable as advanced art, but so far as Conceptual Art is concerned, the question that interests me is just how its modes of dissent are related to the mechanisms of subsequent inflation in advanced art's desirability. Can we speak in terms of cause and effect, and if so are there any implications to be drawn regarding the more general pattern of relations between art and so-called anti-art? I should make clear that my concern is not with the normalities of avant-garde struggle crowned with triumph, but rather with those possibly inherent properties of Conceptual Art that made it congenial to the expansionist drives of art's institutions – and thus, of course, of limited value as an oppositional mode.

Further impetus to these deliberations came shortly after my return home from the meeting at the Clark, when I received a request from the former Getty Fellow Isabelle Tillerot to contribute to an issue of the journal *Museum International*, which she was due to edit. This resulted in a paper written with Michael Baldwin and Mel Ramsden in the name of Art & Language, thus according with a long-established habit of reflection on the conditions that bear on artistic practice.[2] Our aim was precisely to examine possible connections between the oppositional aspect of the Conceptual Art movement and the subsequent expansion in the institutions of the art-world. We were also concerned to ask what resources of necessarily qualified resistance might be available to an artistic practice under conditions that have seen a massive increase in the power of the institution to determine the form of the artist's work.

With those deliberations in mind, the intention of the present paper is to add some detail to the specific case of Conceptual Art and its aftermath, and to review some possible evidence for a wider connection between the virtual iconoclasm of so-called anti-art and real expansion in art-worldly operations – at least as that connection might be accessible to art history. It can be said that an expansive differentiation of the market followed from the loosening of the hold of the church after the Reformation; another during the nineteenth century following the decline in the power of the landed aristocracy. To what kinds of change might our present efflorescence be connected? Though I have an instructive parallel to propose in due course, I do not aim to draw any very large conclusions. From the perspective of Art & Language, I simply mean to offer a partial account of what happened and why.

For the purposes of the workshop at the Clark Institute I was allocated to a session on anti-art as opposition or dismissal – or 'soft iconoclasm' as it was described. My point of departure on that occasion was that anti-art is always a kind of art. I claim no originality for this thought. The argument that iconoclasm and iconophobia presuppose a degree of iconophilia was well made in Tom Mitchell's *Iconology* of 1986[3] and it was more or less taken for granted in those papers at the Clark that touched on relevant matters. Opposition to art presupposes a concept of art – however apparently outlandish or ill-formed. Not only is the aggressive philistine quite as firmly possessed of an aesthetic as the unreflecting art-lover, it is within the world of the philistine rather than the aesthete that the critically positive activity necessary to renewal of the arts tends often to be generated. Those unimaginable English ruffians who pillaged and slighted the churches of northern and western France during the Hundred Years War used the very proceeds to build churches in another genre. To put the point another way, wherever the icon reigns, the discourse of iconoclasm constitutes a kind of second-order discourse, seeking to redescribe and explain the first order and to install itself in its place. Given a degree of adequacy in its redescriptions and explanations, the capacity of this second-order discourse to advance tends to be limited only by such non-cognitive powers and rhetorical resources as may invest and maintain the dominant order. These powers may of course be considerable. The resources are likely to include some persuasively preemptive accounts of the culture of anti-art and iconoclasm – of its dullness, its tendentiousness, its superficiality.

It was in just such terms that Conceptual Art was normally greeted by defenders of the artistic status quo in the late 1960s and early 1970s. As represented by the self-appointed guardians of disinterest, the iconoclasts are always base, with their big feet and their asses' heads. In fact, the Modernist art-history of the twentieth century presents various instances in which the disparagement of some generic candidate for art status serves to establish the authenticity of the select – numerous staged encounters between apparently competing concepts of art, and between specific works in which the relevant contrasts are rendered particularly vivid. In the hall of mirrors of the Cold War, for example, the stereotypes of Socialist Realism and of modernist abstraction were made to confront each other as though the anathematisation of the one was a necessary condition of the virtue of the other.

It was the entertaining thought that détente between these stereotypical representations was practically implausible that motivated Art &

Language's *Portraits of V. I. Lenin in the Style of Jackson Pollock* (see fig. 31), in which a kind of 'monstrous détente' was indeed given artistic form. That the flagrantly expressive aspect of these works was flagrantly inauthentic made them hard for the more self-important institutions of the art-world to stomach. Reflexive consciousness of this order offends against the persistent romanticism on which the link between artist and capital still depends. (It took the Tate more than twenty-five years to admit one of the *Portraits* into its collection.) But among the intuitions to which Art & Language's paintings are responsive is the thought that the relations between the authentic and the disqualified are fixed by thoroughly defeasible protocols. In fact it is the very instability of those relations that secures the possibility of vitality in the world of the aesthetic.

The origins of Art & Language lie in the Conceptual Art movement, and in that moment in the late 1960s and early 1970s when Modernism came to be identified in rapid succession as a sustained and describable body of critical theory about art and as a dominant and restrictive cultural ideology. It was within the Conceptual Art movement that this dual perception of Modernism was most clearly given practical effect. On the one hand the reductive tendency theorised by Greenberg was pursued into a literalist *reductio ad absurdum*, as artists queued up to attach the next most minimal object to Modernism's historicistic train; on the other various mostly quixotic attempts were made to circumvent or to challenge the curatorial and distributive powers vested in the culture of the unique fine-art object.

Conceptual Art's opposition to the high abstract painting and sculpture of the time was built on two perceptions. The first was that the art in question stood in a relation of clienthood to the theory that ratified it, and that it was thus aesthetically sterile or unoriginal according to the theory's own precepts, which required that the self-criticism of modernist art be 'immanent to practice and never a topic of theory' (Greenberg).[4] The second perception was that an adequate critique of the material-object character of late modernist painting and sculpture must resolve at some point into a critique of capital. In its militant early phase Conceptual Art stood for opposition not only to the visual imagery of painting and to the space-occupying configurations of modernist sculpture, but also to the entire theoretical and critical apparatus supporting the idea of a 'visual' art that was beyond the reach of language. The coincidence of a quasi-political critique of modernist culture with a quasi-philosophical critique of modernist aesthetics was conveyed in an Art & Language slogan of the early 1970s: 'Not Marx or Wittgenstein, but Marx *and* Wittgenstein.' To say that the critique of capital entails opposition to what capital supports – that art done for money to be hung in banks is not art, to paraphrase Richard Wollheim – is also to say that any would-be aesthetic meaning in the work in question is liable to be remaindered by its instrumental use.

It had been a foundational principle of modernist criticism that the virtue of the aesthetic lay in its independence from the actualities of socio-economic existence. That principle had never gone unopposed, however. Indeed, its articulation tended always to assume an actual or potential countering argument that art should be relevant, implicated, instructive, correctly tendentious and effective. Ironically, it was in part the practical association of this counter-argument with the doctrine of Socialist Realism that seemed to license systematic amnesia concerning the actual grounding of the modernist tradition in the critique of bourgeois life, and that enabled the alignment of modernist critical theory with the cultural politics of the West during the Cold War, with consequences ultimately fatal to claims for the moral independence of modernist art. The more the high abstract art of America was touted as evidence of the virtues of individualism, of free enterprise, of liberal capitalism and of the American way, the greater the pressure of scepticism that accumulated round the practical tokens of its supposed autonomy. The resulting attention paid to the significance and functions of art's physical and ideological framing left the medium of painting particularly vulnerable. Further, as the edges and boundaries that served to contain the work of art ceased to be marked or embodied by a physical or virtual barrier, the literalist attack on the frame became for many artists indistinguishable from a critique of the larger institution, whether that institution was identified with capital in general or with any of its specific cultural and superstructural forms – the museum notable among them.

The idea of an art *sans* objects had been gathering in impetus throughout the 1960s. By 1968 it had achieved the status of a virtual compulsion among the members of a broad international avant-garde. There were several contributory tendencies – or symptoms. (It can be as hard to distinguish causes from effects in art history as in any other discipline. We do well to proceed with modesty even when we think we can tell the difference.) One compelling factor was the apparent exhaustion of abstract art in the blank and near-blank canvases of the late 1950s, when to return to figuration would effectively have been to beat a retreat. The 'three-dimensional work' proposed by Don Judd seemed briefly to offer an alternative by replacing painting and sculpture altogether – a move that helped create the conditions for art with no fixed connection to these traditional forms, and consequently no use for the aesthetic baggage that encumbered them. Minimalism also came both practically and theoretically prepared for the modern museums and galleries that would house it. For those with an eye to the institutions in question, it thus served to advertise the potential attractiveness of a generic art – one, moreover, that would be free from the intractable untidiness of happenings.

And there was plenty of theoretical support to be had if one knew where to look. In 1964, in the face of Andy Warhol's silk-screened *Brillo Boxes* (fig. 35) – or of a constructive misunderstanding of them – Arthur Danto announced the end of art; the end, that is to say, of art as an honorific category that could be decided on the basis of discernible differences between one kind of object and another.[5] In fact the point might have been better extrapolated from Duchamp's snow shovel (fig. 34) of some half a century earlier. In the thus long-overdue promotion of institutional aesthetics that Danto's announcement served to encourage, the artist was presented with considerable prospects for career development. With liberation from the tedious requirements of craftsmanship came new opportunities for upward social mobility as an agent in the art-world; opportunities to order belt-way technology by telephone, to exploit the distributive potential of the institution and to develop the kinds of managerial and organisational skills that previous generations had treated, at least publicly, as quite incompatible with the morale of artistic practice.

The apparently positive implications of this iconoclastic moment included erosion of the privilege associated with the autonomous and contained art work and the consequent displacement of the Wollheimian gentleman – the 'adequately sensitive, adequately informed spectator' – from his role as prime arbiter of significance and value in the experience of art.[6] Among the boundaries that fell in the process of overthrow of the authority of modernist criticism were some that had served to maintain a fiction of disinterest, and thereby to marginalise certain actual interests on the part of Others – whether the exclusions in question were defined in terms of class, of race or of gender. Further positive consequences included a weakening of the system of values under which the commodity status of works of visual art was secured by their autographic character, in contradistinction to the allographic products of literature and written music. As the status of the authentically inarticulate artist was at least temporarily undermined, it also seemed possible to recover a measure of the intellectual breadth and sharpness that were associated with the lost tradition of figurative painting, but discoverable in most abstract art only by virtue of some ingenious special pleading. In the words of one enthusiast writing in 1969, 'With this new movement art is liberated from all its fetters.'[7] I even contributed some over-excited stuff myself about the prospect of radical changes in consciousness.

That was almost forty years ago. In apparent accordance with the tendency recounted by Tom Crow, the intervening period has seen massive expansion in the cultural and physical extent as well as the geographical distribution of the art-world, of the art-market and of the art-press. There has been a concomitant increase in the numbers of artists living by their work, and in the public institutions devoted to the curating and exhibition of modern art. If any one phenomenon truly captures the character of this expansion it is perhaps the proliferation of art fairs, the increasing improbability of their locations contradicted by the consistently high volumes of trade they seem to attract. Testifying to the power exerted by the fantasy of globalisation, they are visited by instant celebrities drawn to the noise of excess, by newly enriched consumers avid for the profits of lucky investment and no doubt by a percentage of discerning collectors. In London, the Tate is the beneficiary of a special fund set up by one caucus of upmarket shoppers specifically to acquire works from the Frieze Art Fair. The institution of Tate Modern itself furnishes further compelling evidence of the expansionist tendency. Opened after the millennium in the former Bankside power station on the Thames in London, it is now established as one of the world's major tourist attractions, with architecturally and financially ambitious plans already in place for a sixty per cent increase in its accommodation. From a modest Victorian foundation run by self-effacing civil servants and scholars, Tate has swollen over the course of a mere half-dozen years into a global brand with a staff of thousands – rather like the Getty.

That contemporary art institutions conceive of themselves as expansive now appears a necessary condition of their continued existence. As varieties of film and multimedia join the objects paraded in the exhibition space of the museum, new technical and real-estate requirements emerge. Even relatively august institutions historically concerned with pre-modern art become subject to the fascination of the contemporary and to pressures to accommodate it in one way or another, if not by expanding their field of acquisition, then through artist-in-residence schemes or by means of archly staged 'encounters' in temporary displays. In attributing cause and effect there are no clear distinctions to be made between the expansionist pressures of the institutions themselves and the demands and productions of artists in so far as these may be relatively independent of the promptings of the institution. Rather, there is a powerful sense of blurring of the lines of demarcation between art and anti-art, and of convergence of the interests at stake. As the autonomising barriers between work and institution have been eroded, the dominant tendency has been for the artist to be remade in white-collar mode. While opportunities for creative intervention have increased for the curator, commensurate curatorial and managerial opportunities have increased for the artist. In the kinds of compact that result the horrors of alienation and deflation tend to remain unrepresented, save in the staged picturesque of the abject and its cognates. The institution demonstrates its democratic power and, abandoning all memory of enlightenment, deflation and critical negativity, procures the artist as a minor enabler of its status as celebrity venue.

Unquestionably, there are art practices that see themselves as socially and politically 'critical' or 'oppositional', for which the expansive museum and the expansionist view of art that it harbours represent opportunities exploitable for non-Wagnerian purposes. These are practices whose oppositional voice is dependent on the institutional frame at its limit. In the case of the Critical Art Ensemble, for example, the targets attacked have been for the most part corporate (and they have certainly paid for it with the scandalous and brutal persecution of Steve Kurtz by the U.S. authorities). The principal reason for the practice's identification of itself as 'artistic' is precisely that the art museum or high-profile gallery as institutional frame provides a source of funding and a platform of sorts. The privilege associated with this frame is thereby put to oppositional use. But the same conditions provide structurally similar opportunities for practices that could be regarded as oppositional only in the mind of the most primitive of curatorial casuists: consider the Guggenheim Museum in New York playing host to Armani.

The institution's capacity to accommodate these two contrasting types of display is indicative both of its liberal self-image and of its power. And it is the necessity for expansion under conditions that harness liberality to power that defines the life of the modern institution. Once this process of expansion is set in train, failure can only lead to a fatal ebbing of sponsorship and support. Capital, whose interests have previously been served by expansion, will simply bestow its largesse elsewhere.

It should be clear that for artists of the once iconoclastic Conceptual Art generation there have been considerable advantages to be drawn from these circumstances. Increased opportunities for display and distribution have been particularly beneficial for the authors of those identifiable avant-garde brands that require nothing so much as constant reiteration and reinforcement in the consciousness of the art-world. It is by now a virtual truism that artistic practices that had their origins in the aesthetics of liberation have generally been happily accommodated to the orthodoxies of the free market, and that this has been achieved in large part through the agency of the art museum. No real irony is entailed by the observation that the supposedly critical engagement with institutional cultures of display that distinguishes such avant-garde veterans as

Marcel Broodthaers, Daniel Buren and Hans Haacke has been a clear condition of their institutional success. In the age of what has been called post-medium art it seems that the institution has acquired a near-irresistible power to prompt developments in the form of the artist's work.

There have been negative effects associated with the reverse side of the same coin. Expansion in the ratifying power of the curating institutions has been inhibiting to self-change on the part of the artist, entraining as this does the risk of apparent inconsistency in production. The more the signifying power of the art work and the morale of its production has been identified with the life of the institution itself, the greater the dissuasion from those types of internal complexity that fare badly under conditions of rapid distribution, circulation and consumption. It is perhaps because painting as traditionally conceived has been a medium demanding concentration, exertion and silence from the spectator that the organising principles at work in recent displays have so often entailed the marginalisation of certain canonical works, or their effective misrepresentation as mere celebrity spectacle. The liability now courted by any art work emerging from a social or intellectual world in some way independent of the controlling ambit of the institution is that it will be derogated as a hapless failure. The site of production moved long ago from the studio to the institution. The artist has as a result been left bereft of that productive privacy and relative independence without which institutional critique tends actually to be implausible – and is at worst the result of connivance in fraud. The pervasiveness of these inescapable conditions is such as to bring despair to the most resolute of Theodor Adorno's supporters.

It has not been the position of Art & Language that it is possible in practice to mount an absolute and unqualified resistance to the determining powers. Our understanding has rather been that there can be no prospect of independence where there is no comprehension of the mechanisms at work. I return finally, then, to the question of the relations between the iconoclastic tendencies of the Conceptual Art movement and the real expansion of the ensuing decades – an expansion that has seen 'Conceptualism' popularly applied as a category covering more or less any art work with apparent avant-garde pretensions that is neither painting nor sculpture. On the one hand this might be seen as testimony to the sheer extent of Conceptual Art as an avant-garde tendency and to the necessity on the part of the institutions of the art-world that it be accommodated; on the other hand it suggests that the predominant art-historical image of Conceptual Art is one in which the movement is divested of a crucial negativity – and that the real critical import of its iconoclasm has thus been defused. The conclusion implied is that some element in Conceptual Art's critical operation was beneficial if not necessary to entrenchment and expansion of the very cultural apparatus to which the criticism was addressed.

I promised an instructive parallel, which may help to identify the element in question. It derives from the field of higher education, in which I have largely earned my living. In the university in which I have been employed a persistent pressure has for some years now been directed from the executive at academic departments and faculties. It comes in two modes. The first concerns the need to avoid 'over specialisation' in teaching materials, to direct our attention rather to the inculcation of generic 'study skills' and to avoid the 'over-assessment' of students – or, in plain English, to avoid making demands that might lead the weaker ones to drop out. The second mode of pressure concerns the division of academic units. These are generally considered to be too narrowly defined, and thus to leave the operations of management hostage to potentially divisive and unworldly academic interests. Groups of departments are to be re-assembled into more comprehensive 'schools' and so on. There is a need, we are told, for greater interdisciplinarity, leading to the erosion of obstructive intellectual boundaries and enabling more rapid response to the evidence of interest and demand on the part of potential student customers. So far as research work is concerned, rather than exploiting the distinctiveness of disciplinary subject-matter and pursuing the detailed study this tends to require, we should seek topicality with collaborative thematic projects responsive to the promptings of the market. I should make clear that I remain firmly committed to the open-door policy by which the Open University has been distinguished. But it does not follow that I have a comfortable answer to those who warn that more means worse.

I do not know how far similar pressures are to be found at work in American institutions, though the tendency since the war has certainly been for those successive waves of influence that are the workings of capital to break on British shores only after they have gathered sufficient force across the Atlantic. I do know that the pattern I have described is repeated in one form or another throughout the British educational system, where a continual government-directed requirement that capacity be increased acts as a servo-mechanism on the inherent tendency of cultural management to behave as though its institutions will die if they do not expand.

In case the point of my parallel is not already clear I will spell it out. In both educational and art-world institutions suppression of the demands of specialisation tends to be justified by talk of the democratic enlargement of constituencies in need of enlightenment and enjoyment – whether what is effectively denigrated is the capacity to respond to the difficulties of an internally complex work of art, or the competence required to read a novel in the language in which it was written. The suppression is in fact determined by the demands of distribution and business, and by capital's self-serving cant that what the customer requires is that which is consumable without critical exertion. The higher-educational institution fears the difficulty attendant on disciplinary specialisation and responds accordingly. The contemporary art institution fears the absorbing and deflationary power that art tends to possess where practical and intellectual demands are imposed by a medium. The resulting tendency is to camouflage difficulty with trivial topicalisation.

In part through its iconoclastic attack on the values enshrined in the 'visual', the Conceptual Art movement was effective in establishing the critique of specialisation and privilege as a virtually obligatory function of avant-garde practice. But more crucially, it was in the name of Conceptual Art that the advocates of a kind of apostate modernist historicism promoted a generic 'art' in place of the medium-specific categories of painting and sculpture. To the extent that these moves were representative, Conceptual Art served if it did not actually initiate the removal of those boundaries between curatorial categories that stood in the way of institutional claims to liberalism and institutional drives for expansion. This is to say far more than that a once oppositional Conceptual Art got co-opted after a normal interval. The point is rather that the naturalisation of the generic art work by Conceptual Art opened up specific opportunities for institutional art production – both for the production of art under the aegis of the institution and for the production of art congenial to an institutional aesthetics. Expansion of art's institutions was thereby encouraged and supplied. In that case the alternatives were either to connive at Conceptual Art's own co-option or to abandon it altogether as an avant-garde genre.

For my Art & Language colleagues and myself, it seemed that if some independent awareness of art's situation in the world was to be maintained, what was required was a continuing conversation addressed to art's internal processes and situation. What emerged was what has been called an essayistic practice – one not easily rendered transparent and efficient where the needs of the institution are concerned. What gets forgotten or written out both in the art-historical celebration of the original Conceptual Art movement and in the subsequent triumph of Conceptualism as ur-spectacle is that a different and at least equally intense demand for medium-specificity was raised and pursued in the wake of Conceptual Art along the unstable boundary between text and picture – a demand that what is called 'art' be so by virtue of some *internal* argument, and not simply as a measure of its positioning. I suggest that it is only where the persistence of this demand can be admitted that the oppositional impulse of the Conceptual Art movement may still possibly be felt.

A final question remains to be addressed. On the basis of this specific case, is there a pattern to be observed that might be tested for similarity against other instances of expansion in the wake of iconoclasm? If so, I assume it will be recognisable only at the level at which relatively basic changes are effected – down where the tectonic plates of socio-economic life continue to grind against one another. It is presumably to changes in the distribution of power between classes – and perhaps, with the thought of a coming crisis in mind, between whole cultures and religions – that we should look to understand the mechanisms that connect iconoclastic moments to subsequent periods of cultural and economic expansion. From a European perspective at least we may understand the long regime of Modernism as the superstructural manifestation of a struggle for dominance between the hereditary educated bourgeoisie and those whose claims to social standing were supported by the economic fruits of industry and entrepreneurship. It was the achievement of the former to maintain a system of values favourable to the self-images of those who claimed an innate and disinterested taste – those whose mission in life was to keep vulgarity at bay. By the same token the moment of post-modernism in the late 1960s and early 1970s might be seen as symptomatic of an overdue redistribution of powers between the relevant class factions, in favour of those formerly caricatured as the mere prisoners of their own commercial interests and appetites. At a deeper level, perhaps, this redistribution of cultural hierarchies may be seen as securing the instruments necessary for a further expansion in the determining power of capital – a process under which cultural and educational institutions require rebranding in the image of thrusting commercial corporations, properly subject to the instrumental rationality of professional management.

We should not assume of course that the iconoclasts of the Conceptual Art moment were any more the intentional agents of the changes that ensued than were the religious reformers of the sixteenth century. That one can mount a successful redescription of a dominant regime does not commit one to all the values of the order that replaces it. The realism of the Conceptual artists lay in the relative acuteness of their response to determining conditions and in the contingent appositeness of their critiques. But by the time it finally became clear that there existed virtually nothing so base as to have the doors of the culture's institutions closed against it – say by the early 1980s – Conceptual Art had been virtually effaced by the Conceptualism it had in part enabled, and iconoclasm's power to threaten significant change had been altogether exhausted in the world of art, if not in the world at large.

# 12 COMPLEXITY AND DISINTEREST

In its original form this essay was a paper written for a conference on 'Art and Learning' held under the auspices of Arteleku in San Sebastián, Spain, in 2003. Its initial point of departure is a 'position paper' circulated in advance of the conference by Juan Luis Moraza. It offers a case for the revaluation and reinstatement of disinterest as an obligation in criticism. It was revised in 2008 for inclusion in the present collection and is previously unpublished.

If I understand matters correctly, the speakers in the 'Art and Learning' symposium were gathered to consider how these two terms might be related under the conditions of the present, and how the potential of that relationship might be maximised. For such an enterprise to succeed, there is a need to be sure of some common ground – some negotiable value for the respective terms – if the resuting exchanges are not to be conducted at cross-purposes. For all the supposed globalisation of culture, agreement on these matters cannot be taken for granted. I leave aside for the moment the matter of how learning is to be understood. What immediately concerns me is the likelihood that views on art will diverge significantly.

Perhaps it has always been like this. It is quite possible that we face no greater problems in establishing consensus than did those who may have gathered to discuss such issues in the past. After all, it is a truism that differences in age, in residence and nationality, in profession and so on will be reflected in divergent views on art. But my intuition is that the circumstances of the present conversation are distinctive in other ways; that when it comes to discussions about which have been and are the most significant recent developments, there are historically specific problems that may tend to obstruct agreement. Of course we might get together to compile a register of the hundred artists whose work attracts the highest prices, is most widely represented in museums, most frequently exhibited, most often written about in the most widely distributed art magazines and so forth. But I would not give much for the chances of agreement over any diagram that purported to represent the tendencies to which those artists belonged and the relations between them – after the fashion, say, of Alfred Barr's much-reproduced flow chart, originally issued on the occasion of the exhibition *Cubism and Abstract Art* in 1936.[1] Things have changed. The art-world has not only grown hugely since then, it has fragmented. There is no single centre such as Paris or New York could once claim to be, nor is there any appropriate position from which an overview might be achieved.

But however variously we may describe the current state of affairs in art, it does not follow that we must altogether disagree in our accounts of recent history. In fact I believe that any adequate art-historical narrative of the past forty years must accord priority to two particular sets of circumstances. The first is the sharp decline in the authority of modernist art and criticism that occurred between the mid-1960s and the early 1970s, the approximate period of the original Conceptual Art movement. As a mark of that decline, I think of the publication of Fried's 'Art and Objecthood' in the journal *Artforum* in the summer of 1967, where it was besieged by the texts of Robert Smithson, Robert Morris, Sol LeWitt and others. Where Fried was concerned to affirm the abiding 'presentness' of modernist painting and sculpture, Morris wrote of painting in general that 'the mode has become antique', while LeWitt's 'Paragraphs on Conceptual Art' proposed that 'what the work of art looks like isn't too important'.[2]

The second circumstance is the widespread deregulation of financial market practices in Western economies that took place during the 1980s, roughly coinciding with the collapse of the former Soviet empire. My symbolic event in this case would be the fall of the Berlin Wall in 1989, and the ensuing establishment of what is called free-market capitalism as universal economic nature. If we can now conceive of the post-modern as a historically specific period, then we might think of these two sets of circumstances as coinciding respectively with its approximate beginning and its end. I mean to argue that the decline in the status of Modernism and the deregulation of financial markets are connected in other respects, that their conjoint legacy largely explains the difficulty of establishing consensus where recent art is concerned, and that that legacy is of direct relevance to our inquiry into the relations of art and learning.

⁘ ⁘ ⁘

In a position paper circulated in advance of the seminar on 'Art and Learning', Juan Luis Moraza notes the tendency of recent artistic practice to adopt 'productive and interpretative models characteristic of the businessman, the cultural manager, media communicator or political activist'. The evident spirit of these remarks is consonant with a diagnosis offered by the philosopher Alasdair MacIntyre in his book *After Virtue*. Writing at the beginning of the 1980s, MacIntyre identified the manager and the therapist as key figures in the modern culture of bureaucratic individualism. What distinguishes their respective roles, he argued, is that they operate in a world where manipulative conduct is identified with effectiveness, and where effectiveness is the highest of measures, whether the goals in question are organisational or individual.[3] However we are to judge such worldly operations as those referred to by Moraza and MacIntyre, they are clearly not disinterested in the sense intended by Immanuel Kant – that is to say the relevant criteria of success and failure do not assume a success or failure good for all.[4] Moraza goes on to observe that while there have been consequent gains in social status for the practice of art, these have been bought at a certain cost. What has been abandoned, he suggests, is 'the complexity that characterised universal art'.

I take it that the implication of this argument is that a loss of complexity discernible in current art is connected – historically if not logically – to a shift in the self-identification of those involved in practice, that the nature of this shift is such that disinterestedness is relatively devalued, and that the disparagement of disinterest and the loss of complexity are thus mutually implicated. We might say that while disinterest is a dialectical idea, loss of complexity tends to be associated with instrumentality and its material implications. This may not be a novel argument – we have long been accustomed to thinking of crudely tendentious art as transparent, and in that sense as lacking in complexity – but I think it deserves some exploration in the light of the art of the recent past.

I should first try to clarify the implicit suggestion that complexity was a feature of what Moraza describes as 'universal art'. We need to be particularly careful regarding those concepts that may have different connotations in different languages. In this case a great deal hangs on the sense in which the term 'universal art' is understood, and on the kind of complexity that is ascribed to it. As I understand it, the concept of a universal art means little unless it is associated with a voice that aspires to speak for that art's virtue on behalf of everyone – in that sense to speak universally. This is the enlarged voice of Kantian enlightenment, the voice that articulates what ought to be valid for all.

By universal art I therefore take Moraza to mean art as conceived and approved under the long regime of modernist aesthetics. This is the art of the canon – or rather it is art singled out under an aspect that renders its canonisation possible. It is the art that 'speaks for itself' to those that can hear, in the words of Clive Bell,[5] and that establishes itself through what Greenberg later described as a 'consensus of taste' among 'the people who've seen most . . . and who've worked most on what they've seen'.[6] This is the sense in which the art in question could be conceived of as universal. Though disinterested contemplation is primarily a condition of the Kantian aesthete, it was not only the critics who thought like this. If we ask what specifically qualified an artist for consideration as a modernist artist, the answer might be that he or she subscribed to the belief articulated by the sculptor Barbara Hepworth in 1937: that 'the language of colour and form is universal and not one for a special class . . . it is a thought which gives the same life, the same expansion, the same universal freedom to everyone'.[7]

As this quotation suggests, it was an item of faith among artists and writers in the modernist tradition that the aesthetic virtue they associated with the art in question was not simply independent of economic or utilitarian values; it offered a model of difference from the life in which such values were constitutive. Roger Fry referred to art as 'an expression and a stimulus of [the] imaginative life . . . a life freed from the binding necessities of our actual existence'.[8] And this is his colleague Clive Bell, writing in 1914:

> The artist and the saint do what they have to do, not to make a living, but in obedience to some mysterious necessity. They do not produce to live – they live to produce. There is no place for them in a social system based on the theory that what men desire is prolonged and pleasant existence. You cannot fit them into the machine, you must make them extraneous to it.[9]

Almost sixty years later, Greenberg responded in similar terms to a suggestion from T. J. Clark that the American Abstract Expressionists were ruled by straightforward art-market ambitions: 'They wouldn't do a thing just for the money. Good God, that was unthinkable.'[10]

According to this framework of ideas, artists' freedom from commercial interests and market ambitions is the guarantee of their independence and thus of the disinterested character of their production. Disinterest is in turn what sets the art loose from those contingencies in which it may be practically rooted, assuring it of potentially universal significance. The argument is of course circular, as modernist aesthetic theories so often are. Significantly, there is a suggestion that what is practically entailed by the process in question is a decrease in dependence on the appearance of things in the world and an increase in the priority accorded to decorative or abstract properties. Where complexity is conceived as a value within this framework of ideas, what is meant is thus not an increase in the figurative detail and density of paintings and sculptures, but rather an intensification of the demands made on the spectator – a stepping-up of the apperceptive competences required in response to the work of art. It is not the variety of the observed world that generates complexity as thus conceived; rather it results from some significant lack of fit between the world as lived and the imaginary world the work of art proposes. To refer back to Kant again, where the conventional work may adhere to existing rules, it is characteristic of the work of genius that it creates new ones. It is, as it were, the moment of an epistemological crisis. Viewed in this light, a black square in 1915 becomes a possibly more complex thing than a nude on a patterned background. The typical heroes in the modernist narrative as thus conceived are ascetics, mystic seers and *idiots savants*: Cézanne alone with the Mont Sainte-Victoire, Mondrian in his monastic cell in Paris, Pollock in the barn at Springs.

⁘ ⁘ ⁘

My purpose in citing what is by now a fairly standard account of modernist theory has been to emphasise both the familiarity and the relative antiquity of the ideas at issue. We need some sense of the rootedness and pervasiveness of a system of ideas that has actually been under constant attack since the 1960s. A clearer view of the defences our intellectual instruments were initially adopted to assail may help us to understand the deployment of those instruments in the critical discourse of the intervening years. It may also help us to explain why art might subsequently have become subject to the 'crisis of legitimacy' that Moraza refers to at the outset of his paper.

Of all the modernist positions undermined in the revisionist art history and criticism of the late 1960s and early 1970s, none was subject to so sustained an assault as the claimed connection between disinterestedness and universality. Renascent as it was in the cultural and historical studies of the time, the Marxist intellectual tradition provided a powerful resource of scepticism in the face of such claims. Given the idealisation of the artist as one who lives to work, historical materialism reminds us that what defines humans as a species with a history is that we have to work to live – that we must provide the means of our own subsistence. And given the idealisation of the critic as the organ of a disinterested taste, the same resource of theory invites us to consider the highly specific position of the modernist critic within class society, as spokesperson for the advanced interests and preferences of the educated bourgeoisie. The consequence of pursuing analyses along such lines as these was to reinsert the artists into the social history from which standard modernist theory had abstracted them, and to make clear not only that they too 'did it for the money', but that their avant-garde interests were bound to those of an avant-garde constituency of writers, connoisseurs, dealers and collectors.[11] If it could be shown that the art in question was in some significant sense *for* that constituency, the claim to universality would clearly be vulnerable; while if the values promulgated by the critics could be justifiably associated with one class or social section rather than another, the claim to disinterest would seem to be unsupportable.

To arguments such as these, feminist art historians subsequently added an account of Modernism as a patriarchal system. In their view, any claims for the universality of artistic values were liable to be undermined by the female fifty per cent of the human population that went unconsidered when universality was defined. The chorus of critical voices was swelled again during the 1980s and 1990s, when writers claiming to represent the interests of the formerly colonised pointed to the imperialistic character of the modernist canon, and to its tendency to exclude, to patronise, to disparage or to exploit the artistic productions of non-Western peoples. In this revisionist art history the traditional heroes were supplemented or even supplanted by others. First to be elevated were men whose exaggerated worldliness appeared suddenly as an interesting virtue: Marcel Duchamp, dandy, manipulator and entrepreneur; Francis Picabia, cynic and socialite; and Andy Warhol, who, when advised to paint what he was most fond of, produced a silkscreened picture of dollar bills. Joined to these was a quota of women seen as victorious in the face of patriarchy: Lee Krasner emerging from the shadow of her husband, Louise Bourgeois from the shadow of her father. More recently we have seen the perplexing art of native Australians advanced as evidence of the sheer inadequacy and irrelevance of traditional modernist values.

At their inception during the late 1960s and the 1970s, revisionist ideas such as these were pursued concurrently with that internal crisis in the development of modernist art that was the Conceptual Art movement. With that movement the fifty-year adventure of abstract art was effectively brought to a close, except in so far as an ahistorical eclecticism might sustain it. More generally, the prominence of Conceptual Art entailed a sharp decline in the status and plausibility of the high-art media of painting and sculpture in particular and of the autographic object in general. From now on, it seemed, the identification of something as an art work could be made independently of any reference to traditionally sanctioned genres or media, nor need it involve any expectation of physical stability or permanence.

The pursuit of revisionist ideas within the small world of art history also coincided with much larger theoretical programmes that announced the failure of the Enlightenment project, the collapse of the grand narratives and the general onset of the post-modern condition – a condition in which it seemed that disinterest was implausible or unattainable or both. The marked tendency of post-modernist theories was to look sceptically at any claims to cultural dominance or centrality, to think rather in terms of patterns of difference, and to advance the cause of the marginal, the excluded and the hybrid in place of the mainstream typically celebrated in modernist criticism.

It is in the light of these circumstances and of their consequences that I anticipate some difficulty in reaching agreement where developments in recent art are concerned. To put the matter crudely, if art can be anything, if its development is unrestrained by any intrinsic and medium-specific nexus of problems, and if critical judgements are reducible to the reflections of different interests on the part of different constituencies, then the best we can hope for in our deliberations on the theme of 'Art and Learning' is that there will be some purely arbitrary convergences. As I understand it, the 'crisis of legitimacy' referred to by Moraza is consequent on just such a circumstance. If *anything* is allowed to be art, then we will need to make a further distinction if we are to keep going to some critical purpose.

✣ ✣ ✣

I mean in due course to moderate this rather pessimistic conclusion. First, though, I would like to revisit this account of Modernism and its supposed overthrow, and to draw some threads together by means of a kind of anecdote. It concerns a project in the broad area of art and learning that I was personally involved in some twenty-five years ago. I was then working for the British Open University, a distance-teaching institution that runs courses for students who study principally at home in their spare time. The courses consist of extensive written and printed materials accompanied by radio and television broadcasts. A normal course is produced by a team of academics, working with editors and producers. It is designed to run for nine months at a time, with an examination at the end. A given course may be presented annually over a period of about ten years. Some courses require cohorts of students to come together for a week in residence during the summer.

Soon after I first joined the Open University in the late 1970s I was involved in the design and production of a new course on modern art. In a spirit of post-modernist retrospection, we called it 'Modern Art and Modernism: from Manet to Pollock'. It was to have a summer school as an important component, with students coming to London for seminars and for visits to the principal museums. Those of us in intellectual charge of the course had a particular aim in mind. We meant to characterise the modernist narrative of art history that we saw as morally exhausted but still dominant, and to subject it to critical and sceptical scrutiny. We identified Greenberg as that narrative's most sophisticated and influential exponent. The beliefs we aimed specifically to undermine were those that connected claims for the disinterestedness of aesthetic judgements to claims for the universality of artistic values. We attributed these beliefs to a kind of paradigm modernist aesthete. Opposed to this figure in our somewhat Manichaean imaginings was the social historian of art, whose principal weapons were those of historical materialism and class analysis. To put the matter crudely, if an artist such as Degas was represented in standard modernist accounts as a radical innovator in the representation of the human form, we would note the tendency to anti-Semitism suggested by his support for the case against Dreyfus and ask how much he paid his models. We saw ourselves as engaged on a project of constructive demystification. Some of those involved in the writing and teaching of 'Modern Art and Modernism' saw themselves with some justice as representatives of a working class whose cultural interests had been betrayed by a modernist aestheticisation of modern art.[12]

We had expected controversy. In many ways the course succeeded beyond our wildest dreams. Some five hundred students enrolled in the first year, and they were dramatically divided in their responses. One large component saw us as politically motivated philistines, who were abusing our positions as teachers to mount a Marxist assault on the values of high culture. But another large component rejoiced in the fact that the snobbery associated with high culture was being brought out into the open, and that art was being discussed as a social practice subject to the same kinds of basic considerations as any other. A minority so small as to be virtually invisible understood that the two positions might perhaps be dialectically related. (It has to be said that this was not an understanding that the course altogether encouraged.) In any event, in the early years of the course, we were more or less assured of heated argument within any given student group, and of a rapid exposure of class differences in the process of debate. We took this as a measure of the success of our project.

As the 1980s progressed and the course aged, the atmosphere of controversy was gradually dissipated. In the larger academic world the social history of art was fast being established as the new conventional wisdom, and the kinds of objection we had been levelling at modernist criticism and theory were becoming common currency. Our own work was in turn subjected to criticism from feminist colleagues, who wondered how we could devote so much attention to the class-character of modernist culture while ignoring its palpably patriarchal aspect. Others remarked on the relative conservatism of our concentration on painting and sculpture at the expense of photography and print, and so on. Finally, around the time the course was brought to a close in the early 1990s, we were beginning to hear critical comments on the Eurocentrism of our regard. By then, of course, the tide had turned and the critique of Modernism had become accepted as a kind of common sense – especially by those who had never really grasped the theoretical aspect of Modernism in the first place. The student body now knew what to expect and those who signed up for the course were generally content with what they received.

To return to the early 1980s, however, during the first few annual presentations of 'Modern Art and Modernism' there were some students who were made deeply uncomfortable by the approach we took. It should be borne in mind that the Open University is a national institution and that its operations are relatively public. Our printed materials are widely available, and the television programmes we made for the course were broadcast over the national BBC network. Some of the discomforted students dealt with their sense of affront by complaining to their parliamentary representatives. At a certain point the Minister for Education in Margaret Thatcher's Conservative government warned the Vice-Chancellor of the university that a potential problem was brewing in one of its courses. We were unrepentant. If anything, we were encouraged. About a year later, however, in 1985, we received from the Head of Art History a large professionally produced document, complete with apparently scholarly apparatus of references and bibliography. It came under seal of absolute confidentiality, accompanied by an instruction to read it carefully and to prepare our response. The Head of Art History had received this document from the Dean of Arts, who had received it from the Vice-Chancellor. It had come to him from the government Department of Education and Science, with a covering note describing it as 'an apparently well-researched and substantiated piece of criticism' to which the university would need to respond.

The document opened with the statement that the aims of the course 'Modern Art and Modernism' were 'both revolutionary and subversive', that its 'method of procedure' was derived from Leninism, and that its 'ultimate objective' was 'the destruction of the democratic parliamentary system' – a matter about which the government ought surely to be concerned.[13] It continued for some fifty closely typed pages in the same style, driven by the absurd logic of the self-righteously paranoid. At least in the form in which the university received it, the document was unsigned. Internal evidence suggested that it had been produced by a semi-autonomous right-wing organisation, which had funded at least two people to follow the entire nine-month course, including the week of residence at the summer school, with the explicit aim of producing a written critique.

Our response was that the authors were clearly unhinged and that if they would like to identify themselves, we would be happy to debate with them in any public forum of their choice. But the management of the university would not allow this response to go forward. They were perhaps worried that there might be some truth in the allegations. Over the next six months a series of grey-suited persons subjected us to various forms of inquisition, and crawled all over the drafts of course materials and the minutes of course-team meetings, before finally responding to the Minister for Education to the effect that all was in order and that this was just a case of disagreement on academic issues. On the one hand we felt deeply compromised by the institution that employed us. On the other, some of my colleagues felt powerfully vindicated in their understanding of the undemocratic character of modernist culture. Specifically, they took the attack on the course as conclusive evidence that claims for disinterest in aesthetic judgement and for the universality of artistic values were the effective means by which oppressive powers naturalised their actual and thoroughly political interests.

⁂

My own response to these events was more mixed. I think there were two reasons for this. The first was my abiding involvement with the artistic practice of Art & Language. Not only had Art & Language been involved in the Conceptual Art movement of the late 1960s and early 1970s but it had also tended to treat the radical pretensions of the social history of art with at least as great a scepticism as it did the modernist aesthetics of Greenberg and others. Art & Language's work of the 1970s addressed an artistic culture forgetful or grown complacent with respect to its own radical history. It offered a strategic resistance both to the prevailing modes of consumption of art and to the primordial spectator proposed in modernist theory. But in occupying the space of painting with works that were texts of one kind or another, Art & Language was not necessarily disparaging the notion of a primarily visual art; rather we were seeking to re-establish a notion of art as a dialectical practice of *thought*, and of spectatorship as an activity that might require assiduous effort. We were highly sceptical of any mode of interpretation for which virtue was claimed in the terms of a practical politics.[14]

The second reason for my mixed response was a chance reading of an editorial statement which appeared in one of the British tabloid newspapers at about the time that 'Modern Art and Modernism' was first launched. According to the writer's argument, notions of disinterest and of the universality of cultural values are the deceptions by means of which a self-appointed elite restricts competition, prevents the evolution of more efficient systems and undemocratically imposes its taste on the population. The author of this text was the global press baron Rupert Murdoch, whom no one could have mistaken for a Marxist-Leninist revolutionary. His real target was the licence fee levied on all those in Britain who possess a television set, the proceeds of which go to fund the BBC and to preserve its precarious independence from commercial and political pressures. In the Darwinian economic world of Murdoch and his ilk, a guarantee of independence such as this amounts to unfair protection from competition. Murdoch was one of those whose empire was enlarged dramatically under the regimes of Ronald Reagan and Margaret Thatcher, and as a consequence of the economic policies they espoused and implemented. Understood very crudely, what those policies amounted to was that the brakes should be taken off capitalism; that systems of regulation were simply inhibiting to economic vitality and to modernisation.

Belief in the need for regulation in the economic field tends to imply some faith in the possibility of disinterest – or at least of principle. That is, it presupposes that there are certain kinds of decision that ought not to be taken by those who have a stake in their outcomes. Such notions may be associated with the gentlemanly ideals of the Kantian Enlightenment. In the era of the post-modern, however, the Enlightenment project was seen as finally exhausted – the ideal of disinterest exposed as a cover for the controlling agency of self-appointed and sluggish elites.

For all that our Western economies may still retain a formal disapproval of insider trading, what we have actually seen over the past twenty-five years or so is a massive professionalisation of the economic field. At the same time, the competitive ethos of commercial enterprise has been insinuated into virtually all areas of public life. In my own sphere of higher education, students have been recast as customers, with rival institutions competing aggressively for their attention. Those of us who previously assumed a willing responsibility for deciding what ought to be taught and learned are now advised by a marketing department about what it is that is desired by the university's potential consumers. I see an inescapable parallel with the kind of hectic trading in short-term commodities that has become the typical mode of life in the international art-world.

⁂

I will try to extract a kind of moral from my anecdote. My main point, of course, is that in discounting the principle of disinterest we risk leaving the arts as wide open as our other social practices have become to the manipulative models of operation remarked by Moraza: those of the businessman, the cultural manager, the media communicator and the political activist. In the sphere of education we remove a traditional safeguard against manipulation masquerading as teaching. Those anonymous authors who attacked the Open University's course were repellent, deluded and potentially sinister. In so far as they spoke for a kind of authority vested in high culture, that authority thoroughly deserved to be undermined. But it does not follow from our status as their targets that our own motives were unimpeachable, nor that our teaching was free from the urge to manipulate. It is a sobering thought that it may have been our inflated sense of ourselves as left-wing intellectuals that prevented us from perceiving how much our arguments against the claim to disinterest had in common with those of rapacious free-market capitalists like Rupert Murdoch.

It was always a mistake, I think, to conceive of Modernism as an ideology of art opposed to the interests of the working class. The real target of the modernist aesthetes, from the mid-nineteenth century to the mid-twentieth, was the rising commercial faction of their own bourgeois class. For all their efforts, this is the section that has effectively been in power for the past quarter century. It appears in its typical form as modern management. It is busy remaking culture in its own image. Art schools used once to be populated by interesting misfits. Now every student has a business plan. This is a world in which disinterest has entirely lost its Kantian meaning. As the result of a kind of journalistic transformation, to say that one is disinterested is now understood as meaning that one is *un*interested. In the managed culture of artistic spectacle, disinterest has come to signify boredom.

So far as art is concerned, in denying the possibility of a disinterested regard, we risk transforming the work of interpretation into a constant and anxious search for issues and tendencies. To the extent that we do this, we traduce the art in question, reducing the difficult and exceptional to the status of evidence. We should not mistake academic arguments about art for what it is that art may have to teach us. If art is in some sense a mode of thought, it is not simply translatable or interpretable – not separable from its content. It is significant, I think, that none of the major theorists of Modernism was an academic or an art historian. All were either artists or practising critics or both, and they were for the most part reluctant to deal in the kinds of issue-mongering that preoccupy many of today's writers on art. It is also significant that the formal analysis of works of art – by which I mean the difficult enterprise of description, apart from the mere tracking of anecdotal detail – went out of fashion with Modernism itself. Indeed it is now widely assumed that Modernism and formalism are interchangeable terms, both or either serving to connote a culpable indifference to social and historical reality.[15]

Yet it is at the level of form that the complexity of art is actually recognised – when art is indeed complex, and when that complexity is indeed sensed. Or perhaps the point should be put another way: what is complex in art may in part be revealed in the enterprise of description, but it will also be acknowledged as a kind of remainder at the point where description runs out; we need a term by which to refer to whatever unity it is that is both contained within the limits of description and sensed beyond them; 'form' is the term we are accustomed to use. Of course any object will present a kind of remainder – an ineffable whole substance – in the face of description. The point is that that remainder is not ordinarily of much concern to us. In the case of art it is. We do not often know why. But if it is indeed the case that art is a kind of learning, then this is presumably the reason. We might say that art is complex in knowing something about the world that we do not, but that *how* it knows it is a technical matter; that is to say it is a matter specific to the use of a given medium.

And so, finally, I return to a connection I noted earlier, the connection between devaluation of disinterest and loss of complexity that I see as implied in Moraza's paper. In so far as that paper describes a cultural situation in the present, I take it that it suggests a certain deficiency in art now: one that the connection in question serves to indicate. And yet the project in whose name this paper was invited speaks of turning difficulties into opportunities, and proposes that we recognise art as a significant producer of learning – and as a field of activity in which the learning of our period may achieve its highest and most problematic aspect. The missing ingredient, it seems to me, is the exemplary art by reference to which this project can be sustained.

In making this observation I mean neither to suggest a failing in Moraza's paper nor to play the old fool and bemoan the current state of art. I take it that the search for an art capable of bearing the weight of our expectations is both a central and an inviting part of the project of Art and Learning. No one should be surprised if my own expectations are set by reference to the practice of Art & Language, given that my association with that practice is a matter of record. It is in the studio of Art & Language, in the presence of its production and in occasional contribution to that production that much of my own learning gets done. That association apart, however, I cannot nowadays claim to keep myself well informed about the plethora of work that is available to view in the art centres of the world; and since I can only speak with any confidence about the little that I have seen at first hand, I am clearly in no position to prescribe the art that we ought to be looking at. What I can do, however, with a mind to the arguments I have tried to represent here, is imagine what I might hope for from a work of art that was the deserving object of some significant process of learning.

First some negative considerations. Though I cannot speak securely about writing in other languages than English, I am aware of a recent tendency for commentary on art in the English language to fall into one or other of two modes. The first is the valedictory. Here the critical essay effectively represents artists' reasons and rationales as if they were adequate definitions of the enterprise, with no attempt to take account of what might under other cultural conditions be seen as external measures of significance or defining problem fields. In this mode the critical essay is virtually indistinguishable from the press release. The second mode is the radical. Possessed by a sense of their own oppositional status, writers in this mode tend to divide the objects of their scrutiny into the complicit and the subversive, critical approbation being reserved entirely for the latter. All too often, however, the requirement of subversiveness is seen as satisfied by mere postures of dissent from the prevailing order, by an untidy experimentalism in the use of unconventional materials, or by some combination of the two.

We have to do better than this. I would therefore be suspicious of an art that in any sense rendered itself client to the interpretive models mentioned by Moraza: those of the businessman, the cultural manager, the media communicator or the political activist – and to these I would add the self-enchanted curator. And I would be equally suspicious of an art that wore its oppositional testimonials on its sleeve, or that seemed grounded in the fallacy that messing about with unconventional media is a guarantee of critical effect. I would also be suspicious of art that edged too close to the typical manners of the mass media. During the 1970s it was believed by many that a progressive breakdown of technical barriers between the fine arts and the media of mass-communication would lead to a constructive infiltration of the symbolic order and a subversion of its prevailing codes. My impression is that the traffic has mostly been in the other direction. Subversiveness is now a career choice. Think of the entertaining squibs of Banksy.

To speak more positively, I would look for complexity in the sense I have tried to expound; that is, I would look for an art that teaches us about the problems of representation, and by virtue of doing so teaches us something about the world represented; an art that requires of its spectators – of us, the potential community of learners – that we do not, cannot, put it to use for our own established ends. In the cultural economy of managed desire, it is disinterest that is radical. We should not make the mistake of assuming that disinterest implies a masterful understanding. On the contrary. If we recognise this art as somehow good, it will not be because we know how to consume it. We may well be deeply confused by it. The art I have in mind will be internally complex, but in such a manner as to provoke external reference. It will be highly exceptional, as art at its most demanding always is. This is to say that there will not be much of it. I have no idea what it might look like. But in so far as I can imagine what the encounter with it might be like, I imagine learning.

# NOTES

## 1 SCULPTURE'S RECENT PAST

1 This and the following quotations are from Herbert Read, 'Introduction' to *Sculpture: Open-air exhibition of contemporary British and American works*, London County Council, Battersea Park, 1963.

2 The term 'Middle Generation' was first used by the painter Patrick Heron for an exhibition of work by himself, Roger Hilton and Bryan Wynter (all artists associated with St Ives in Cornwall) at the Waddington Galleries in May 1959. 'It expressed the awareness of painters aged between 30 and 45 in 1956 [the year the exhibition *Modern Art in the United States* was shown in London] that they were no longer the youngest generation. They had lost valuable years in the war, had been laboriously building something out of the remnants of modern art left in Europe in the late forties, and now had to come to terms with American painting.' Alan Bowness, 'The American Invasion and the British Response', *Studio International* 173, 890 (June 1967): 290.

3 Alan Bowness, 'Introduction' to *Sculpture in the Open Air*, Greater London Council, Battersea Park, 1966.

4 Ibid.

5 Clement Greenberg, 'The Decline of Cubism', *Partisan Review* 15 (March 1948): 366–9.

6 The phrase is Michael Baldwin's from his script for 'Beaubourg', a television programme for the Open University, in *A315: Modern Art and Modernism; Manet to Pollock*, TV 32, Milton Keynes, Open University, 1983.

7 This is a conflation of the titles of two relevant articles: Bowness, 1966, and Patrick Heron, 'A Kind of Cultural Imperialism?' *Studio International* 175, 897 (February 1968): 62–4.

8 Two large exhibitions at the Tate Gallery were of particular importance in alerting British audiences to the quality of 'first generation' (Abstract Expressionist) American painting: *Modern Art in the United States*, 5 January–12 February 1956, and *New American Painting*, 24 February–22 March 1959.

9 See n. 2.

10 *Situation* was held at the R.B.A. Galleries in London in September 1960. The members of the organising committee were Lawrence Alloway, Bernard Cohen, Roger Coleman, Robyn Denny, Gordon House, Henry Mundy, Hugh Shaw and

William Turnbull. The exhibitors were Gillian Ayres, Bernard and Harold Cohen, Peter Coviello, Denny, John Epstein, William Green, Peter Hobbs, House, John Hoyland, Robert Law, Mundy, John Plumb, Ralph Rumney, Richard Smith, Peter Stroud, Turnbull, Mark Vaux and Brian Young.

11 *New London Situation* was held at the New London Galleries in 1961 and included Caro's painted steel sculpture *The Horse* (collection of Mr and Mrs David Mirvish, Toronto), completed that year.

12 Though there was a considerable representation of American sculpture in the Tate's 1956 show *Modern Art in the United States*, no work by David Smith was included. The first considerable showing of his work in England came in August 1966, when the Museum of Modern Art's touring retrospective arrived at the Tate Gallery.

13 Patrick Heron, 'The Americans at the Tate Gallery', *Arts* 30, 6 (March 1956): 15–17.

14 The organisers of the *Situation* exhibition had excluded the St Ives painters from consideration on the grounds that works should be 'without explicit reference to events outside the painting – landscape, boats, figures' (from Roger Coleman, 'Introduction' to 'Situation' catalogue, 1960). In such terms the younger artists of the 1960s recognised that division between the generations which the older artists had sensed at the close of the previous decade (see n. 2).

15 In 1963–4 and during the spring of 1965, Caro taught sculpture at Bennington College, Vermont. He continued teaching part-time at St Martin's on his return to London, with a break in 1967. Many of those first subject to his teaching at St Martin's had enrolled in evening classes. The main business of the sculpture department was the provision of a three-year course leading to the award of a diploma. Alongside this an 'advanced sculpture course' had developed in response to the conservatism of the official syllabus during the late 1950s. At a time of government reorganisation of art education, the school's application for accreditation as a postgraduate centre for sculpture was rejected in favour of the Chelsea School of Art (where both David Nash [1969–70] and Richard Deacon [1977–8] were to complete their studies). The advanced course at St Martin's therefore remained 'vocational' and relatively independent of institutional requirements. As a consequence of this, and of its growing reputation, it attracted many students from abroad. In the early and mid-1960s, during a period of relative financial ease, the tendency was for promising ex-students to be taken on as part-time tutors, thus maintaining continuity and a line of succession.

16 In Lawrence Alloway, 'Interview with Anthony Caro', *Gazette* (London) 1 (1961): 1.

17 Phillip King, 'Phillip King talks about his sculpture', *Studio International* 175, 901 (June 1968): 300.

18 Clement Greenberg, 'Anthony Caro', in *Arts Yearbook 8: Contemporary*

*Sculpture* (1965); reprinted in *Studio International* 174, 892 (September 1967): 116–17.

19 As quoted by Philip Leider, the reason given was 'the high quality of the work he made in this country and the influence he exerted on the new American sculpture'. Philip Leider, 'American Sculpture at the Los Angeles County Museum of Art', *Artforum* 5, 10 (Special Issue, Summer 1967): 80. Leider commented, 'one looks about in vain for the Caro-influenced sculpture. For the truth is that most of Caro's influence has been in England, among a promising group of younger English sculptors.'

20 Originally published as 'The pasted-paper revolution', *Art News* 57, 5 (September 1958). Greenberg restored his own title when printing the essay in substantially revised form in his *Art and Culture*, Boston, Mass., Beacon Press, 1961.

21 Quotation from the original 1958 version, reprinted in Francis Frascina and Charles Harrison, eds, *Modern Art and Modernism: A Critical Anthology*, London and New York, Harper and Row, 1982: 107.

22 William Tucker, 'An Essay on Sculpture', *Studio International* 177, 907 (January 1969): 13.

23 Anthony Caro in Alloway, 1961.

24 Tim Scott, 'Reflections on Sculpture: A Commentary by Tim Scott on Notes by William Tucker', in *Tim Scott: Sculpture 1961–67*, London, Whitechapel Art Gallery, 1967.

25 'I cannot conceive a work and buy material for it. I can find or discover a part. . . . Rarely the Grand Conception but a preoccupation with parts. I start with one part, then a unit of parts, until a whole appears. . . . The order of the whole can be perceived but not planned. Logic and verbiage and wisdom will get in the way. I believe in perception as the highest order of recognition. My faith in it comes as close to an ideal as I have. When I work there is no consciousness of ideals – but intuition and impulse.' David Smith, 'Notes on My Work', *Arts* 34, 5 (February 1960); reprinted in *First* 2, a magazine published in 1961 by members of the advanced sculpture course at St Martin's and edited by William Tucker, p. 34. 'This whole operation for me doesn't come out of a concept in the mind, it comes out of some vague idea, plus the stuff.' 'Anthony Caro, interviewed by Andrew Forge', *Studio International* 171, 873 (January 1966): 6–9.

26 King, 1968.

27 William Tucker, statement in *First* 2 (1961): 23. In an editorial in the same issue, Tucker wrote, 'The problems here implied for sculpture are immense and serious, but open. Everything has yet to be done, and soon' (p. 4).

28 Greenberg, September 1967: 117.

29 Annesley, Waddington Galleries, 1966; Bolus, Waddington Galleries, 1965; King,

Rowan Gallery, 1964; Scott, Waddington Galleries, 1966; Tucker, Grabowski Gallery, 1962, Rowan Gallery, 1963 and 1966; Witkin, Rowan Gallery, 1963, Waddington Galleries, 1966.

30 Edward Lucie-Smith, ed., 'An interview with Clement Greenberg', *Studio International* 175, 896 (January 1968): 117. That this was not a conclusion recently arrived at is demonstrated by a letter addressed in February 1964 to Frank Martin, head of the sculpture department at St Martin's. The advanced sculpture course was threatened with closure and Greenberg, who had visited the department the previous October, now responded to a request for support:

> St Martin's under the present dispensation should be one of the prides of England, and not just because some of its faculty and some of its graduates are producing the most distinctive, the strongest new sculpture done anywhere in the world at this time. . . .
>
> No other art school I know of can match what St Martin's is doing in fruitfulness. No other art school I know of can achieve such results of such importance either pedagogically or artistically. No other art school manifests a spirit nearly so invigorating and at the same time mature; no other art school demands so much of its students.
>
> All this . . . has . . . to do with the ambitious seriousness St Martin's appears to instil in its students, and with the entire absence of artiness and dilettantism in the atmosphere of the school.

The letter was published in facsimile in *Going* 1 (1964): 8. *Going* was a magazine printed and published by the St Martin's school of Art Students Union.

31 Quoted by Nena Dimitrijevic in *Bruce McLean*, London, Whitechapel Art Gallery, 1981.

32 I have attempted elsewhere to fill out this view of the development of modernist art since Pollock. See the following articles: 'Modernism and the "Transatlantic Dialogue"', in Francis Frascina, ed., *Pollock and After: The Critical Debate*, London and New York, Harper and Row, 1985: 217–32; and 'Expression and Exhaustion: Art and Criticism in the Sixties', *Artscribe* 56 (February–March 1986): 44–9, and 57 (April–May 1986): 32–5.

33 Michael Fried, 'Art and Objecthood', *Artforum* 5, 10 (Special Issue, Summer 1967): 12–23.

34 As well as the article cited in n. 33, see Michael Fried, 'New Work by Anthony Caro', *Artforum* 5, 6 (February 1967): 46–7; 'Two Sculptures by Anthony Caro', *Artforum* 6, 6 (February 1968): 24–5; 'Caro's Abstractness', *Artforum* 9, 1 (September 1970): 32–4; and 'Introduction' to *Anthony Caro*, London, Arts Council of Great Britain, Hayward Gallery, 1969.

35 See esp. Michael Fried's *Three American Painters: Kenneth Noland, Jules Olitski, Frank Stella*, Cambridge, Mass., Fogg Art Museum, Harvard University, 1965.

36 'When it's sculpture, it's to be looked at. Sculpture, for me, is something outside of which you are. It's not something you can get inside; it's not architecture or environment. I put this limit on sculpture and I think that by doing so, I gain more freedom, not less.' Anthony Caro in Phyllis Tuchman, 'An Interview with Anthony Caro', *Artforum* 10, 10 (June 1972): 57.
37 Fried, February 1968: 25.
38 Anthony Caro in Tuchman, June 1972.
39 The classic formulation of this dilemma is to be found in Walter Benjamin's address, 'The Author as Producer'; for an edited version see Frascina and Harrison, 1982: 213–16. See also Art & Language, 'Author and Producer revisited', in Charles Harrison and Fred Orton, eds, *Modernism, Criticism, Realism: Alternative Contexts for Art*, London and New York, Harper and Row, 1984: 251–9.
40 Tucker, January 1969.
41 Flanagan attended as a student 1964–6, Long 1966–8, Woodrow 1968–71, and Deacon 1969–72. The two former were in the 'advanced' course, the latter in the three-year diploma course. Flanagan taught part-time at St Martin's from 1967. Both Woodrow (1971–2) and Deacon spent time as postgraduate students at the Chelsea School of Art. Deacon also attended the Royal College of Art as a student from 1974 to 1977, where he was the near contemporary of Tony Cragg.
42 Sculptors working at Stockwell Depot in 1968–9 were Alan Barclay, Roland Brener, David Evison, Roger Fagin, John Fowler, Gerard Hemsworth, Peter Hyde and Roelof Louw.
43 Roland Brener, 'The Concerns of Emerging Sculptors', *Studio International* 177, 907 (January 1969): 25.
44 Turnbull showed with the Middle Generation sculptors at the Venice Biennale in 1952. His work of the 1950s was marked by an interest in Giacometti, and later in Brancusi, which served to distinguish it from those working in a line of clear succession from Moore. In the late 1950s and early 1960s, his interest in a totemic and animistic kind of sculpture distinguished him from Caro and the New Generation. Despite their superficial resemblance to other contemporary British works, his abstract, painted sculptures of the mid-1960s were actually closer in spirit to his own painting, and to the work of Barnett Newman, by which he had been considerably affected.
45 'Anthony Caro's work: A Symposium by Four Sculptors', *Studio International* 177, 907 (January 1969): 20.
46 Clement Greenberg, 'After Abstract Expressionism', *Art International* 6, 8 (October 1962): 28.
47 Fried, Summer 1967: 21.
48 Donald Judd, 'Specific Objects', *Arts Yearbook* 8: *Contemporary Sculpture* (1965): 74–82.

49 Robert Smithson, 'Entropy and the New Monuments', *Artforum* 4, 10 (June 1966): 26–31.

50 Robert Morris, 'Notes on Sculpture', *Artforum* 4, 6 (February 1966): 40.

51 Robert Morris, 'Notes on Sculpture, Part 3: Notes and nonsequiturs', *Artforum* 5, 10 (Special Issue, Summer 1967): 29. 'Part 2' was published in *Artforum* 5, 2 (October 1966): 20–23, and 'Part 4' in the same journal in April 1969 (7, 8): 50–54.

52 Material for the April 1969 *Studio International* was largely assembled by the American writer Barbara Reise, who had published a two-part 'exposé' of 'Greenberg and the Group' the previous year, *Studio International* 175, 900 (May 1968): 254–7, and 175, 901 (June 1968): 314–15. The editors of *Studio* were not unaware of the advantage to be gained by importing a faction-fight started in American publications. Judd's 'Complaints part I', published in the *Studio International* special issue, 177, 910 (April 1969): 82–4, was in part a response to adverse criticism from Greenberg (especially his essay 'The Recentness of Sculpture') and to Fried's 'Art and Objecthood'. Judd also addressed their estimation of Caro:

> Caro is a conventional, competent second-generation artist. I don't understand the link between Noland and Caro, since wholeness is basic to Noland's work and Cubist fragmentation is basic to Caro's. I think Caro had his first show in New York in December 1964. Di Suvero first showed his somewhat similar but far better sculpture in October 1960; by 1964 di Suvero had a tiresome number of followers and Caro's work looked like that of just another of them.

Judd had the excuse of provocation but the concluding imputation was certainly unjust.

53 Tate Gallery, April–June 1969. *The Art of the Real* was a crowded and incoherent exhibition which did little to satisfy those impatient for a representative showing of Minimal Art in England – and even less to interest those inclined to dismiss it.

54 The phrase is taken from Noam Chomsky, *Reflections on Language*, London, Fontana, 1976, excerpted in Harrison and Orton, 1984: 263:

> Suppose that the social and material conditions that prevent free intellectual development were relieved, at least for some substantial number of people. Then, science, mathematics and art would flourish, pressing on towards the limits of cognitive capacity. At these limits . . . we find various forms of intellectual play, and significant differentiation among individuals who vary little within the domain of cognitive capacity. As creative minds approach the limits of cognitive capacity, not only will the act of creation be limited to a talented few, but even the appreciation or comprehension of what has been created. If cognitive domains are roughly comparable in complexity and potential scope,

> such limits might be approached at more or less the same time in various domains, giving rise to a 'crisis of modernism', marked by a sharp decline in the general accessibility of the products of creative minds, a blurring of the distinction between art and puzzle, and a sharp increase in 'professionalism' in intellectual life, affecting not only those who produce creative work but also its potential audience. . . . It may be that something of the sort has been happening in recent history . . .

55 Anthony Caro, from an interview with Noel Channon, broadcast on Granada Television, September 1974, printed in Diane Waldman, *Anthony Caro*, Oxford, Phaidon, 1982: 34.

56 See e.g. the (somewhat euphoric) testimony of David Annesley as given in the *Studio International* symposium (January 1969):

> Other people said, 'Oh, you can do that Tony? I mean is it all right to do that?' He said, 'Yes, you don't have to look at all that other stuff, enough time for that later, that's all been done. Let's look at some of these new things. How about making sculpture out of feathers? Can we make it out of a balloon? Ooh, would it be nice out of cushions?' All these lovely ideas he had. 'What can you do with it? Can you make it out of anything? What are the rules? Are there any rules at all?' It was like he was jumping around in a thousand different directions at once.

57 Tucker in Scott, 1967.

58 Though the immediate impression conveyed by *Prairie* is of a visually integrated whole, one element (composed of one of the four horizontal and parallel poles, the vertical plate which supports it and another smaller plate joined to this at floor level) is physically separate and free-standing. Realisation of this comes as something of a surprise. Caro has paid tribute to the role of his assistant in the making of the sculpture; interview in Waldman, 1982: 50–52:

> *Prairie* is not merely an artwork – but my goodness, it's a work of engineering. Underneath *Prairie*, inside *Prairie*, is first of all a cradle which holds the wings together. The wings are two separate parts; they're held together underneath; and on top of that sits the corrugated steel and they're held together on top, to stop them flopping down, by a single tie. The whole thing comes to pieces, it's all spiggoted. It was clever of Charlie to make that, terribly clever of him to think out how that would work . . .

59 See Greenberg, September 1967: 'By opening and extending a ground-hugging sculpture laterally, and inflecting it vertically in a way which accents the lateral movement, the plane of the ground is made to seem to move too; it ceases being the base or foil against which everything else moves, and takes its own part in the challenge to the force of gravity.'

60 This seemed to be a particularly important issue as regards Phillip King's work of 1966–8, in which he tried out various means to extend his sculptures spatially by making them of separated components. Some of the results appeared dangerously close to architectural and environmental installations. The impression created by individual works varied dramatically according to viewing conditions. His *Call* of 1967 (Tate Gallery, London) seemed plausible in its occupation of a single bay of the Whitechapel Art Gallery during his retrospective there in 1968, but the same sculpture had previously failed completely to hold its own outside the British pavilion at the Venice Biennale. Since the experimental and interesting *Blue Blaze* of 1968 (collection of Mrs John D. Murchison, U.S.), King has largely relied on actual physical integration to hold individual works together.

61 Barry Flanagan, 'From notes '67/8; dating from observations made in March '67 about three sculptures for Paris Biennale', *Studio International* 177, 907 (January 1969): 37. The colour photograph of the three works was reproduced, together with a statement by Flanagan, in *Studio International* 174, 892 (September 1967): 98–9.

62 Quoted in Charles Harrison, 'Some Recent Sculpture in Britain', *Studio International* 177, 907 (January 1969): 32.

63 A story current at the time told of Caro confronted by an arrangement of twigs in the exhibition hall of the St Martin's sculpture department. A conversation ensued. Caro: 'What's this?' Long: 'It's one part of a two-part sculpture.' Caro: 'So show me the other half.' Long: 'It's on top of Ben Nevis' (the mountain in Scotland). Caro: 'So how can I assess it when I can't see all of it?' The story is no doubt apocryphal. It is representative, however, of a host of similar conversations which certainly did take place in art schools all over Britain during the late 1960s and early 1970s. At one point, in 1971, a government official was required to rule that only 'tangible visual art objects' would be acceptable for submission for the diploma in Art and Design, at the time the national qualification awarded for satisfactory completion of a three-year course of study. See 'Some Concerns in Fine Art Education', *Studio International* 183, 937 (October 1971): 120–22, and 183, 938 (November 1971): 168–70. The question whether 'not producing objects' entailed 'not working' was one that bedevilled and divided British art education for some years after.

64 'On the Material-Character/Physical-Object Paradigm of Art' is the title of an article by Terry Atkinson and Michael Baldwin, published in *Art-Language* 2, 1 (February 1972): 51–5. The article was written in response to the publication of Richard Wollheim's lecture 'The Work of Art as Object' in *Studio International* 180, 928 (December 1970): 231–5 (see also the edited reprint in Harrison and Orton, 1984: 9–17). Wollheim had asserted that 'for the mainstream of modern art, the appropriate theory is one that emphasizes the material character of art,

a theory according to which a work is importantly, or significantly, and not just peripherally, a physical object'. Atkinson and Baldwin commented, 'If the statement is supposed to be retrospective, it's not so bad: we have been stuck with reism etc. Assume, however . . . that there is some predictive intent behind it. . . . What we may have here is a law-like statement which has been immunized against possible future experience insofar as, if an experience does not fit, so much the worse for the experience – rather than "so much the worse for the law-like statement."'

65 The termination of Latham's part-time contract at St Martin's coincided with his response to a request from the library for the return of *Art and Culture: Critical Essays*, Greenberg's collected essays. Latham returned a small phial of liquid distilled from chewed-up pages of the book. Some of the chewing had been done by sculpture students. The phial with its container – *Art and Culture* – is now in the collection of the Museum of Modern Art, New York.

66 John Latham in 'Where does the collision happen: John Latham in conversation with Charles Harrison', *Studio International* 175, 900 (May 1968): 259.

67 Flanagan to Caro, letter of June 7, 1963, printed in *Silâns* 6 (January 1965): n.p.

68 *Silâns* was a duplicated magazine edited in the St Martin's sculpture department by Barry Flanagan, Alistair Jackson and Rudi Leenders and circulated internally. Sixteen issues were published between September 1964 and June 1965.

69 For discussion and a bibliography on the relations between modernist critical theory and Cold War cultural policy, see Frascina, 1985.

70 See Harrison, 'Some Recent Sculpture in Britain', January 1969: 31

71 The other exhibitors were Bernhard Hoke, Konrad Lueg, Charlotte Posenenske and Peter Roehr. The exhibition was organised by Paul Maenz.

72 Artists included were Alice Adams, Louise Bourgeois, Eva Hesse, Gary Kuehn, Bruce Nauman, Don Potts, Keith Sonnier and Frank Lincoln Viner.

73 Robert Morris's article 'Anti Form' was published in *Artforum* 6, 8 (April 1968): 33–5.

74 *Prospekt* was co-organised by Konrad Fischer. Long's first one-person show was running concurrently at Fischer's gallery in Düsseldorf. This conjuncture must have helped to get Long's name spread around the international art community.

75 The other exhibitors in *Op Losse Schroeven* were Anselmo, d'Armagnac, Boezem, Bollinger, Buthe, Calzolari, Dekker, Dibbets, van Elk, Engels, Hoke, Icaro, Jalass, Kaks, Koetsier, Mario and Marisa Merz, Nauman, Panamarenko, Prini, Ryman, Simonetti, Viner, Weiner and Zorio. The other exhibitors in *When Attitudes become Form* were Andre, Anselmo, Artschwager, Bang, Bark, Berry, Beuys, Boetti, Bochner, Boezem, Bollinger, Buthe, Calzolari, Cotton, Darboven, De Maria, Dibbets, van Elk, Ferrer, Glass, Haacke, Heizer, Hesse, Huebler, Icaro, Jacquet, Jenney, Kaltenbach, Kaplan, Kienholz, Klein, Kosuth, Kounellis, Kuehn,

LeWitt, Lohaus, Merz, Morris, Nauman, Oldenburg, Oppenheim, Panamarenko, Pascali, Pechter, Pistoletto, Prini, Raetz, Ruppersberg, Ruthenbeck, Ryman, Sandback, Saret, Sarkis, Schnyder, Serra, Smithson, Sonnier, Tuttle, Walther, Wegman, Weiner, Wiley and Zorio. Victor Burgin was included in the London showing.

76 Grégoire Muller in *When Attitudes become Form*, Kunsthalle, Bern, 1969; original in French, my translation.

77 Printed as an opening slogan on the title page of the *Attitudes* catalogue.

78 Morris, 'Notes on Sculpture, Part 3' (Summer 1967): 25. Morris continued, 'Specifically, what is antique about it is the divisiveness of experience which marks on a flat surface elicit.'

79 For example, whatever visual delights may have been offered at the time by the works of, say, Daniel Buren, Sol LeWitt, Robert Ryman, Mel Bochner or Hanne Darboven, they were not such as to compete on equal ground with the paintings of Kenneth Noland, Jules Olitski or Larry Poons.

80 The original members, Terry Atkinson, David Bainbridge, Michael Baldwin and Harold Hurrell, had variously collaborated in the two years previous to the formal constitution of Art & Language in 1968. Baldwin had visited New York while a student in 1966 and had been interested in Judd. Atkinson went to New York the next year and made contact with LeWitt, Andre and Smithson. Both were then associated with Coventry College of Art, which became the principal British centre of interest in Minimal and Conceptual Art and art theory. Bainbridge studied in the sculpture course at St Martin's in the early 1960s. The nature of his relationship with the ethos of the institution is suggested by the title of an article he contributed to *Silâns* 8 (February 1965): 'The Artist/Intellectual as an Ineffective (Hypocritical?) Idealist.' Hurrell worked briefly as a part-time tutor in the St Martin's sculpture department. Bainbridge and Hurrell jointly staged the *Hardware* show at the Architectural Association, London, in February 1967.

81 *Art-Language* 1, 1 was published in May 1969, with the subtitle 'The journal of Conceptual Art' (a designation dropped from all subsequent issues). Contributors included Dan Graham, Sol LeWitt and Lawrence Weiner.

## 3 BEN NICHOLSON AND THE DECLINE OF CUBISM

1 Clement Greenberg, 'The Decline of Cubism' (1948), reprinted in Charles Harrison and Paul Wood, eds, *Art in Theory 1900–2000*, Oxford, 2003: 579.

2 '"American-Type" Painting' (first published, *Partisan Review*, Spring 1955), in J. O'Brian, ed., *Clement Greenberg: The Collected Essays and Criticism*, Vol. 3, Chicago, 1993: 219–20.

3 In the paper 'England's Climate', printed in B. Allen, ed., *Towards a Modern Art World: Studies in British Art 1*, New Haven and London, 1995 (proceedings of a conference held at the Tate Gallery, December 1989).

4 The two phrases express respectively the negative and positive aspirations of current artistic practice as Judd conceived it. The first, referring to Anthony Caro's sculpture, appears in his 'Complaints Part 1', *Studio International* 177, 910 (April 1969): 82–4, the second in his 'Barnett Newman', ibid. (February 1970), an essay originally written in 1964.

5 'No possible set of notes can explain our paintings. Their explanation must come out of a consummated experience between picture and onlooker.' From a statement originally published in the *New York Times*, 13 June 1943, signed by Adolph Gottlieb and Mark Rothko, though written with the collaboration of Barnett Newman; reprinted in Harrison and Wood, 2003: 569. 'If I must place my trust somewhere, I would invest it in the psyche of sensitive observers who are free of the conventions of understanding. I would have no apprehension about the use they would make of my pictures for the needs of their own spirit. For if there is both need and spirit, there is bound to be a real transaction.' Rothko, from a letter to Katharine Kuh, 1954, printed in *Mark Rothko*, London, Tate Gallery, 1987: 58.

6 Rothko, letter to Kuh, p. 58.

7 From the interview 'Newman, in Conversation with David Sylvester', taped in 1965 and published in *The Listener* (10 August 1972): 169–70.

8 Statement by Rothko published in *Tiger's Eye* (New York), December 1947; reprinted in Harrison and Wood, 2003: 573.

9 From Rothko, 'The Romantics were prompted . . .', originally published in *Possibilities* 1 (New York), 1947; reprinted in Harrison and Wood, 2003: 573.

## 4 ROGER HILTON: THE OBLIGATION TO EXPRESS

1 *Oh Yoi Yoi* was purchased by the Tate Gallery in 1974. Hilton dictated an account of the painting's origin in response to a questionnaire from the compiler of the gallery's catalogue in May of that year. See *Biennial Report and Illustrated Catalogue of Acquisitions 1972–74*, London, Tate Gallery, 1974.

2 The additional information about the fire was given to David Brown, during a visit to Roger and Rose Hilton in the winter of 1974.

3 Hilton would not be the first or the last artist to protect the generative conditions of his art by fobbing off content-mongers with trivial but appealing causal explanations. For discussion of another notable example see Charles Harrison and Fred Orton, 'Jasper Johns: meaning what you see', *Art History* (March 1984).

4 When asked why in this exceptional case he had painted more than one version of the same composition, Hilton replied, 'I did this because I thought it was a good picture and because I wanted to use different colours.' *Biennial Report*, 1974.

5 Mark Rothko, in a lecture at the Pratt Institute, as recorded by Dore Ashton and published in the *New York Times*, 31 October 1958.

6 'I think an artist is born by some accident. I mean, I think they're born not bred. That's what the art schools are trying to do, breed the fuckers.' From 'Every Artist is a Con-Man', Hilton in interview with Alan Green, *Studio International*, (March 1974).

7 I am only too well aware that within the conventional wisdom of art history, realism and Modernism are generally regarded as antithetical dispositions or aspirations. It is an assumption basic to this essay that they are mutually implicated, if not identical. I believe that that assumption – or some assumption capable of being reconciled to it – was also basic to the establishment of Hilton's own mature practice. In what follows I seek to represent as a form of argument a series of intuitions by which I take Hilton to have been motivated in the late 1940s and early 1950s at a crucial stage in his development as a painter. I do not pretend, however, that these intuitions were likely to have been formulated at the time as an argument in the terms I offer.

8 Robin Ironside, *Painting Since 1939*, London, 1947. This small book was commissioned and published by the British Council. If it was not influential in forming cultural policy, its judgements were certainly consonant with what soon became the governing representation of modern British art.

9 The *locus classicus* for analysis of the relationship between depicted shape and literal shape in painting is Michael Fried's 'Shape as Form: Frank Stella's New Paintings', first published in *Artforum*, November 1966, reprinted in edited form in Charles Harrison and Paul Wood, eds, *Art in Theory 1900–2000*, Oxford, 2003.

10 From Hilton's statement written for the publication *Nine Abstract Artists*, edited and introduced by Lawrence Alloway, London, 1954. The quotation is taken from the complete version of this statement, printed in *Roger Hilton: The Early Years 1911–55*, catalogue by Adrian Lewis, Leicester Polytechnic Gallery, 9–30 November 1984.

11 See e.g. the work surveyed in *Paris Post War: Art and Existentialism 1945–55*, London, Tate Gallery, 9 June – 5 September 1993.

12 *Hilton*, 1984.

13 It is significant that Hilton came to view Nicholson, the senior English proponent of abstract art, as 'far too finicky and tidy'. *Biennial Report*, 1974.

14 Barnett Newman, 'The Sublime is Now', first published in *Tiger's Eye* (New York), December 1948; reprinted in Harrison and Wood, 2003.

15 *Hilton*, 1984.

16 Hilton wrote in 1958, 'The result of all the intensive experimentation of the last 50 years and the throwing off of so many of what Clement Greenberg so aptly calls "expendable conventions" has left us free to take up again the whole resources of the accumulated technique of the past and to use them in the utmost freedom without fear of being caught up in the conventions with which this technique has come to be associated.' (From a statement for the catalogue, 'Paintings 1953–1957', London, ICA, 12 February – 8 March 1958.)

17 In a footnote to his essay 'Roger Hilton', *Artscribe*, 34 (March 1982), David Nicholson refers to 'an anecdote told by a nonplussed newspaperman' to whom Hilton related 'how he had painted the picture as a total abstract but years later came to see it as a big red woman'.

18 Hilton, 'About Painting', statement written for the catalogue of an exhibition at the Galerie Lienhard, Zürich, in 1961, reprinted in Harrison and Wood, 2003.

This essay benefited from the painstaking work done by Adrian Lewis in documenting the artist's career, and from comments on the first draft made by the late John Hilton, Rose Hilton, Elizabeth Knowles and the late David Brown.

## 5 'ENGLISHNESS' AND 'MODERNISM' REVISITED

1 *English Art and Modernism 1900–1939*, first edition, London and Bloomington, Ind., 1981; second edition, New Haven and London, 1994.

2 It would be disingenuous to assume that this distance could be maintained without some reciprocal effects. The proceedings of the 'Rethinking Englishness' conference were due to be published by Manchester University Press. At the request of the organisers I provided the original version of the paper for inclusion in the proposed volume. After a decent interval I was informed that a decision had been taken to exclude it from the publication on the grounds that it was 'out of keeping with the interests of the other contributors' and that it 'effectively mounted a challenge to the rationale of the collection', My conclusion at the time was that limits had clearly been set to the reach of 'rethinking' allowable in academic publications on the national culture. I was grateful for the more sympathetic response of the editors of *Modernism/Modernity*. The revised and supplemented proceedings of the conference were finally issued under the title *English Art 1860–1914: Modern Artists and Identity*, ed. David Peters Corbett and Lara Perry, Manchester, 2000. In their introduction to this volume, the editors hold me responsible for arguing 'that the category of the modern does not pertain to the art of England and that English art has little claim on our attention', Further, 'Harrison's attack on any claims for the modernity of English

art is only the latest of a long series of dismissals which deny the importance of English art to any history of modernism'. These are strange accusations to level at the author of a book on *English Art and Modernism* and of more than twenty subsequent articles on art and artists in Britain, leaving aside my engagement with and publications on the practice of Art & Language over the past thirty-five years. The original publication of the present essay seems particularly to have irritated Corbett and Perry. Yet, as in all my previous contributions to the subject, my concern has simply been to ensure that sentimental or professional investment in the products of the national culture neither privileges nor insulates those products where it is their Modernism that is at issue.

3 Bell's views, as expounded in his *Art*, London, 1914, find an American echo in the writing of Sheldon Cheney, whose *Primer of Modern Art* was first published in 1924, achieving ten printings before the issue of a revised edition in 1939.

4 See e.g. Michael Baldwin, Charles Harrison and Mel Ramsden, 'Art History, Art Criticism and Explanation', *Art History*, 4, 4 (December 1981); reprinted in Eric Fernie, ed., *Art History and its Methods*, London, 1995; and 'Author and Producer Revisited', in *Art-Language*, 5, 1 (October 1982).

5 Bell, 1914: 261.

6 'Our sense of the relative orders of discourse is as follows. Within any practice a first-order discourse characterises the normal terms in which discussion, business, exegesis etc., is conducted. A second-order discourse is conventionally understood as conducted in a type of metalanguage by which the terms and concepts etc. of the first may be related, analysed etc. and their referents explained. The requirement upon a second-order discourse is that it should be capable of "including" the first (i.e., describing what it describes and explaining what it explains), but that it should also furnish an explanation of *how* (and perhaps *why*) that describing and explaining is done. A second-order discourse thus presupposes a position somehow "outside" but engaged with the contexts of the first. It is suggested that a cognitively defensible discourse for the recovery of meaning from art will have a second-order character with respect to the normal and current means of interpretation. To the extent that this is true, the second-order discourse might be expected to supersede the first, except insofar as it is prevented from doing so by the agency which invests and maintains the normal order.' From Michael Baldwin, Charles Harrison and Mel Ramsden, 'Manet's *Olympia* and Contradictions: Apropos Timothy J. Clark's and Peter Wollen's Recent Articles', *Block*, 5 (Autumn 1981).

7 See Tom Phillips, 'Echoes', *London Review of Books* 3, 6 (2–15 April 1981); my response is printed in 3, 8 (7–20 May 1981).

8 The course in question – 'A316: Modern Art: Practices and Debates' – was based around four volumes of essays by members and associates of the Department of Art History at the Open University (Francis Frascina, Nigel Blake, Bryony

Fer, Tamar Garb and Charles Harrison, *Modernism: French Painting in the Nineteenth Century*; Charles Harrison, Francis Frascina, Gill Perry, *Primitivism, Cubism, Abstraction: The Early Twentieth Century*; Bryony Fer, David Batchelor and Paul Wood, *Realism, Rationalism, Surrealism: Art between the Wars*; and Paul Wood, Francis Frascina, Jonathan Harris and Charles Harrison, *Modernism in Dispute: Art since the Forties;* all New Haven and London, 1983). In none of the thirteen essays is there any explicit address to English art.

9 See e.g. Geoffrey Grigson and John Piper, 'England's Climate', *Axis*; 7 (Autumn 1936); Myfanwy Piper, editorial introduction to *The Painter's Object,* London, 1937, and 'Paul Nash, 1937', *Axis*, 8 (early Winter 1937); Robin Ironside, *Painting Since 1939*, London, British Council, 1947.

10 See my 'England's Climate', in B. Allen, ed., *Towards a Modern Art World: Studies in British Art i,* New Haven and London, 1995.

11 Transcript of an interview with Myfanwy Piper, February 1993, in David Masters, 'Constructions of National Identity: British Art 1930–1990', PhD, Open University, 1996, appendix: 304–5. Both Nicholson and Hepworth published texts in *Circle.*

12 The first Art & Language *Index* was shown at *Documenta 5* in Kassel in 1972. I have written about this work and about the longer project it initiated in my *Essays on Art & Language*, Oxford, 1991, and Cambridge, Mass., 2001.

13 Triplets had been born to Hepworth and Nicholson in October 1934. In a subsequent statement Hepworth wrote of her abstract work of the mid-1930s that it 'initiated the exploration' in which she hoped 'to discover some abstract essence in sculptural terms giving the quality of human relationships'. *Barbara Hepworth: Carvings and Drawings*, with an introduction by Herbert Read, London, 1952.

14 Mark Rothko, letter to the *New York Times,* 8 July 1945.

15 For Rothko's letter see Ch. 3 n. 5.

16 I think in particular of the following statement from 'Can Taste be Objective?', the third of Greenberg's Seminars on Aesthetics. 'Certain works are singled out in their time or later as excelling, and these works continue to excel: that is they continue to compel those of us who in time after look, listen or read hard enough. And there's no explaining this durability – the durability that creates a consensus – except by the fact that taste is ultimately objective. The best taste, that is; that taste which makes itself known by the durability of its verdicts; and in this durability lies the proof of its objectivity. (My reasoning here is no more circular than experience itself.)' Published in Greenberg, *Homemade Esthetics,* New York and Oxford, 1999: 26.

17 'Everything of naturalistic significance would indicate that there is indeed one world, one reality "out there", the source of our perceptions if not their total determinant, the cause of our expectations being fulfilled or disappointed, of our

endeavours succeeding or being frustrated. But this reality should not be identified with any linguistic account of it, or, needless to say, with any way of perceiving it, or pictorial representation of it. Reality is the source of *primitive causes*, which, having been pre-processed by our perceptual apparatus, produce changes in our knowledge and the verbal representations of it which we possess. All cultures relate symmetrically to this reality. Men in all cultures are capable of making reasonable responses to the causal inputs they receive from reality – that is are capable of learning. That the structure of our verbal knowledge does not converge upon a single form, isomorphic with what is real, should not surprise us. Why ever should we expect this to be a property of our linguistic and cognitive capabilities?' Barry Barnes, *Interests and the Growth of Knowledge*, London, 1977: 26.

18 At the time when this paper was delivered, my interest in this 'current of concerns' had been explored in a number of papers and published articles. Since then it has formed the animating thread of my book *Painting the Difference: Sex and Spectator in Modern Art*, Chicago, 2005. I have attempted in that publication to repair my omission in respect of Gwen John.

19 In considering this question I have three specific paintings in mind: Paula Modersohn-Becker's *Nude Self-Portrait* of 1906 (Kunstmuseum, Basle); Gwen John's *Self-Portrait* of 1900 (National Portrait Gallery, London); and Sophonisba Anguissola's highly complex painting, *Bernardino Campi paints Sophonisba Anguissola*, of c. 1559 (Pinacoteca, Siena). All three are reproduced and discussed in *Painting the Difference*.

20 I have attempted to argue for this connection in a chapter on Mark Rothko in *Painting the Difference*.

21 Bell, 1914: 98.

22 Ibid: 97.

23 Greenberg, 'Complaints of an Art Critic', *Artforum* (October 1967): 38.

24 In 'Greenberg on Art Criticism', televised interview with T. J. Clark; TV32 in *A315: Modern Art and Modernism: Manet to Pollock*, Milton Keynes, Open University, 1982.

## 6 THE POWER OF MODERNISM

1 George Dondero, 'Modern Art Shackled to Communism', speech to the American Congress, 16 August 1949, printed in *The Congressional Record* for 1949: 11584–7; edited version printed in Charles Harrison and Paul Wood, eds, *Art in Theory 1900–2000*, Oxford, 2003: 665–8.

2 First published in *Forum Lectures*, Washington, D.C. (Voice of America), 1960; reprinted in *Arts Yearbook*, 4, New York, 1961; see John O'Brian, ed., *Clement*

*Greenberg: The Collected Essays and Criticism*, Chicago, Vol. 4, 1993: 85–94.

3 See O'Brian's Introduction to ibid., Vol. 3: xv–xvi. O'Brian's conclusion that Greenberg's essay was 'heard by millions around the world' seems to me insecure – at least to the extent that hearing implies attention or comprehension. Some people no doubt tuned in to Voice of America for news, probably far more for the latest light music. O'Brian acknowledges that 'Over the agency's airwaves "Modernist Painting" kept company with the likes of Perry Como.' How many of those far-flung millions were likely to *listen* to more than a few sentences of Greenberg's patrician exercise in modern art theory? There is certainly little evidence of European response to 'Modernist Painting' before its 1965 reprinting in *Art and Literature,* an English-language journal published in Paris.

4 'Modernist Painting', as reprinted in Harrison and Wood, 2003: 774–8.

5 The most concise summary of the processes at issue is given by Fred Orton in 'Footnote One: the Idea of a Cold War', in David Thistlewood, ed., *American Abstract Expressionism,* Liverpool, 1993: 179–92. I have benefited considerably both from this specific essay and from more wide-ranging conversations with its author.

6 The statement was made during the unrecorded portion of an interview, 'Greenberg on Pollock', televised interview with T. J. Clark, University in connection with *A315: Modern Art and Modernism: Manet to Pollock*, Milton Keynes, Open University, 1983.

7 For further discussion of this series of works and of the issues raised by them see 'On *A Portrait of V. I. Lenin in the Style of Jackson Pollock*', in my *Essays on Art & Language*, Oxford, 1991 and 2001: 129–49; see also Art & Language, 'Portrait of V. I. Lenin in the Style of Jackson Pollock', *Artforum* (February 1980), and Art & Language, 'Joseph Stalin Gazing Enigmatically at the Body of V. I. Lenin as it Lies in State in Moscow in the Style of Jackson Pollock', *File*, 4, 4, (Toronto, 1980).

8 See *Modern Art and Moderism*, 1983.

9 From a notebook of the late 1930s, now in the collection of the Getty Research Institute, Los Angeles, cited in James Breslin, *Mark Rothko: A Biography*, Chicago, 1993: 124.

10 See Ch. 3 n. 5; reprinted in Harrison and Wood, 2003: 568–9.

## 7 FEELING THE EARTH MOVE

1 Rosalind Krauss, 'A View of Modernism', *Artforum* (September 1972); edited reprint in Charles Harrison and Paul Wood, eds, *Art in Theory 1900–2000*, Oxford, 2003: 976–9.

2 Bell, *Art*, London, 1914: 98.

3 'Three New American Painters: Louis, Noland, Olitski', catalogue essay for an exhibition at the Norman Mackenzie Art Gallery, Regina, Saskatchewan; reprinted in J. O'Brian, ed., *Clement Greenberg: The Collected Essays and Criticism,* Chicago, Vol. 4, 1993: 153.

4 'Complaints of an Art Critic', *Artforum* (October 1967); reprinted in O'Brian, Vol. 4, 1993: 265.

5 *Artforum* (Summer 1967). This was the issue that included, among other things, Michael Fried's 'Art and Objecthood', Sol LeWitt's 'Paragraphs on Conceptual Art', the third of Robert Morris's 'Notes on Sculpture' and Robert Smithson's 'The Development of an Air Terminal Site'.

6 Charles Harrison, 'Morris Louis', *Studio International* (April 1969).

7 Benjamin Buchloh, 'Hans Haacke: Memory and Instrumental Reason', *Art in America* (February 1988); reprinted in Buchloh, *Neo-Avant Garde and Culture Industry*, Cambridge, Mass., 2000: 212.

8 Arthur C. Danto, 'The Artworld', *Journal of Philosophy,* 61, 19 (1964): 571–84.

9 George Dickie, 'Defining Art', *American Philosophical Quarterly*, 6, 3 (1969), and *Art and the Aesthetic: An Institutional Analysis*, Ithaca, N.Y., 1974.

10 Hans Haacke, 'Statement', *Art into Society, Society into Art,* Institute of Contemporary Arts (ICA), London, 1974; reprinted in Harrison and Wood, 2003: 930–31.

11 Ibid: 931.

12 Victor Burgin, 'Situational Aesthetics', *Studio International* (October 1969); reprinted in ibid: 895.

13 Quoted from an interview between Mary Kelly and Laura Mulvey in *Afterimage* (March 1986), in Buchloh, 2000: 220.

14 Ibid: 218.

15 Haacke quotes from a text by Brecht from 1934, in Harrison and Wood, 2003: 931 n. 10.

16 Michael Baldwin in conversation; see also Michael Baldwin, Charles Harrison and Mel Ramsden, 'Emergency Conditionals', in Peter Goldie and Elisabeth Schellekens, eds, *Philosophy and Conceptual Art,* Oxford, 2007 (published form of a paper delivered to a symposium at King's College, University of London, June 2004).

17 Baldwin, letter to the author, December 2001.

18 Ibid.

19 Delacroix, journal entry, Paris, 3 September 1857, *The Journal of Eugène Delacroix,* trans. Walter Pach, London, 1938; reprinted in Harrison and Wood, 2003: 331.

## 8 A PLACE OF WORK: CONCEPTUAL ART AS REALIST PRACTICE?

1 In a paper circulated by the convenor of the panel, David Raskin, in advance of the conference.

2 Donald Judd, as expressed, for instance, in his 'Complaints, Part 1', *Studio International* 177, 910 (April 1969): 82–4.

3 Greenberg, 'Modernist Painting', 1961, reprinted in Charles Harrison and Paul Wood, eds, *Art in Theory 1900–2000,* Oxford, 2003: 778.

4 *When Attitudes become Form* was installed at the ICA, London, in September 1969.

5 The slogan 'Live in your head' is attributed to the American artist Keith Sonnier.

6 Grégoire Muller in *When Attitudes become Form*, Kunsthalle, Bern, 1969; original in French, my translation.

7 Kosuth's 'Art after Philosophy' was originally published in three parts in *Studio International* in October, November and December 1969. It was commissioned by the present author.

8 Haacke's statement is reprinted in Harrison and Wood, 2003: 931.

## 9 DRAWING: COMPETENCE AND INCOMPETENCE

1 Roger Hilton, 'Remarks about Painting', 1961, first published in the catalogue of an exhibition at Galerie Lienhard, Zurich, June 1961; reprinted in Charles Harrison and Paul Wood, eds, *Art in Theory 1900–2000,* Oxford, 2003: 772.

2 Roger Fry, 'The French Post-Impressionists' (1912), in *Vision and Design* (1920), Harmondsworth, 1961: 190.

3 Clement Greenberg, 'Avant-Garde and Kitsch' (1939), in Harrison and Wood, 2003: 540.

4 T. J. Clark, 'Preliminaries to a Possible Treatment of *Olympia* in 1865', *Screen*, 21, 1 (Spring 1980).

5 Art & Language (Michael Baldwin, Charles Harrison, Mel Ramsden), 'Manet's *Olympia* and Contradiction (apropos T. J. Clark's and Peter Wollen's recent articles)', *Block*, 5 (Middlesex), 1981.

6 In Charles Harrison, *Painting the Difference: Sex and Spectator in Modern Art,* Chicago, 2005.

7 Cézanne, letter of 26 September 1874, reprinted in Charles Harrison, Paul Wood and Jason Gaiger, eds, *Art in Theory 1815–1900,* Oxford, 1998: 549.

8 Clive Bell, *Art*, London, 1914: 253.

9 Roger Fry, 'The Art of the Bushmen' (1910), in *Vision and Design* (1920), Harmondsworth, 1961: 74.

10 Hanz Prinzhorn, *The Artistry of the Mentally Ill* (1922), in Harrison and Wood, 2003: 123 and 122.

11 Rothko, 'The Romantics were prompted . . .' (1947), in ibid: 572.
12 Barnett Newman, 'The First Man was an Artist' (1948), in ibid: 576.
13 For example, consider the following. 'It is to Benjamin Buchloh that we owe the most developed analysis of the symbiotic relation between abstraction and photography during the second decade of the twentieth century. Far from forming an opposition around the contrasting poles of their strategies of depiction . . . these two ways of working set in motion, at the level of their mode of production, wholly parallel changes in the technology of the image. For both photography and abstraction involve a radical "deskilling" of the artist/producer, a flight from the traditional beaux-arts techniques into the mechanically produced photographic negative on the one hand, and, on the other, the automated execution of an abstract painting, as for example with a pencil and ruler or – even more radically – a roller. And, as a corollary to this deeply impersonal, mechanical fabrication, both abstraction and photography accommodate themselves to the industrial condition of serialized production.' Rosalind Krauss, 'Picasso/Pastiche', *The Picasso Papers*, New York, 1998: 127–8. The reference is to Buchloh's PhD dissertation, 'Gerhard Richter: Painting after the Subject of History', Graduate Center, City University of New York, 1993.
14 Gustave Courbet, letter to Champfleury, 1854, in Harrison and Wood, 2003: 370.
15 'There has been a lot of naively revisionist "instability" noticeable in the artworld recently. New Wave "Americans", young "Italians" and Born Again "German" Neo-expressionists have moved in to occupy a territory formerly held by the cosmopolitan and progressively secure artists of the Sixties and Seventies. Many of the latter have rightly pointed to the Natopolitan interests of "new" Euro-art and to the axis of dealer interests lying behind this art. What has not been noted is that its discourse is hysterical.' Art & Language, 'Letter to a Canadian Curator', January 1982, in *Mannerism: A Theory of Culture*, Vancouver Art Gallery; reprinted in *Style* (Vancouver), March 1982: 11.
16 Art & Language went on to produce a further six large versions of *Index: The Studio at 3 Wesley Place*, of which four are extant. One was destroyed and a second was recycled into a later painting, *Index: Incident in a Museum XXI*, 1987. Each version was preceded by at least one large drawing, though not all of these were made by mouth.
17 The formula is Richard Wollheim's, from his *Painting as an Art*, London and Princeton, 1987: 22.
18 Hilton, 1961, in Harrison and Wood, 2003: 773.
19 Charles Baudelaire, from 'The Painter of Modern Life' (section IV, 'Modernity'), first published 1863 from a text of 1859, in Harrison, Wood and Gaiger, 1998: 497.

## 10 KEEPING UP

1 From 'On the Surface of Painting', in my *Essays on Art and Language* (1991), Cambridge, Mass., and London, 2001: 202. The chapter was based on a paper of the same title given to the 'Visions and Revisions' conference of the Mid-America College Art Association, in Minneapolis in 1987.

2 See Clive Bell, *Art*, London, 1914: 19–20: 'Of course "The Doctor" is not a work of art. In it form is not used as an object of emotion. This alone suffices to make it nugatory; it is worse than nugatory because the emotion it suggests is false. What it suggests is not pity and admiration but a sense of complacency in our own pitifulness and generosity. It is sentimental.'

3 Thierry de Duve, *Kant after Duchamp*, Cambridge, Mass., 1996.

4 See Rosalind Krauss, 'Art & Language Turns to Painting: A Strange Quirk in the Fate of Conceptual Art', *Art Press*, hors série, 16 (1995): 'The conditions of reproduction, as they seep across the boundary into high art . . . have turned every gesture and every seemingly resistant surface of painting, into the glitteringly transparent sign of its own subordination to a spectacle world in which it no longer operates in relation to values like spontaneity or authenticity, but functions as a pure token of sign-exchange.'

5 See the article of this title by Lucy Lippard and John Chandler, first published in *Art International*, (February 1968). The notion of Conceptual Art as dematerialisation was subject to considerable criticism: see e.g. Mel Bochner, 'Excerpts from Speculation (1967–1970)', *Artforum* (May 1970). The criticism did not appear to abate the influence of the notion over journalistic accounts of Conceptual Art.

6 Donald Davidson, 'What Metaphors Mean', in Sheldon Sacks, ed., *On Metaphor*, Chicago and London, 1979: 45.

7 Matthew Jesse Jackson, 'Artists and Repertoires: Notes on the A & R Aesthetic and the Problem with Art', paper delivered to the College Art Association Conference, Atlanta, February 2005. Revised version published as 'Para-performative Practices and Late Modernism: On Contemporary Art and the Museum', *Museum International*, 235, special issue on 'The Stakes of the collection in the 21st Century' (September 2007).

## 11 VIRTUAL ICONOCLASM AND REAL EXPANSION

1 Thomas Crow, *The Rise of the Sixties*, London, 1996: 12.

2 Art & Language (Michael Baldwin, Charles Harrison and Mel Ramsden), 'A Place to Work', *Museum International*, 235, special issue on 'The Stakes of the Collection in the 21st Century' (September 2007).

3 W. J. T. Mitchell, *Iconology: Image, Text, Ideology*, Chicago and London, 1986.
4 Clement Greenberg, 'Modernist Painting' (*Forum Lectures*, Washington, D.C., 1960), in Charles Harrison and Paul Wood, eds, *Art in Theory 1900–2000*, Oxford, 2003: 778.
5 See Arthur C. Danto, 'The Artworld', *Journal of Philosophy*, 61, 19 (October 1964): 571–84. See also Danto, *After the End of Art: Contemporary Art and the Pale of History*, Princeton, 1997.
6 Wollheim's paradigm spectator is so described in his *Painting as an Art*, London and Princeton, 1987: 22 and *passim.*
7 Grégoire Muller, introduction to *When Attitudes become Form*, Kunsthalle, Bern, 1969; original in French, my translation.

## 12 COMPLEXITY AND DISINTEREST

1 Barr's graphic chart was originally printed on the dust jacket of a book published to accompany the exhibition *Cubism and Abstract Art* at the Museum of Modern Art, New York, March–April 1936. It represented the patterns of flow in artistic influence, and the relations of diverse movements, during the period 1890–1935.
2 The summer 1967 issue of *Artforum*, 5, 10, was labelled as a special issue on American sculpture; see Ch. 7 n. 5.
3 Alasdair MacIntyre, *After Virtue: A Study in Moral Theory*, Notre Dame, Ind., 1981.
4 In his *Critique of Judgement*, §40, Kant lists three 'Maxims of common human Understanding'. These are, '1. to think for oneself; 2. to put ourselves in thought in the place of everyone else; 3. always to think consistently. The first is the maxim of *unprejudiced* thought; the second of *enlarged* thought; the third of *consecutive* thought.' He later adds, 'Taste is then the faculty of judging *a priori* of the communicability of feelings that are bound up with a given representation (without the mediation of a concept). If we could assume that the mere universal communicability of a feeling must carry in itself an interest for us with it . . . we should be able to explain why the feeling in the judgement of taste comes to be imputed to every one, so to speak, as a duty.' The relevant passage is reprinted in Charles Harrison and Paul Wood, eds, *Art in Theory 1900–2000*, Oxford, 2003: 782–3.
5 Clive Bell, *Art*, London, 1914: 98.
6 'A Conversation with Clement Greenberg; part I', ed. Trish Evans, *Art Monthly*, 73 (February 1984): 8.
7 Barbara Hepworth, 'Sculpture', originally published in J. L. Martin, Ben

Nicholson and Naum Gabo, eds, *Circle: International Survey of Constructive Art*, London, 1937; reprinted in Harrison and Wood, 2003: 395.

8 Roger Fry, 'An Essay in Aesthetics', first published in *New Quarterly* (London), 1909; reprinted in ibid: 77.

9 Bell, 1914: 261.

10 'Greenberg on Pollock', a televised interview with T. J. Clark, in *A315: Modern Art and Modernism: Manet to Pollock*, Milton Keynes, Open University, 1983.

11 Among the notable paintings that might be cited in support of this suggestion are Manet's portrait of Zola, Degas's of Duranty, Picasso's of Kahnweiler, Bonnard's of the Bernheim Jeune brothers, and portraits of Vollard by Renoir, Cézanne, Picasso and others.

12 'Modern Art and Modernism: Manet to Pollock' was first offered to students of the Open University in 1983, with the course code *A315*. It was replaced in 1993 by *A316*: 'Modern Art, Practices and Debates', a pluralistic course (co-produced with Yale University Press) that worried no one and that was in turn replaced in 2004 by *AA318*: 'The Art of the Twentieth Century'.

13 The quotations are taken from a copy of the original document in the possession of the author.

14 See, e.g., the text 'Art for Society?' published in *Art-Language*, 4, 4 (June 1980): 1–25.

15 Fortunately the vagaries of fashion have their limits. Here is what was said recently by the art-historian who above all others writing in English gave a renewed impetus to the social history of art during the 1970s and 1980s:

> Certain works of art . . . show us what it is to 'represent' at a particular historical moment – they show us the powers and the limits of knowledge. That is hard to do. It involves the artist in feeling for structures of assumption and patterns of syntax that are usually (mercifully) deeply hidden, implicit and embedded in our very use of signs; it is a matter of coming to understand, or at least to articulate, what our ways of world-making most obviously (but also most unrecognizably) amount to. I think that such work is done with real effectiveness – and maybe can only be done – at the level of form.

T. J. Clark, *Farewell to an Idea: Episodes from a History of Modernism*, New Haven and London, 1999: 165.

# COPYRIGHT ACKNOWLEDGEMENTS

In most cases images of works of art have been supplied by the owners or guardians of those works and are reproduced courtesy of them. Those images for which further credit is due are as follows:

9, 11, 12, 34, 44, 45, 46, 47: author; 28: Photo CNAC/MNAM, Dist. RMN; 29: Image © The Metropolitan Museum of Art; 30: courtesy Art & Language and Lisson Gallery, London © Bill Dodwell Photography; 31, 36, 37: courtesy Art & Language; 38, 39: Ashmolean Museum Photo Studio; 42: Photo © Kunstmuseum, Basel – Martin Bühler; 49: Photo © RMN, Paris; 50: Photo © Lady Lever Art Gallery, National Museums Liverpool / The Bridgeman Art Library; 53: courtesy Art & Language and Lisson Gallery, London

Works by Roger Hilton are © Estate of Roger Hilton, All rights reserved, DACS 2009

Works by Ben Nicholson are © Angela Verren Taunt 2009. All rights reserved, DACS

25: © Estate of Gwen John. All Rights Reserved, DACS 2009

28: © ADAGP, Paris and DACS, London 2009

29: © The Pollock-Krasner Foundation ARS, NY and DACS, London 2009

34: © Succession Marcel Duchamp / ADAGP, Paris and DACS, London 2009

35: © The Andy Warhol Foundation for the Visual Arts / Artists Rights Society (ARS), New York / DACS, London 2009

43: © Judd Foundation. Licensed by VAGA, New York / /DACS, London

# INDEX

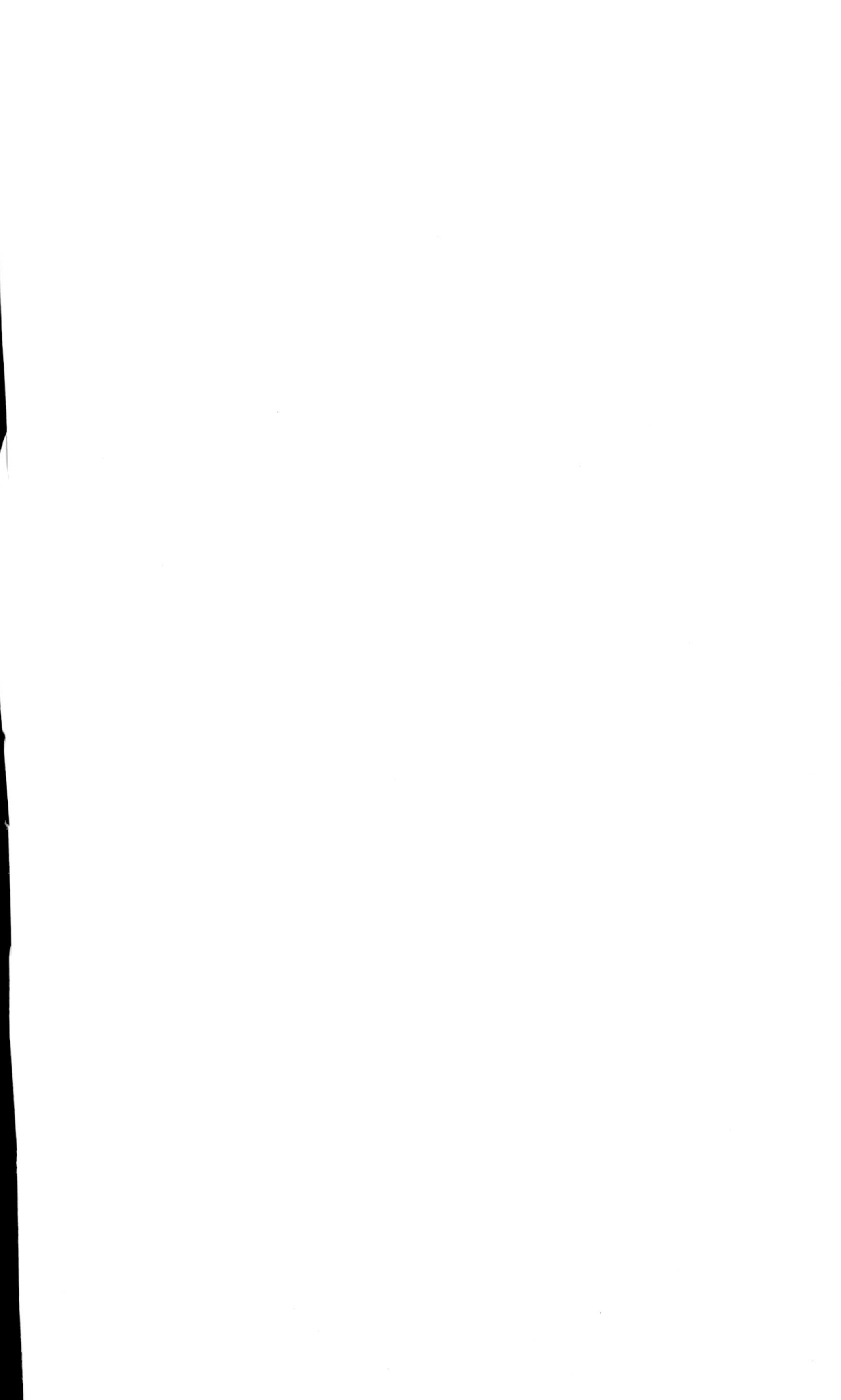

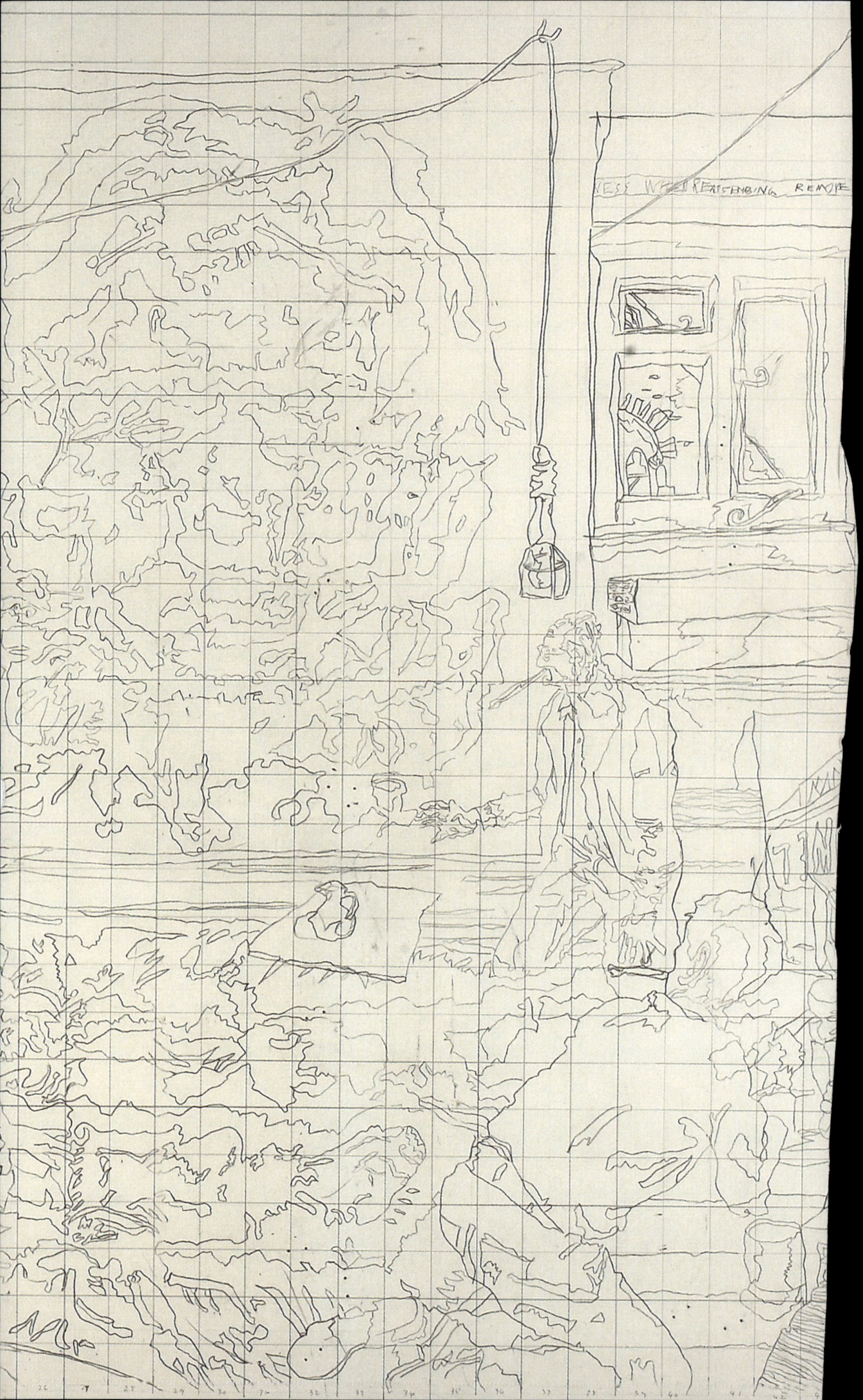